"On Everyone's Lips": Humanists, Jews, and the Tale of Simon of Trent

MEDIEVAL AND RENAISSANCE
TEXTS AND STUDIES
VOLUME 418

ARIZONA STUDIES IN THE
MIDDLE AGES AND THE RENAISSANCE

VOLUME 36

"On Everyone's Lips": Humanists, Jews, and the Tale of Simon of Trent

Edited and introduced by
Stephen Bowd

Latin texts edited and translated by
J. Donald Cullington

ACMRS
(Arizona Center for Medieval and Renaissance Studies)
Tempe, Arizona
in collaboration with
BREPOLS
2012

Research for this book was made possible through the generous support of the Gladys Krieble Delmas Award for Venetian Research

Published by ACMRS (Arizona Center for Medieval and Renaissance Studies)
Tempe, Arizona
and Brepols Publishers, n.v., Turnhout, Belgium.

ASMAR Volume 36: ISBN 978-2-503-54664-3   D/2012/0095/141

Library of Congress Cataloging-in-Publication Data

"On everyone's lips" : humanists, Jews, and the tale of Simon of Trent / edited and introduced by Stephen Bowd ; Latin texts edited and translated by J. Donald Cullington.
     pages. cm. -- (Medieval and Renaissance texts and studies ; volume 418) (Arizona studies in the Middle Ages and the Renaissance ; volume 36)
  ISBN 978-0-86698-466-9 (alk. paper)
1. Judaism--Controversial literature--Early works to 1800. 2. Antisemitism--Early works to 1800. 3. Jews--Persecutions--Early works to 1800. 4. Blood accusation--Early works to 1800. 5. Simon, of Trent, d. 1475--Early works to 1800. I. Bowd, Stephen D. II. Cullington, J. Donald. III. Series: Medieval & Renaissance Texts & Studies (Series) ; v. 418.
  BM585.2.O54 2012
  870.8'038296--dc23

                                                                    2012011950

Cover Image:
The Torture of Simon by the Jews of Trent. Woodcut in Giovanni Mattia Tiberino, *Die geschicht und legend von dem seyligen kind und marterer genannt Symon von den Iuden zu Trientt gemarteret und getoettet* (Augsburg, c. 1475).
By Permission of the Trustees of the National Library of Scotland.

Contents

Section I.

SECTION II.

SECTION III.

ILLUSTRATIONS

Cover. The torture of Simon of Trent by the Jews of Trent. Woodcut from Giovanni Mattia Tiberino, *Die geschicht und legend von dem seyligen kind und marterer genannt Symon von den Iuden zu Trientt gemarteret und getoettet* (Augsburg, c. 1475), [Edinburgh, National Library of Scotland, Newb. 5019, courtesy of the Trustees of the National Library of Scotland]

Fig. 1. The corpse of Simon is examined by Johannes Hinderbach, prince-bishop of Trent, Giovanni de Salis, podestà of Trent, Giovanni Mattia Tiberino, and other doctors while the Jews of Trent look on. Woodcut from *Historie von Simon zu Trient* (Trent: Albrecht Kunne, 6 Sept. 1475), fol. 8v [Munich, Bayerische Staatsbibliothek, 2 Inc.s.a. 62/1, available digitally at www.gateway-bayern.de]

Fig. 2. Simon's body is held in a cruciform pose while he is strangled with his cloak, his arms and right leg are attacked with pincers or needles, his penis is circumcised and the blood collected for ritual use by the Jews of Trent. *Ubertini Pusculi Brixiensis duo libri Symonidos* (Johannes Ot[h]mar: Augsburg, 11 April 1511), sig. iiiv [BL, IA.51138, ©The British Library Board. All rights reserved.]

Acknowledgments

I am immensely grateful to Stephen Bowd for introducing me to this fascinating (if unsavory) aspect of Renaissance humanism, for unearthing the relevant texts, for remedying many of the gaps in my knowledge, and for valuable assistance with my annotations. For help of sundry kinds I thank John Barsby, Andrew Collins, Christian DeLisle, Karen Edwards, Ennio Ferraglio, Estelle Haan, Robert Hannah, James Harding, Leofranc Holford-Strevens, Paul Morris, Ben Outhwaite, and especially John Hale, who kindly critiqued much of my work on Pusculo's epic. I am also very grateful for the many helpful comments and suggestions made by the publisher's two anonymous readers. Finally, for her moral support and encouragement my wife Stella deserves more than words can say.

JDC

It has been a pleasure to work with Donald Cullington on this, our second, project together. The research for this book has been made possible by the generosity of the Carnegie Trust for the Universities of Scotland, the Gladys Krieble Delmas Award for Venetian Research, and the British Academy. I am grateful to Martin Korenjak for generously making his work on Ubertino Pusculo's *Simonis* available to me before publication, and to the copyeditor for the publisher for some very helpful suggestions and bibliographical references. Donald and I are once again indebted to Robert Bjork, Todd Halvorsen, and Roy Rukkila for their aid in bringing about the publication of this volume.

SDB

ABBREVIATIONS

ASB	Archivio di Stato, Brescia
ASC	Archivio Storico Civico [in ASB]
BL	British Library, London
Goff	F. R. Goff, *Incunabula in American Libraries: A Third Census* (New York, 1964)
GW	*Gesamtkatalog der Wiegendrucke.* Vols. 1–7 (Leipzig 1925–1940). Vols. 7–9 (Stuttgart, 1972–1985)
H	Ludwig Hain, *Repertorium bibliographicum.* 4 vols (Stuttgart, 1826–1838)
HC	W. A. Copinger, *Supplement to Hain's* Repertorium Bibliographicum. 2 vols. (London, 1895–1902)
ISTC	*The Incunabula Short-Title Catalogue* www.bl.uk/catalogues/istc/
IGI	*Indice generale degli incunaboli delle Biblioteche d'Italia.* 6 vols. (Rome, 1943–1981)
PL	*Patrologiae Cursus Completus, Series Latina*, ed. J.-P. Migne (Paris, 1844–1864)

The Texts

The two complementary principles guiding this edition have been fidelity to the original texts—the sources of which are detailed below—and helpfulness to the modern reader. Thus, eccentricities and inconsistencies of spelling have been kept where no confusion could arise (e.g., in proper names), but where it could (e.g., in the representation of diphthongs), classical Latin usage has been followed; as a further aid to comprehension, consonantal *v* has always been distinguished from vocalic *u* in the texts themselves, although not in the text-notes. Punctuation, capitalization, quotation-marks, and paragraphing are all editorial; and editorial additions are indicated either by square brackets (in the case of single letters) or by text-notes (in the case of whole words). Those notes also list all other emendations, which have been made only when necessary for reasons of scansion, sense, or grammar, but are sometimes quite numerous—as in Pusculo's *Simonis.* Where two or more copies of a text have been consulted (as with Pusculo's epic and Tiberino's long letter), the available versions have been collated; but in a few cases (usually involving proper names) minor deviations from the spellings of the main source have been ignored.

The texts themselves are seen here as primarily historical documents, but they are also examples of humanist literature. The translations therefore aim above all at accuracy, clarity, and completeness, while taking into account the claims of literary style. Contextual notes mostly aim to give the reader any necessary background information, but may occasionally mention points arising from the translations. All biblical quotations in Latin are taken from the Vulgate, but for citations of the Psalms the King James Version's numbering is given first.

The manuscripts, incunabula, early sixteenth-century printed edition, and eighteenth-century text which form the basis of the three sections of this book are listed below, preceded by the letters used to identify them in the textual notes and followed by the location and press-mark of each text consulted. Information relating to the incunabula is taken with adjustments from *ISTC*.

Section I:

P = Giovanni Mattia Tiberino, *Relatio de Simone puero tridentino* [addressed to Raffaele Zovenzoni. Inc. '(R)em maximam'], *Miraculum* [Inc. 'Sayth iudeorum causam protector adortus']; Raffaele Zovenzoni, *Carmen ad Gabrielem Petri; Carmen ad Johannem Hinderbachium* [Inc. 'Surgite pontifices tuque o sanctissime caesar']; Johannes Hinderbach, *Epistola Raphaeli Zovenzonio* [Venice: Gabriele di Pietro, after 30 Apr. 1475] [BL, IA.19916]

T = Giovanni Mattia Tiberino, *In beatum Symonem novum sanctissimae passionis christi lumen & martirem: epigram[m]a* [Inc. '(S)um puer ille Symon']; *Divo Iohanni Hinderbach, quarto pontifici ac domino Tridentino, Iohannes Matthias s[alutem] p[lurimam] d[icit]* [Inc. '(C)um tua sancte symon lux sempiterna tridenti']; *Deprecatio* [Inc. '(S)alve sancte symon christi pendentis ymago']; *Deprecatio* [Inc. '(S) um memor alme symon cum te iudaea necasset']; *Iohannis Matthiae Tyberini liricum carmen ad beati Symonis Tridentini com[m]endationem feliciter incipit* [Inc. 'Sacro sancta fides christi']; *Divo Iohanni Episcopo Tridentino: de sabino lacu; Carmen* [Inc. 'Corticibus prisci numeros scripsere poetae']; *Ad laudem assumptionis beatae Mari[a] e semper virginis;* Raffaele Zovenzoni, *Divo Iohanni Hinderbacchio* [sic] *antistiti Tridentino dignissimo* [Inc. '(S)urgite pontifices tuque o sanctissime c(a)esar']; [Trent: Giovanni Leonardo Longo, 5 Sept. 1482] [BL, IA.51136]

B = Giovanni Mattia Tiberino, *S. Simonis martiris* [Inc. '(R)em maximam'], Brescia, Biblioteca Queriniana, MS G. IV. 10 (c.1475), fols. 84r–87v.[1]

A = *De S. Simone puero*, in *Acta Sanctorum martii, III* (Giovanni Battista Albrizzi and Sebastiano Coleti: Venice, 1736), 494–98.

O (for details see below under Section III)

---

[1] This manuscript has been edited and published by Ennio Ferraglio, "Due esemplari bresciani della *Passio* di Simonino da Trento di G. M. Tiberino," *Civis: studi e testi* 77 (2002): 91–108.

Section II:

L = Giovanni Calfurnio, *Mors et apotheosis Simonis infantis novi martiris*; *Elegia Calphurnii poetae Brix[iensis] ad Franciscum Tronum, patricium Venetum clarissimum et Mecoenatem suum*;[2] *Ad librum*; Raffaele Zovenzoni, *Divo Simoni martiri Tridentino innocentissimo Raphael Romeus Hister, poeta laureatus, dedicavit* [Inc. 'Dic age sancte puer christi inocentis (sic) imago']; [Verse inc. 'Obductis tenebris occulos (sic) iam morte propinqua'] [Trent: Z. L. (Giovanni Leonardo Longo), c.1481] [BL, IA.51138]

O (for details see below under Section III)

Section III:

O = Ubertino Pusculo, *Duo libri Symonidos. De iudaeorum perfidia* . . . ed. Johannes Kurtz von Eberspach (Johannes Ot[h]mar: Augsburg, 11 April 1511) [BL, C.133.e.8][3] [with additions by Othmar Nachtigall, Giovanni Piniciano, Giovanni Mattia Tiberino (inc. 'Sum puer ille Simon quem nuper in urbe tridenti'), Raffaele Zovenzoni (inc. 'Dic age sancte puer christi morientis ymago'), Johannes Kurtz von Eberspach, and Johannes Vögelin Heilbrunnen]

V = *Ubertini Pusculi Brixiensis Simonidos* . . . : Vienna, Österreichische Nationalbibliothek, Codex Vindobonensis Palatinus, series nova 12,822.

---

[2] Also published at Vicenza in 1481. We have not consulted this edition.

[3] A faulty Latin version of this text was published in Franco Bontempi, *Il ferro e la stella: presenza ebraica a Brescia durante il Rinascimento* (Boario Terme: Circolo culturale S. Alessandro, 1994), 236–57.

INTRODUCTION

In 1475 news of the murder of a young child called Simon shocked the inhabit-ants of the city of Trent as they commemorated Easter. Suspicion fell on three Jewish households in the city, and the gentile narrative of events quickly assumed a consistent form: according to the confessions extracted under torture, the Jews had abducted Simon and attacked his body with needles and pincers in order to cause bloodshed, before strangling him and throwing his mutilated corpse into a ditch. This was shocking but not particularly surprising news, for most medi-eval Christians were familiar with comparable cases of Jewish child murder and shared a presumption that the Jews were a perfidious and savage race instrumen-tal in the death of Jesus Christ.

However, the case of Simon of Trent was exceptional as the first such inci-dent to receive extensive press coverage: over thirty separate editions of verse and prose accounts of Simon's supposed murder are known to have been issued dur-ing the last quarter of the fifteenth century (for a complete list see Appendix 1). Just as the loss of Christian Negroponte to the Muslim Turks in 1470 prompted a dozen or so texts from the new presses of Europe,[1] so the death of Simon was turned by jobbing poets and humanists from Nuremberg to Naples into a sensa-tional and instructive moral tale. The publication of several texts in vernacular suggests that the story of Simon resonated with popular fears of Jewish blood-lust, but equally the preponderance of Latin versions of the case,[2] some of which are presented here in English for the first time, serves as an indication of political and religious priorities at the highest level, and should remind the modern reader of the darker uses of Renaissance learning.[3]

---

[1] Margaret Meserve, "News from Negroponte: Politics, Popular Opinion, and In-formation Exchange in the First Decade of the Italian Press," *Renaissance Quarterly* 59 (2006): 440–80.

[2] M. Korenjak, "Latin Poetry about Simon of Trento," in *Acta Conventus Neo-Latini Budapestensis*, ed. R. Schnur et al., MRTS 386 (Tempe: ACMRS, 2010), 397–406.

[3] Two Italian accounts were published in Treviso, while four German texts were issued at Trent, Ulm, Augsburg, and Nuremberg. A German text may also have been printed at Sant'Orso. See Appendix 1; Alison Knowles Frazier, *Possible Lives: Authors and Saints in Renaissance Italy* (New York: Columbia University Press, 2005), 468–70; Wolf-gang Treue, *Der Trienter Judenprozess: Voraussetzungen, Abläufe, Auswirkungen (1475–1588)* (Hannover: Hahnsche Buchhandlung, 1996), 285–308; Paul Oskar Kristeller, "The

I. Murder at Trent

On Easter Sunday, 26 March 1475, the corpse of Simon, twenty-eight-month-old son of the worker Master Andreas Garbarius (or Unferdorben, meaning 'uncorrupted') and his wife Maria, was found floating in a ditch in the city of Trent (see Appendices 2 and 3 for a list of those involved in the case, and a chronology of events).[4] Simon had been missing for several days, and during that time rumors implicating the local Jewish community in the child's disappearance had circulated. Accordingly, the house of Samuel, the leader of the small Jewish community, had been investigated by the local *podestà* (chief magistrate) Giovanni de Salis, and it was in a ditch running through the cellar of Samuel's house that the boy's body was finally discovered. According to statements extracted at their subsequent trials, this discovery was made by the Jews themselves who immediately reported it to the *podestà*. However, by some other accounts the body was found by one of the *podestà*'s men, and, observing that it bled in their presence, a sure sign of guilt, six Jews were promptly arrested. The body was examined in the hospital of St Peter's church by two doctors in the service of the local prince-bishop Johannes Hinderbach. The Brescian doctor Giovanni Mattia Tiberino (or Taberino), who sent an account of the case to his native city, stated that the boy had been dead since Good Friday and that the absence of water in his body indicated that he had not drowned. To make matters worse for the Jews, one witness came forward to give an account of hearing Simon's cries from Samuel's house, while another alleged that her son had been found injured in Samuel's shed fourteen years earlier.

As the interrogations under torture proceeded at the castle of the prince-bishop during March and April, the *podestà*, via a German-speaking interpreter, was instrumental in directing the prisoners towards admissions of guilt for the ritual murder of the child in order to obtain Christian blood for use in the Jewish ceremonies of Passover—a rite which Giovanni de Salis learned about from a Jewish convert.[5] In a series of intensive sessions over two weeks the *podestà* hung the accused men by ropes from the ceiling and repeatedly threatened them with the dislocation

---

Alleged Ritual Murder of Simon of Trent (1475) and its Literary Repercussions: A Bibliographical Study," *Proceedings of the American Academy for Jewish Research* 59 (1993): 103–35; and F. Hamster, "Primärliteratur zu Simon von Trient: Drucke und Handschriften vom 1475 bis 1500 mit Standortnachweisen," in *Frumenzio Ghetta O.F.M.: Scritti di storia e cultura ladina, trentina, tirolese* (Trent: Comune di Trento, 1991), 311–19.

[4] The following relies on R. Po-chia Hsia, *Trent 1475: Stories of a Ritual Murder Trial* (New Haven: Yale University Press, 1992); Iginio Rogger and Marco Bellabarba, eds., *Il principe vescovo Johannes Hinderbach (1465–1486) fra tardo Medieovo e Umanesimo*, Atti del Convegno promosso dalla Biblioteca Comunale di Trento (2–6 ottobre 1989) (Bologna: Edizioni dehoniane, 1992), 383–496.

[5] Below, 181; Hsia, *Trent 1475*, 40.

of their limbs. In this way he dragged out the details of Simon's final hours: the ritual Hebrew curses and gestures that accompanied the torture of the child with needles and pincers, and finally the collection and use of blood.

At this point in the grim process played out in the dungeons of the prince-bishop's castle in Trent a superior local power, Archduke Sigismund of Tirol, stepped in and suspended the trial until June 1475. When the prosecution subsequently resumed against some of the accused their confessions contained a marked emphasis on the role of Simon as a Christian martyr whose blood was especially desirable for use in religious rites, magic, and cures.[6] Blood demanded blood, and on 21 June Samuel was executed—the *podestà* ordered his flesh torn by hot pincers before he was burned outside the city walls. Two more of Trent's Jews followed him to the stake, while two others converted and were therefore beheaded before being burned. One man committed suicide.

In September 1475 envoys from the archduke and Battista dei Giudici, an apostolic commissioner appointed by Pope Sixtus IV, arrived in Trent to begin an investigation of the conduct of the trial, the position of the remaining prisoners, and the cult of the 'martyr' Simon which had quickly sprung up around the body on display in St Peter's church. The commissioner examined the body, sought to obtain the trial records, attempted to interview the remaining prisoners, and gathered evidence on a Christian suspect for the murder known as 'Schweitzer' (the Swiss). The commissioner's work was not easy, and he accused Prince-Bishop Hinderbach of hindering his interviews with the accused and with witnesses sympathetic to them, and generally of impeding his investigations. Dei Giudici also found the local populace credulous and hostile to any doubts about the miraculous nature of Simon's corpse, and he observed that they had used fraudulent means to preserve the body, and had also lied about the supposed miracles associated with Simon.[7] For his part, the prince-bishop assiduously promoted the cult of Simon, gathered evidence of Jewish ritual murder in German lands, and accused the commissioner of succumbing to Jewish bribery and of making an unwarranted interference in secular jurisdiction.

The next series of interrogations under torture began once the archduke had expressed his support for Hinderbach's actions. In the course of these the Jewish women of Trent were drawn into the web of accusations, their need for Christian blood was explored, and links with other ritual child murders in German lands were established. Pope Sixtus IV, who prohibited sermons about the martyrdom of Simon, appointed a special committee of cardinals to look into the whole affair in Rome. In 1478 a papal bull cleared Hinderbach of presiding over illegal proceedings, but it enjoined the prince-bishop not to promote the cult of Simon

---

[6] Hsia, *Trent 1475*, 65.

[7] See Battista dei Giudici, *Apologia Iudaeorum; Invectiva contra Platinam: Propaganda antiebraica e polemiche di curia durante il pontificato di Sisto IV (1471–1484)*, ed. and trans. Diego Quaglioni (Rome: Gestisa, 1987).

and, in line with medieval papal decrees, warned Christians against harming Jews, extorting money from them, or preventing them from practicing their rites. However, by this point the Jewish community had been eradicated from Tridentine society, and Simon was the focus for an international cult boosted by an array of texts and images.

II. The Blood Libel

During the later Middle Ages the flowing blood and body of Christ were the objects of increasingly intense Christian devotion, especially in northern Europe.[8] Christ's passion marked the New Covenant between men and God and it superseded the Old Covenant established by the animal sacrifices of the Jews.[9] The flow of blood from Christ's punctured body was therefore the "price and confirmation of salvation" for Christians and was repeated in the sacrifice of the Mass (or Eucharist) in which the host played a crucial role.[10] According to some Christian interpretations of Scripture the Jews were instrumental in this bloodletting, and it was thought that their beliefs and practices were marked by a desire to torture and martyr Christ (in the form of the host) and even to cause the flow of Christian blood by means of physical assaults.[11] Stories of host desecration spread through central Europe from the end of the thirteenth century and followed a fairly stereotypical pattern. A group of Jews, or a single Jew leading others, might be accused of procuring and keeping the host by means of bribery. Acording to "gentile tales" these attacks most often occurred at Easter when the Jewish feast of Passover was also usually celebrated. The Jews proceeded to abuse the host with metal instruments such as needles and knives. However, these attacks were normally frustrated by the miraculous indestructibility of the host, which might only bleed and survive immersion in boiling water. The host occasionally took on the shape of an infant or emitted child-like sounds, and this child-like innocence "paralleled the child-like persona of Christ, the innocence of Christ, and raised the level of compassion and drama in the narrative."[12] The tales often concluded with the discovery and punishment, or conversion, of the

---

[8] Caroline Walker Bynum, *Wonderful Blood: Theology and Practice in Late Medieval Northern Germany and Beyond* (Philadelphia: University of Pennsylvania Press, 2007).

[9] David Biale, *Blood and Belief: The Circulation of a Symbol between Jews and Christians* (Berkeley and Los Angeles: University of California Press, 2007), 56–57.

[10] Bynum, *Wonderful Blood*, 42–43.

[11] Ariel Toaff, *Pasqua di sangue: Ebrei d'Europa e omicidi rituali* (Bologna: Il Mulino, 2007); Miri Rubin, *Gentile Tales: The Narrative Assault on Late Medieval Jews* (New Haven: Yale University Press, 1999).

[12] Rubin, *Gentile Tales*, 77.

Jews whose homes were destroyed and became a 'site of memory' commemorated by public inscriptions.[13]

The accusation of host desecration explicitly intersected with an accusation of child torture and murder in Wrocław in 1453, and this association was made in several subsequent German cases.[14] These accusations drew on the theological tradition outlined above, but also on tales about the Jewish need for the blood of Christians — especially children and martyrs — as a cure for the wound of circumcision, or for other ailments such as body odor or male menstruation, with which Jewish men were said to be cursed.[15] This accusation of ritual child murder was well known throughout medieval Europe and had led to a number of infamous cases of persecution and expulsion. As Ubertino Pusculo noted in his poem about the Trent case, printed here, a boy called Richard was killed by Jews in Paris in the twelfth century and consequently all Jews were temporarily expelled from France by royal edict. A cult grew up around Richard and around the other supposed child or adolescent victims of the Jews, including William of Norwich (1144), Herbert of Huntingdon (c. 1180), Dominic of Val (1250), Hugh of Lincoln (1255), Lewis of Ravensburg (1429), Andrew of Rinn (1462), two unnamed children in Endingen (1470), and Simon of Trent. In each case the victims became martyrs venerated for the miracles associated with their remains. Their innocence combined with the violence of their deaths prompted strong local feeling which drew on widespread distrust of Jews and provoked localized hostility usually checked by a local power.[16]

Trent presented a deadly cocktail of suspicion and persecution unrestrained by local powers. By 1475 the traditional association of Jews with the torture and death of Christ, the desecration of the host, and the murder of Christian children must have been well known in Trent from printed accounts and tales of such cases in neighboring German lands such as Endingen and Regensburg.[17] It is clear that these general stereotypes were shaped by local circumstances and promoted by the local elite in the form of the prince-bishop, his doctor, his humanist clients and friends, and the town's *podestà*. In the course of the interrogations under torture or threat of torture the Tridentine Jews seem to have adopted a single

---

[13] The Jewish house in Trent, which housed the synagogue, was demolished, and the two relief sculptures set in the wall of the building which replaced it show Simon's murder and his apotheosis as a martyr: Hsia, *Trent 1475*, 134, fig. 10.

[14] Rubin, *Gentile Tales*, 121–26; R. Po-chia Hsia, *The Myth of Ritual Murder: Jews and Magic in Reformation Germany* (New Haven: Yale University Press, 1988), 56.

[15] Biale, *Blood and Belief*, 99, 100–1, 105; Bynum, *Wonderful Blood*, 239–44; Hsia, *Myth of Ritual Murder*, 2, 8–9, 20–22, 75.

[16] André Vauchez, *Sainthood in the Later Middle Ages*, trans. Jean Birrell (Cambridge: Cambridge University Press, 1997), 149–54.

[17] The Endingen and Regensburg cases are outlined in Hsia, *Myth of Ritual Murder*, chaps. 2, 4.

script provided by their persecutors: they explained how they scorned Christ using insulting gestures and uttering curses from the *Haggadah* (which provided
the order for the Passover *seder*). They also admitted that they tortured and killed
Simon in imitation of the crucifixion, and used the young boy's blood to make
matzo for use in their Passover rituals. In their confessions the Jews asserted
that Simon's blood, and indeed the blood of other Christian children obtained
through an illicit trade, was a cure for their bodily stench, prevented menstruation in women, and could be used in magic. As R. Po-chia Hsia has remarked of
this process: "Thus, the unique event, Simon's death, and the historicity of past
child murders are subsumed in the eternal structure of repeated Jewish rituals.
And the narrative imperative, the official story of ritual murder, the trial record
of 1475–76, represents [sic] nothing less than a Christian ethnography of Jewish
rites."[18] The advocates for the Jewish cause were well aware of this, and declared
to the apostolic commissioner that they wished to defend the truth: in this way
defending not only those Jews detained in the dungeons of Trent, but also Jews
throughout the world, against the 'blood libel'.[19]

III. The Cult of Simon

News of the discovery of the body of Simon and the circumstances of his martyrdom spread very quickly.[20] Trent was well placed for communications with the
archducal court at Innsbruck to the north via the Alpine passes, and to Verona
and Venice to the south along established trade routes. Moreover, the death of
Simon took place at the end of a Jubilee year when many pilgrims were traveling to and from Rome.[21] Miracles associated with the body were noted within
days of its discovery, and by June the following year almost a hundred and thirty

---

[18] Hsia, *Trent 1475*, 48, 63, 88–94, 97, 107, 115–16, quotation at 94.

[19] Dei Giudici to Hinderbach, Rovereto, 24 Sept. 1475, in Dei Giudici, *Apologia Iudaeorum*, 132, 133.

[20] Before he left for a pilgrimage to Rome on 19 April 1475 the Brescian Corradino Palazzo noted in his diary: "Fo la novella di Giudei da Trento." See "Il Diario di Cor-radino Palazzo," in *Le Cronache bresciane inedite dei secoli XV–XIX*, ed. Paolo Guerrini, 5 vols. (Brescia: Editrice Brixia Sacra, 1922–1932), 1: 227. In general, see Anna Esposito, "Il culto del 'beato' Simonino e la sua prima diffusione in Italia," in Rogger and Bella-barba, *Il principe vescovo*, 429–43.

[21] The full title of Tiberino's account of Simon's death published in Rome on 24 July 1475 runs: *De infantulo in civitate Tridentina per Iudeos rapto atque in vilipendium Christiane religionis post multas maximasque trucibationes* (sic) Anno Iubileo *die Parasceve crudelissime necato ac deinde in flumen cadavere dimerso Hystoria feliciter incipit*. Digitized version at http://inkunabeln.ub.uni-koeln.de/vdib-info/kleioc/it00487**000** [accessed 16 Aug. 2008] (emphasis added).

miracles had been attributed to Simon.[22] Pilgrims flocked to Trent from all over
Italy and the German states to view the corpse and to donate money. Miracles
associated with Simon continued to occur in large numbers after the papal bull
of 1478,[23] and pilgrims were visiting Simon's corpse as late as 1517.[24] In short,
there is every sign that the case and its miraculous consequences resonated widely
for many decades.[25]

Prince-Bishop Johannes Hinderbach was very keen to ensure that news of
Simon's martyrdom reached as many Christians as possible, and he probably
encouraged the writing and dissemination of the first major text about the case
from his own doctor. As he wrote to his friend the Istrian poet Raffaele Zovenzoni, many Brescians "had come here in large numbers because of this affair."[26]
For example, the nobleman Gasparo Martinengo was miraculously cured of a fe-
ver and consequently made a donation to Simon in gratitude.[27] Hinderbach went
on to explain to Zovenzoni that in response to this surge of interest Giovanni
Mattia Tiberino, the Brescian doctor who had examined the body, had decided
to send "the city of Brescia's magistrates a very lucidly and elegantly phrased
letter" describing the murder of Simon. The Latin text of this missive, which
was written as early as 4 April 1475, survives in no fewer than sixteen separate

---

[22] Hsia, *Trent 1475*, 52; Treue, *Trienter Judenprozess*, 225–84. A list of the miracles
is printed in Giovanni Mattia Tiberino, *Hystoria completa de passione et obitu pueri Simonis*
([Albrecht Kunne for] Hermann Schindeleyp: Trent, 9 Feb. 1476). The first miracles are
described by Pusculo below, 168–71, 176–77.

[23] Raffaele Zovenzoni's daughter Bartolomea was saved from death when he made a
vow to Simon. See his verse below, 106–7. Giovanni de Salis noted miracles taking place
in the Bresciano in a letter to Hinderbach dated at Brescia, 10 July 1480: *Processi contro gli
ebrei di Trento (1475–1478)*, vol. 1: *I Processi del 1475*, ed. Anna Esposito and Diego Quaglioni (Padua: CEDAM, 1990), 448–54 (at 451–52).

[24] Palazzo, "Il Diario," 302. Also note the visit made by a Vicentine in 1479: James
S. Grubb, *Provincial Families of the Renaissance: Private and Public Life in the Veneto* (Bal-
timore: Johns Hopkins University Press, 1996), 193, 195–97.

[25] In *c.* 1530 Pandolfo Nassini mentioned in his personal register of Brescian matters "uno Ms. Zoan di Sale Dottore il quale fu Podestà della Città di Trento, il quale Ms.
Zoan fu al tempo che era Podestà che fece morire li zudei li quali feno morire lo beato Simone, quale è anche in detta Città di Trento." Quoted in Fausto Lechi, *Le dimore bresciane
in cinque secoli di storia*, 8 vols. (Brescia: Edizioni di storia bresciana, 1973–1983), 4: 452.

[26] Hinderbach to Zovenzoni, Trent, 30 April 1475: below, 36–37; Archivio di Stato,
Trent, archivio principesco-vescovile, capsa 69, no. 10, fol. 1v.

[27] "[M]agnificus Gaspar martinengus: primus brixianae urbis Heros: Febre quotidiana continua graviter iacebat. Et balbutientibus Medicis: statuit Beati Symonis tridentini revisere corpusculum: Emisso voto: subversionem incidit stomaci: et inter maximam
flegmatis quantitatem quod evomuit: xx ontiarum globum: vitreum mirabile visu: per
vomitum eiecit: illico febre remissa: optatam paulo post foeliciter consecutus est sani-
tatem: Tridentumque ingressus: Beatum Symonem argenteo homine donavit": Tiberino,
Hystoria, unpaginated.

printed editions, some of which were illustrated, or carry work, by other writers including Zovenzoni.[28]

The prince-bishop moved to commission other works which would spread the tale of Simon's murder and would boost the fame of the miracles associated with the martyr's corpse. He sent to Zovenzoni in Venice a copy of Tiberino's letter to the Brescians about the case, and expressed his wish for a poetic account of Simon's death. He called on Zovenzoni as follows:

> I ask that in your lyrical poetry you curse this as an utterly impious act, truly perpetrated by the Jews themselves, and that in your words you honor this new little martyr of ours as he deserves, so that this affair may be revealed to all Christ-worshipers and, by being on everyone's lips, may be publicly known and proclaimed—to the praise of almighty God and the heightening of our Christian faith, and to the glorification of this new little martyr and of our city, and a greater appreciation of the blessings, present to us here and now, which God has granted us amongst his other gifts![29]

Zovenzoni duly composed his verses and later that year sent to a certain Michele Pacis in Rome a little book (*libello*) containing poems in which Christ was again crucified by the Jews. Pacis also recorded receipt of a letter from Hinderbach in favor of the cult of Simon and in recommendation of the orators in Rome at that moment pleading the prince-bishop's case before a sceptical curia.[30] Hinderbach's letters to Zovenzoni make it evident that the literary campaign complemented the efforts of the envoys such as Approvinus de Approvinis whom he had sent to Venice and Rome to counter the investigations of the apostolic commissioner.[31] Zovenzoni himself was interested not only in drawing his contemporaries' attention to the case but also in appealing to posterity through the new medium of print. As he addressed the Tridentine printer Gabriel di Pietro: "Print it—you,

---

[28] Tiberino's text is below, Section I. On the different editions of this text see Appendix 1; Frazier, *Possible Lives*, 468–70; Treue, *Trienter Judenprozess*, 285–308; Kristeller, "The Alleged Ritual Murder"; and Hamster, "Primärliteratur." On the diffusion of the image of Simon see Dana E. Katz, *The Jew in the Art of the Italian Renaissance* (Philadelphia: University of Pennsylvania Press, 2008), chap. 5; Treue, *Trienter Judenprozess*, 348–92. See also Anna Esposito, "Lo stereotipo dell'omicidio rituale nei processi tridentini e il culto del 'beato' Simone," in eadem and Quaglioni, *Processi contro gli ebrei*, 53–95, at 81–95.

[29] Hinderbach to Zovenzoni, Trent, 30 April 1475: Archivio di Stato, Trent, archivio princepesco-vescovile, capsa 69, no. 10, fol. 1v. The quotation is from the printed version below, 38–39.

[30] Pacis to Zovenzoni, Rome, 2 Jan. 1476: Archivio di Stato, Trent, archivio princepesco-vescovile, capsa 69, no. 10, fols. 9v–10v.

[31] Hinderbach to Zovenzoni, Trent, 21 May, 1 Oct. 1475: Archivio di Stato, Trent, archivio princepesco-vescovile, capsa 69, no. 10, fols. 3v, 5v.

Gabriele, new glory of our age—print the horrible outrage that the Jews have committed! / Print it, I beg you, O I beg you, print it on a thousand sheets, so that all posterity, alas, can learn about it."[32] He also addressed Nicholas Jenson in nearly identical terms in that German printer's edition of Tiberino's letter issued in Venice.[33]

Prince-Bishop Hinderbach also contacted the Brescian humanist Ubertino Pusculo, who visited Trent and was paid to write an emotionally-charged epic verse account of the case.[34] In 1481 Pusculo sent a unique copy of his poem to the prince-bishop by means of Tiberino, a mutual friend who had urged him to complete it. Pusculo declared that once Hinderbach had approved the text it would be made public.[35] The manuscript was eventually prefaced by an address (suggested by Hinderbach and framed with Tiberino's guidance) to Maximilian, the young son of Emperor Frederick III, in which Pusculo described the Jews' lust for fresh blood and the murder of Simon as a renewal of the memory of Christ's passion, before going on to praise Maximilian's lineage, learning, and virtues.[36] At around the same time the verses about Simon by the humanist Giovanni Calfurnio were published in Trent.[37] It is impossible to judge exactly how popular these works were, but in addition to the printed versions, at least two manuscript copies of Calfurnio's work and six manuscript copies of Tiberino's work survive, and accounts of the case found in contemporary diaries or chronicles seem to owe something to the tenor and substance of these texts.[38]

---

[32] Below, 36–37.

[33] Giovanni Mattia Tiberino, *Relatio de Simone puero tridentino* ([Venice]: Nicholas Jenson, [after 30 Apr. 1475]), unpaginated.

[34] Payments in 1479 and 1480 "pro quodam opere composito" and "pro miniatura et ligatura" noted in Treue, *Trienter Judenprozess*, 300 n. 80.

[35] Pusculo to Hinderbach, Brescia, 29 June 1481: Parma, Biblioteca palatina, MS. Parm. 1583, fol. 55r.

[36] Parma, Biblioteca palatina, MS. Parm. 1583, fols. 55v–7r (prefatory letter), 57v–86v (poem).

[37] For brief individual biographies of all authors see below, Section VI.

[38] Both the Calfurnio manuscripts are in the Vatican Library: Paul Oskar Kristeller, *Iter Italicum: A Finding List of Uncatalogued or Incompletely Catalogued Humanistic Manuscripts of the Renaissance in Italian and Other Libraries; Accedunt alia itinera*, 6 vols. (London: Warburg Institute; Leiden: E. J. Brill, 1963–1991), 2: 448, 461. I have seen manuscript copies of Tiberino's letter in Brescia, Biblioteca Queriniana, MS. G. IV. 10 (*c.* 1475), fols. 84r–87v; and Rovereto, Biblioteca civica, MS. Cod. 22, fols. 3r–5r. Kristeller, "Alleged Ritual Murder," 123–24, lists four other manuscripts. For the separate printed editions see below, Appendix 1. Simon's murder is described in the "Cronaca di anonimo veronese, 1446–1488," in *Monumenti storici pubblicati dalla R. deputazione veneta di storia patria*, ser. 3, *Cronache e diarii*, vol. 4, ed. Giovanni Soranzo (Venice: Libraria Emiliana, 1915), 308–9. For a discussion of other chronicles see Treue, *Trienter Judenprozess*, 318–40.

The visual impact of the tale of Simon's martyrdom was also significant. As
Dana Katz has recently noted, the accusations of ritual murder and host desecration, as well as a range of other alleged Jewish crimes, "had a marked presence in
the visual arts" of Renaissance Europe. She has argued that "Christians defined
themselves and their faith through the production of images that sought to vilify
Jews in order to create a unified Christian social body."[39] Images in the form of
portable prints or frescoes might render localized events such as the Trent case
with universalizing traits and enact a symbolic form of violence which helped reinforce social order.[40] For example, an early vernacular account of Simon printed
in Trent in 1475 was accompanied by twelve woodcuts depicting scenes from
the narrative of Simon's martyrdom—from the conspiracy of the Jews to find a
Christian boy to the decapitation of the condemned Jewish convert [fig. 1].[41]

In 1493 the immensely popular *Weltchronik*, or Chronicle of the World, of
Hartmann Schedel included an account of Simon's martyrdom, and an accompanying woodcut showing the Jews of Trent in the act of torturing the child.[42]
This printed leaf was bound into one copy of Tiberino's letter published in
Nuremberg,[43] and it may also have provided the model for one of the woodcuts
included in the unique printed edition of Pusculo's poem published in Augsburg
in 1511 [fig. 2].

Individual woodcut images and engraved prints were produced as far afield
as Tuscany and Rome. In these the Jews were presented in instantly recogniz-
able and stereotypical fashion as ugly or hook-nosed, sumptuously dressed, and
wearing distinctive hats bearing their names, together with the badges or symbols required by many authorities in medieval Europe. Narrative representations
of Simon being tortured and murdered by the Jews, or votive images of the child
with the pincers, clothing, and other symbols of his martyrdom, were especially common in Brescia or the Bresciano: a painting of Simon in the Carmelite
church of Brescia was said to have wept (prompting one viewer to bear twins
three months apart),[44] and he appeared in dozens of frescoes on the walls of
Franciscan churches the length of the Val Camonica.[45] The fresco image of a

---

[39] Katz, *Jew in the Art*, 7.

[40] Katz, *Jew in the Art*, 125–57.

[41] Katz, *Jew in the Art*, 127–38, figs. 46–57.

[42] Hsia, *Myth of Ritual Murder*, 46–50, fig. 4.

[43] See below, Appendix 1, no. 4.

[44] Palazzo, "Il Diario," 246 (entry for 13 April 1476); Elia Capriolo, *Chronica de rebus brixianorum* (Brescia: Arundo de' Arundi, n. d., but 1505), fol. LXXIXv.

[45] Katz, *Jew in the Art*, 142–57; D. Rigaux, "L'immagine di Simone di Trento nell'arco
alpino per il secolo XV: un tipo iconografico?" in Rogger and Bellabarba, *Principe vescovo*,
485–96; eadem, "Antijudaïsme par l'image: l'iconographie de Simon de Trente († 1475)
dans la région de Brescia," in *Politique et religion dans le judaïsme ancien et médiéval*, ed. D.
Tollet (Paris: Desclée, 1989), 309–18; Gabriella Ferri Piccaluga, "Economia, devozione

FIGURE 1: The corpse of Simon is examined by Johannes Hinderbach, prince-bishop of Trent, Giovanni de Salis, *podestà* of Trent, Giovanni Mattia Tiberino, and other doctors while the Jews of Trent look on. Woodcut from *Historie von Simon zu Trient* (Trent: Albrecht Kune, 6 Sept. 1475), fol. 8v [Munich, Bayerische Staatsbibliothek, 2 Inc.s.a. 62/1].

Ad lectorem Hexastichon Ioan‑
nis Vögelin Haylbrunnen.
Æneam celebrat Maro: Achillem doctus Homerus
Sic Vbertinus ille Symona suum
Illic ficta simul veris confusa videntur
Hic rem sinceram candide lector habes
Quo veris ficta et sinceris oblita fuco
Cędunt: hoc liber hic sit tibi corde magis

Ad Reuerendissimū dñm: dñm Ioannem
Hinderbach Epm Tridentiuū, Vbertini
Pusculi Brixiuēsis .   Oratio

FIGURE 2: Simon's body is held in a cruciform pose while he is strangled with his cloak, his arms and right leg are attacked with pincers or needles, his penis is circumcised and the blood collected for ritual use by the Jews of Trent. *Ubertini Pusculi Brixiensis duo libri Symonidos* (Johannes Ot[h]mar: Augsburg, 11 April 1511), sig. iiiv [BL, IA.51138].

bleeding Simon which was nailed to a board on the busiest gate into Frankfurt-am-Main seems to have been an isolated case of public art outside the Bresciano, although it is reminiscent of some printed images and of the illuminated image of the recumbent Simon in one of the manuscripts of Pusculo's verses.[46]

The texts and images relating to Simon were the accoutrements of a developing cult which was taken up with some vigor by the Franciscans who had long been suspicious of the economic traps into which Jewish moneylenders supposedly lured Christians. The leading Franciscan preacher Bernardino da Feltre had given a sermon in Trent just around the time of Simon's disappearance, and he may well have stirred up hostile feeling towards the Jews. The Franciscan preachers Michele Carcano and Brother Niccolò also preached against the Jews of Trent in Venice and Vicenza respectively. In addition, Francesco Sanson, the new general of the Franciscan order, was in contact with Hinderbach, and he supported the cult of Simon from his base in Brescia. At a meeting of the Venetian province in that city in 1476, Sanson urged all Franciscan preachers to promote Simon's cult.[47]

However, the tension between official Roman Catholicism and "local knowledge" or religious enthusiasm may explain why this cult was deplored by a Franciscan pope, Sixtus IV, and by members of the Roman curia. These clerics were reluctant to endorse or encourage popular veneration of unauthorized local saints and were outraged by the comparisons made between Simon and Christ.[48] The apostolic commissioner, who blasted the Tridentines for the superstition, credulity, and outright lies which lay at the base of Simon's cult, was horrified that

---

e politica: immagini di Francescani amadeiti ed ebrei nel secolo XV," in *Francescanesimo in Lombardia* (Milan: Silvana, 1983), 107–22; eadem, "Iconografia francescana in Vallecamonica," and "Ebrei nell'iconografia lombarda del '400," in eadem, *Il confine del nord: Microstoria in Vallecamonica per una storia d'Europa* (Boario Terme: BIM, 1989), 255–75, 305–34; Gianfranco Massetti, "Il culto di Simonino a Brescia e l'affresco di Santa Maria Rotonda a Pian Camuno," *Ateneo Veneto*, 3rd ser., 190, pt. 2/I (2003): 67–79 [another version of this article is available at: http://www.storiadelmondo.com/20/massetti.simonino.pdf]. All of these essays are illustrated, but some of the images are also in Heinz Schreckenberg, *The Jews in Christian Art: An Illustrated History*, trans. John Bowden (London: SCM Press, 1996), 277–80.

[46] Hsia, *Myth of Ritual Murder*, 61–62, fig. 8; Vienna, Österreichische Nationalbibliothek, Codex Vindobonensis Palatinus, series nova 12,822, fol. 18r.

[47] Esposito, "Il culto del 'beato' Simonino," 440–41, 440 n. 57, 441 n. 61. The Brescian council granted fifty *lire* to Sanson towards the expenses of holding the meeting in the city: ASC 505, 4 Jan. 1476, fol. 193v.

[48] Vauchez, *Sainthood*, esp. 86–87, 154–55, 420–21; Hsia, *Trent 1475*, 126. On "local knowledge" in an ecclesiastical sense see Simon Ditchfield, "'In Search of Local Knowledge': Rewriting Early Modern Italian Religious History," *Cristianesimo nella Storia* 19 (1998): 255–96.

they worshipped Simon as a "second Christ" and preferred him to all the virgins, martyrs, apostles, and saints of the church.[49]

In addition, many secular authorities were reluctant either to tolerate or to stir up trouble against an economically lucrative group, and, as the apostolic commissioner noted, most princes and prudent persons in Italy opposed the Tridentine trials. Indeed, he had high praise for Venice where justice was always exercised, innocent people were not sent to their deaths, and Christians did not attack Jews.[50] In fact, as early as April 1475 the Venetian Doge Pietro Mocenigo wrote to his rectors in Brescia, Padua, and Friuli about the violent actions and threats made against Jews travelling through Venetian territory which had been provoked by the rumors about Trent and inflamed by the sermons of certain, notably Franciscan, preachers. He ordered these rectors to protect the Jews from this violence and to move against these preachers. During the subsequent two years similar admonitions were issued, with additional injunctions against the spread of images of Simon.[51] The papal brief threatening excommunication for anyone who painted or printed accounts of the boy was cited in a ducal letter sent from Venice on 5 November 1475 to governors in the mainland empire.[52] The Brescian *podestà* who received this letter executed the command and issued an order to clergy and laity which was to be posted in the palace and in the other usual places in the city:

> No person, lay and secular of whatever station, must paint pictures on the walls or elsewhere, nor sell such pictures of the martyr or blessed [child]. Nor must anyone preach *per zaratani*[53] or in any other form of verse, nor

---

[49] Dei Giudici, *Apologia Iudaeorum*, 52, 53, 61, 65, 85–91, 112 (quotation), 113. However, Tiberino claimed in *c.* 1478 that Sixtus IV "enrolled in the list of saints this boy who stands next to Christ's throne, Simon, flower of flowers, virgin, martyr, and innocent." See below, 78–79.

[50] Dei Giudici, *Apologia Iudaeorum*, 52, 53, 64, 65–66, 67; note also 106, 107, 108, 109.

[51] Ducal letters of 24 April, 17 July, and 5 Nov. 1475 in ASB, Cancelleria pretoria, atti, reg. 18 (1474–1476), fols. 19v, 32v–33r, 46v–47r; ducal letters of 14 May, 18 Aug. 1476, 22 Aug. 1477 in ASB, Cancelleria pretoria, atti, reg. 19 (1476–1477), fols. 16r, 16v, 64v–65r, 143v, 143v–44r, 144r–v, 241r.

[52] "Scripsit summus pontifex omnibus dominis et potestatibus breve, per quod Declarat & Iubet sub pena excommunicationis ut puer ille qui Tridenti ab Judeis Interfectus dicitur pingi non sinatur, neque illa res ab scriptoribus Imprimi, aut a predicatoribus diffamari Instigarique vulgus contra Judeos, ab ecclesia tolleratos, In testimonium veritatis Dominice passionis": ASB, Cancelleria pretoria, atti, reg. 18 (1474–1476), fols. 46v–47r. A copy of the papal brief dated 10 Oct. 1475 ("Licet inter causas") was included with the ducal letter (fol. 47r–v).

[53] A *cerretano* was a peddler who recited or sang vernacular ballads, often concerning dramatic events, before crowds in public squares in Italian cities. Such peddlers also

write epistles, nor sell anything written about that small child called Simon who has died at the hands of Jews in the city of Trent.[54]

With characteristic literary energy Johannes Hinderbach ignored such injunctions, encouraged the composition and circulation of the texts published here, and worked to reverse Venetian policy. In October 1475 he wrote to Zovenzoni in Venice explaining that he hoped that his case would be heard in the city by the ducal secretaries, senior councillors, and patricians so that the doge and senate might hear of it, and consequently the doge would write to Venice's subject cities making the event known to them, letting all freely preach about it, and post up images ("et imagines affigere").[55]

IV. Toleration and Persecution

In spite of Venetian and papal injunctions, it is clear that ritual and symbolic violence against Jews continued in northern Italy, especially in Lombardy and in the Venetian *terraferma* (mainland empire) for at least a decade after Trent. News of the blood libel spread along established channels of communication, was then conflated with long-standing suspicion of Jewish bankers and money-lenders, and was finally adapted to local circumstances. Accusations of ritual murder were made at Pavia (1479), Bormio (1479), near Treviso at Portobuffolè (1480), Tortona (1482), Vicenza (1486), and possibly Marostica (*c.* 1486).[56] In these areas, as

---

sold copies of the ballads alongside their other goods: Meserve, "News from Negroponte," 454.

[54] "[C]he non dobia penzere ne far penzere in carto, in muro, ne altramente, ne vendere imagine alguna da Martyro ne beato, ne predicar per zaratani, ne per modo de versi, overo epistole scrivere, ne scritte vendere, de quello Fantolino appellato Simono et Morto per le mane de li zudei, ne la cita de Trento": ASB, Cancelleria pretoria, atti, reg. 18 (1474–1476), fol. 47v. English text adapted from Salo Wittmayer Baron, *A Social and Religious History of the Jews: Late Middle Ages and Era of European Expansion, 1200–1650*, vol. 10: *On the Empire's Periphery* (New York, London, and Philadelphia: Columbia University Press and the Jewish Publication Society of America, 1965/5726), 286.

[55] Hinderbach to Zovenzoni, Trent, 1 Oct. 1475: Archivio di Stato, Trent, archivio princepesco-vescovile, capsa 69, no. 10, fols. 5v–6r. Pusculo later accused the secular authorities which made these prohibitions of being bought with Jewish gold: below, 118–19.

[56] Corrado Guidetti, *Pro Judaeis: riflessioni e documenti* (Turin: Roux e Favale, 1884), 280–94; Georgius Summaripa, *Martyrium Sebastiani Novelli trucidati a perfidis iudeis* (Bernardini Celerii de Luere: Treviso, 12 May 1480); *Itinerario di Marin Sanuto per la terraferma veneziana nell'anno MCCCCLXXXIII*, ed. Rawdon Brown (Padua: Dalla Tipografia del Seminario, 1847), [129]; Mariano Nardello, "Il presunto martirio del beato Lorenzino Sossio da Marostica," *Archivio Veneto*, 5th ser., 95 (1972): 25–45.

elsewhere in Renaissance Italy, Jewish communities could be small and well-defined and subject to sporadic persecution. Their marginalization was a function of the toleration afforded to them as "a foil to Christian spiritual and material wealth," and in recognition that, as St Augustine had observed, they had preserved the original laws and prophecies announcing Christ, and that they would be converted at the end of time.[57] Spiritual toleration had economic benefits too for Christian rulers, since Jews had long acted as money-lenders in the place of Christians for whom usury, or the lending of money at interest, was considered a sin and had been condemned by canon law since the thirteenth century.[58]

Economic necessity often led to illicit or semi-licit money-lending in many Italian cities and states. Giovanni Mattia Tiberino asserted that Jews consumed Christians both symbolically and literally, and he thundered:

> Listen, you rulers of peoples, to the unheard-of crime, and watch over your peoples as faithful shepherds should! Let earth's denizens awake and see what snakes they are nurturing in their own bosom! The cruel Jews not only eat up Christians' property in their frenzied craving for interest payments but, conspiring against our lives and for our destruction, they feast on the living blood of our sons, afflicting them with terrible punishment in their synagogues and cruelly slaughtering them in place of Christ.[59]

In the course of the fifteenth century the citizens of Verona, Padua, and Mantua who were in dire need of usurious services consulted their bishops or sought assurances from Rome that the presence of Jews would not lead to excommunication. However, the excommunication of the marquis of Mantua for tolerating Jews in his territory suggests that the papacy could take a hard line toward Jewish money-lenders and Jewish-Christian contact during the fifteenth century.[60] Moroever, the warnings issued by mendicant preachers like Bernardino da Siena, Alberto Berdini da Sarteano, Roberto Caracciolo, and Giovanni da

---

[57] Katz, *Jew in the Art*, 10.

[58] On Jews in Renaissance Italy see Robert Bonfil, *Jewish Life in Renaissance Italy*, trans. Anthony Oldcorn (Berkeley and Los Angeles: University of California Press, 1994), which revises the more optimistic views of assimilation outlined by Moses A. Shulvass, *The Jews in the World of the Renaissance*, trans. Elvin I. Kose (Leiden and Chicago: Brill, 1973); Baron, *Social and Religious History*, 10: 220–96; Attilio Milano, *Storia degli ebrei in Italia* (Turin: Einaudi, 1963); and Cecil Roth, *The History of the Jews of Italy* (Philadelphia: The Jewish Publication Society of America, 1946/5706). On Jews in the Venetian *terraferma* see the essays in G. M. Varanini and R. Mueller, eds., *Ebrei nella Terraferma veneta del Quattrocento* (Florence: Florence University Press, 2005).

[59] Below, 42–43.

[60] Reinhold C. Mueller, "Lo *status* degli ebrei nella Terraferma veneta del Quattrocento: tra politica, religione, cultura ed economia: Saggio introduttivo," in Varanini and idem, *Ebrei nella Terraferma*, 1–22, here 17.

Capistrano were consonant with some papal pronouncements and undoubtedly helped to shape debates in many places.[61] For example, in once again rejecting a proposal by the special council of Brescia to allow the admission of Jews to help relieve poverty in the mid-fifteenth century, the general council explicitly cited the preaching of Bernardino and Alberto, and described Jews as a public disease and waste matter best kept far from the city and from any contact with Christians.[62] Jews were subsequently admitted to the city and acted as money-lenders, but there is evidence of sporadic violence against them in the period after 1475, which can hardly have been discouraged by the letter sent home by Tiberino.[63] As already noted, the Tridentine sermons of the Franciscan Bernardino da Feltre before Easter 1475 were unlikely to have omitted some reflection on the subordinate place of Jews in Christian society.

Therefore, throughout Italy the Jews were routinely subject to generalized moral comments in sermons, Christian abuse, special taxes, and residency and dress requirements. The small Jewish communities were often protected from violence by princes to whom they were directly subject, and some were mobile enough to escape, at least temporarily, from the worst of popular hostility or legislation.[64] In German lands imperial toleration was often extended to Jewish communities in the face of local hostility and served to derail trials for ritual murder or host desecration in 1470, 1476, and 1504.[65] However, when princes or other powers were distant from a locality (as in the case of Venice), or magistrates turned against the Jews (as in the case of Trent) and acted to assert their autonomy from lords, more hostile forces could be unleashed. Some humanists were evidently willing to please their patrons, join the mob, and attack the Jews with their sharpened pens. The hazily positive view of Renaissance Italian toler-

---

[61] On exemplary and moralizing sermons in fifteenth-century Italy see Franco Mormando, *The Preacher's Demons: Bernardino of Siena and the Social Underworld of Early Renaissance Italy* (Chicago: University of Chicago Press, 1999).

[62] "Qui tanquam vere columne fidei nostrae, & vera ecclesiae luminaria Iudeos tanquam publicam luem ac ignem intestinum non modo à civitatibus se ab omnium Christianorum frequentia arcendos & repellendos penitus esse consulebant cum Iudei ipsi non modo omnem ex civitatibus sostantiam exhauriunt: Verum etiam mentes hominum tanquam publica pestis erroribus scismatibus heresibus . . .": ASC 498, 15, 17 April 1458, fol. 27v.

[63] On the position of a small group of Brescian Jews caught between local hostility and Venetian tolerance see Stephen D. Bowd, *Venice's Most Loyal City: Civic Identity in Renaissance Brescia* (Cambridge, MA: Harvard University Press, 2010), chap. 9.

[64] For example, when Jews were expelled from Padua in 1455 they simply moved to the villages in the Padovano where they continued to act as money-lenders for locals as well as for Paduans who travelled out of the city to transact business. See Brian Pullan, *Rich and Poor in Renaissance Venice: The Social Institutions of a Catholic State, to 1620* (Oxford: Basil Blackwell, 1971), 456.

[65] Hsia, *Myth of Ritual Murder*, 15–16, 35, 77, 83, 103–6.

ance must therefore be revised. Just as the limited toleration extended to Jewish communities was often tempered by persecution spurred by a need to define and reinforce the Christian community, so these humanist texts encoded a symbolic violence against Jews which served to highlight Christian faults and point towards reform.[66]

V. Humanists and Jews

In the course of the fifteenth and sixteenth centuries harsh polemics against Jews were bolstered by a number of texts, often composed by converted Jews, lawyers, clerics, and humanists, which employed an array of scriptural proofs, sometimes restricted to Mosaic authorities, and Talmudic references, as the basis for a refutation of Jewish arguments and supposed obstinacy. These texts were sometimes the outcome of public debates, and they reflect a more general tendency toward public, often lay, discussions of theological questions in the courts and urban spaces during the Renaissance.[67] The study of these texts has largely been limited to Germany, but further investigations may reveal their full extent in Italy.[68] It is clear that humanists drawn from the civic or courtly elite, or tied by patronage and employment to towns and princes and other powers, often flattered their paymasters with panegyrics, and some were naturally biddable and willing to be used in support of discriminatory movements and legislation. Others wrote with a sincere Christian hostility toward Jews. Few seem really to have appreciated or valued contemporary Jewish religion and culture and they sought to master Hebrew only in order to understand the correct meaning of Scripture and to refute Talmudic authorities which denied the intimations of Jesus Christ's advent supposedly found there.

For example, the humanists Giannozzo Manetti in Florence, and possibly Lauro Querini in Venice, explored Hebrew literature with a view to showing the Jews the error of their ways.[69] Manetti wrote works faithful to the medieval tradition which emphasized the obstinacy of the Jews, and the Venetian patrician Paolo Morosini described their perfidy, or faithlessness, in a work which

---

[66] On academic discussions of Jews in German lands see Hsia, *Myth of Ritual Murder*, chap. 6.

[67] Gianfranco Fioravanti, "Polemiche antigiudaiche nell'Italia del Quattrocento: un tentativo di intepretazione globale," *Quaderni storici* n.s. 64 (1987): 19–37.

[68] Y. Deutsch, "'A View of the Jewish Religion': Conceptions of Jewish Practice and Ritual in Early Modern Europe," *Archiv für Religionsgeschichte* 3 (2001): 273–95.

[69] Eugenio Garin, "L'umanesimo italiano e la cultura ebraica," in *Storia d'Italia, Annali* 11: *Gli ebrei in Italia*, I: *Dall'alto Medioevo all'età dei ghetti*, ed. Corrado Vivanti (Turin: Einaudi, 1996), 359–83.

was printed in Padua in 1473.[70] The Veronese antiquarian Felice Feliciano tran-
scribed a *Pronosticon* against the Jews dedicated to Johannes Hinderbach and
published in Padua in 1474. Feliciano may also have translated and brought to
the press a work about Simon of Trent.[71] In Pavia the humanist Lateran canon Matteo Bosso preached on an alleged Jewish murder there, and he issued a
stream of anti-Semitic writings which were read by prominent Veronese citizens.[72] In Verona itself, where the Jews were accused of ritual murder in 1481,
three local humanists composed texts on Simon of Trent and the perfidy of the
Jews during 1475–1476.[73] In Vicenza three authors, including the humanist and
suffragan bishop Pietro Bruti, wrote about Simon or penned attacks on the Jews
who were expelled from the city in 1486.

Bruti and some others who wrote about Jews in the aftermath of the Trent
case cited the Talmud and claimed some knowledge of Hebrew texts and Jewish
traditions.[74] Knowledge of the Hebrew language was certainly spreading among
Italian humanists from the middle of the fifteenth century as they sought to understand the meaning of the mysteries in Scripture.[75] However, increased knowledge of the Talmud and Torah did not encourage toleration; in fact, it seems to
have intensified the traditional polemics by pointing up the differences between

---

[70] Christoph Dröge, *Giannozzo Manetti als Denker und Hebraist* (Frankfurt: Peter
Lang, 1987); Paolo Morosini, *Pauli Mauroceni opus de aeterna temporalique Christi gen-
eratione in Iudaicae improbationem perfidiae Christianaeque religionis gloriam divinis enun-
tiationibus comprobata ad Paulum pontificem maximum incipit* (Padua: Bartholomaeus de
Valdezoccho and Martinus de Septem arboribus, 28 April 1473).

[71] [Mattheus Künig], *Tormenti del Beato Simone da Trento* (Sant'Orso: Giovanni da
Reno, 24 June 1475). On the identity of the translator see Agostino Contò, "'Non scripto
calamo': Felice Feliciano e la tipografia," in *L'Antiquario' Felice Feliciano veronese tra epi-
grafa antica, letteratura e arti del libro*: Atti del convegno di studi (Verona, 3–4 giugno
1993), ed. idem and Leonardo Quacquarelli (Padua: Editrice Antenore, 1995), 289–312,
at 308–10; Esposito, "Lo Stereotipo dell'omicidio," 83.

[72] Gian Maria Varanini, "Società cristiana e minoranza ebraica a Verona nella seconda metà del Quattrocento: Tra ideologia osservante e vita quotidiana," in Mueller and
idem, *Ebrei nella terraferma*, 141–62, at 149. His preaching is mentioned in a note in Rovereto, Biblioteca civica, MS. Cod. 22, fol. 5r.

[73] Soranzo, "Cronaca di anonimo," 362–63; Grubb, *Provincial Families*, 196. See
also the account of a "boyish infantry" attacking the papal envoy Giovanni Battista dei
Giudici in Verona: below, 202–5.

[74] Below, 54–57; Pietro Bruti, *Victoria contra Iudaeos* (Vicenza, 30 Oct. 1489), sigs.
[gvr], iiiir, siiir.

[75] Heiko A. Oberman, "Discovery of Hebrew and Discrimination against the Jews:
The *Veritas Hebraica* as Double-Edged Sword in Renaissance and Reformation," in *Ger-
mania Illustrata: Essays on Modern History Presented to Gerald Strauss*, ed. Andrew C. Fix
and Susan C. Karant-Nunn (Kirksville, MO: Sixteenth Century Journal Publishers,
1992), 19–34.

biblical Judaism and its corrosive Talmudic and Rabbinical successors. Thus, the majority of humanists, as well as writers in religious orders or otherwise connected with the church, continued to present the place of Jews in Christian society in largely Augustinian terms: the Jews remained in Christendom as a divine scourge for men's sins and as a spur to renew religious observance.

In a similar fashion, it is clear that the printing press was not an instrument for greater toleration. Indeed, it was the religious orders who recognized the importance of the printing press in spreading a more spiritual way of life: the activity of the Ripoli press in Florence is well known, and the Franciscans in Venice were active as printers during the 1470s.[76] In Venice in 1471 the printer Nicholas Jenson issued a Carthusian spiritual manual containing strongly anti-Semitic elements, the origins of which can be traced not only to the Carthusian prior and ducal confessor Francesco Trevisan, but also to the correspondence of prominent patricians and humanists such as Ludovico Foscarini and his friend Paolo Morosini.[77] Jenson, as already noted, was also happy to publish Tiberino's account of the death of Simon, while a prominent patrician, Francesco Tron, was instrumental in eliciting Calfurnio's poem about Simon's death and 'apotheosis' as martyr.[78]

Finally, it is worth emphasizing that the texts presented in this volume also show the engagement of some humanists with the medieval hagiographical tradition — an aspect of their output which has been neglected until now. Humanists wrote, edited, or translated stories of martyrs and saints, and presented their biographies as passions in imitation of the story of Christ's tormented last days on earth. In a similar way, the authors of texts about Simon presented him as a second Christ who died to redeem Christian society and intercede on its behalf through miracles. Narratives and votive images of Simon also made this point in different iconographic ways: for example, they often included the instruments of his torture and death as if they were the *arma Christi* by which Christ was tortured.[79] As Alison Knowles Frazier has shown, humanists participated in a

---

[76] Melissa Conway, *The* Diario *of the Printing Press of San Jacopo di Ripoli, 1476–1484: Commentary and Transcription* (Florence: Leo S. Olschki, 1999); Martin Lowry, "'Nel Beretin Convento': The Franciscans and the Venetian Press (1474–78)," *La Bibliofilia* 85 (1983): 27–40.

[77] On Foscarini's "furious lobbying" in *c.* 1462 against the admission of Jews to Venice see Martin Lowry, "Humanism and Anti-Semitism in Renaissance Venice: The Strange Story of *Décor Puellarum*," *La Bibliofilia* 87 (1985): 39–54.

[78] Below, 98–105. Martin Lowry, *Nicholas Jenson and the Rise of Venetian Publishing in Renaissance Europe* (Oxford: Basil Blackwell, 1991), 120–21.

[79] On the proliferation of these representations during the fifteenth century see Bynum, *Wonderful Blood*, 13–14. Biale, *Blood and Belief*, 99, also suggests that the implements being used to torture Simon in one woodcut "seem to resemble those of the *mohel*", or ritual circumciser.

veritable "Renaissance of martyrs" which was often motivated by the physical presence of holy relics, well-attested miracles, and the enthusiasm of local communities and patrons; they were also instrumental in universalising these local cults.[80] The texts in this book, as well as many others which we have chosen not to publish in translation here, may be viewed as "humanist ex-votos" of sorts, like the sacred narratives composed and presented by humanists in recognition of heavenly favors.[81] In sum, it is possible to trace in detail the construction of a cult which not only had local political, social, religious, and even emotional resonances but was also consonant with broader debates and concerns in Renaissance Italy over the place of the holy and thaumaturgical in society.[82]

VI. Authors and Texts

The texts presented in English translation for the first time in this volume were written between 1475 and 1482. Although the texts vary in some details, the essential narrative is fairly consistent, and it is clear that the confessions of the Jews were quickly made known by Hinderbach to the humanists and poets whose pens he employed in his campaign in favor of the local cult of Simon.[83] The texts share a number of significant themes and what might be broadly termed belief systems: Christian, rabbinical Judaic, and classical. The authors are all emphatic in their Christian denunciation of the savagery, perfidy, and monstrousness of the Jews of Trent. Equally, they highlight the beauty, innocence, and Christ-like nature of the murdered infant. In addition, like the passion tales and medieval hymns of lament by Mary at the death of Jesus, which invited the audience to identify with her sorrow and maternal mourning, the reader is encouraged to feel grief not only for Simon but also for Christ's sacrifice at the hands of the Jews.[84] For example, Tiberino explicitly recalls the passion and he describes the Jews in the act of "violently stretching out his [i.e., Simon's] most holy arms in place

---

[80] Frazier, *Possible Lives*, 24.

[81] Frazier, *Possible Lives*, 38–39.

[82] Cf. *Images, Relics, and Devotional Practices in Medieval and Renaissance Italy*, ed. S. J Cornelison and S. B. Montgomery, MRTS 296 (Tempe: ACMRS, 2006).

[83] On Hinderbach making a copy of a confession available to the bishop of Regensburg, with terrible consequences for the Jews of Regensburg implicated in ritual murder, see Hsia, *Trent 1475*, 97–98. On the circulation of trial records or confessions in manuscript elsewhere see Hsia, *Myth of Ritual Murder*, 53, 72. One confession of host desecration was printed, probably in Magdeburg, in 1492: Bynum, *Wonderful Blood*, 69.

[84] James H. Marrow, *Passion Iconography in Northern European Art of the Late Middle Ages and Early Renaissance: A Study of the Transformation of Sacred Metaphor into Descriptive Narrative* (Kortrijk: Van Ghemmert Publishing Company, 1979); Carol Lansing, *Passion and Order: Restraint of Grief in the Medieval Italian Communes* (Ithaca: Cornell University Press, 2008), 148–52.

of the crucified [Christ's]," and declares: "Behold, Christian, Jesus crucified between thieves again!" Zovenzoni recalls the Jewish attacks on Christ just before
describing the attacks on Simon by the Jews of Trent. Pusculo declares that "the
Lord God wished to encourage the minds of his faithful people by a new symbol
of his passion," and he later dwells on Christ's death. According to Calfurnio the
kidnapping and torture of Simon was "a mighty misdeed . . . prepared in mockery of Christ!"[85]

The authors also include details of supposed Jewish rites for which Simon's
body and blood were indispensable. All of the authors, except for Zovenzoni,
claim that the consumption of Simon's blood in pure form or as matzo was a cure
for Jewish body odor. Tiberino and Pusculo, who provide the greatest detail of
Jewish ceremonies and (erroneously) cite the Talmud, argue that the Jews curse
Christ and his followers daily, and Pusculo explains that the sacrifice of an innocent child was instituted at a (spuriously identified) Jewish council to replace
the sacrifice of a calf. All of the writers, with the exception of Calfurnio, mention
the attack on the "tip" or foreskin of Simon's penis, and in this way a specifically
Jewish practice is conflated with the bloodletting and torture of Simon by these
"dogs", "tigers of Hyrcania" (Vergil, *Aeneid* 4.367), and "wolves" as they are vari-
ously described.[86]

In their detailed descriptions of Simon's suffering body the authors intended
not only to draw the reader's attention to Jewish savagery but also to highlight the
Christ-like nature of Simon. In general, meditation on Christ's torments was a
central feature of late medieval piety and found expression in art and literature. In
particular, the attack on Simon's penis would remind the pious reader of Christ's
circumcision which had foreshadowed his own crucifixion and the redemptive flow
of blood offered as salvation for all suffering mankind. Just as Christ's bleeding
flesh in the form of the consecrated eucharistic wafer was thought to be attacked
by the Jews, so Simon's body is pierced and the blood drained off for ritual use. By
elaborating the curses and gestures employed by the Jews in this supposed rite the
writers of these tales must have sought—consciously or unconsciously—to deflect
scepticism about such alarming, and in many respects illogical, details and to con-
vince readers of the veracity of the case.[87]

---

[85] Below, 50–51, 54–55, 60–61, 90–91, 116–17.

[86] Below, 46–49, 92–93, 136–37.

[87] One early reader of Tiberino's tale underlined the prayer against Christians included in a copy of Giovanni Mattia Tiberino, *Relatio de Simone puero tridentino* (Augsburg: Monastery of SS. Ulrich and Afra, after 4 Apr. 1475), 15, now in the Bayerische
Staatsbibliothek, Munich (Inc.s.a.1891), and available digitally at www.bsb-muenchen.
de/ [consulted on 27 Feb. 2011]. This is one of only two manuscript annotations in this
copy. On Christian interest in Hebrew curses see Deutsch, "'A View of the Jewish Religion'," 282–85.

It is important to note that while the authors drew on scripture and medieval tales of Jewish host desecration and child murder, they also applied classical poetic meter, imagery, and style to heighten dramatic effect. Tiberino, Calfurnio, and Pusculo provide a plethora of classical phrases or images drawn from Lucretius, Vergil, Horace, and others. For example, both Tiberino and Calfurnio contrast the peacefulness of night with the anguished events of Simon's last hours in a way which recalls a key scene in the Vergilian story of Dido and Aeneas. Pusculo's lengthy work owes much to ancient epic, especially Vergil's *Aeneid* as its title suggests.[88] The classicization of the gruesome events of Trent served to bolster the authority of these tales and to raise them above vernacular trial records and vulgar discussion. The effect was carefully calculated to appeal to the educated elite of Renaissance Italy for whom classical Latin embodied the Roman virtues which they aimed to imitate. Tiberino praises Hinderbach as a patron of poets, while Calfurnio answers his question "Where now is antiquity?" with reference to Hinderbach's patronage and classical virtues; moreover, Francesco Tron is characterized as a Maecenas with the virtues of a Cato from whose lips "nothing that is not of Socratic depth falls." In this way the writers also flattered both their readership and themselves, and in doing so they increased the chances of success for the contested cult of Simon.[89]

In general, the authors seized on the details of Simon's torture and death and took pious pleasure in recounting his soul's migration to heaven and the miracles which were associated with his corpse. It should not be assumed that the authors simply intended to thrill a popular lay audience, but by writing in Latin they had in mind a more learned and elite readership—men and women whom they encountered in the course of their intellectual activities and active political roles. It is difficult to establish exactly who read these texts, but in Rome, as noted above, Michele Pacis was one early reader, and so too in all likelihood were the papal nephew Cristoforo della Rovere, the jurist Giovanni Francesco de Pavini, the humanist Pomponio Leto, the Venetian Cardinal Barbo, and the papal librarian Platina who was described as a supporter of Hinderbach and promoter of his cause at the papal court.[90] Hinderbach's letters to Zovenzoni in Venice were in circulation in Rome by October 1475, and the prince-bishop had to apologize to Zovenzoni for their publication, which had been far from his intention.[91] In Trent one unknown per-

---

[88] On this point see Korenjak, "Latin Poetry."

[89] On the antiquarian and classical interests shared by Hinderbach and Tiberino see Giovanni Dellantonio, "Felice Feliciano e gli amici del principe vescovo di Trento Iohannes Hinderbach: Raffaele Zovenzoni e Giovanni Maria [sic] Tiberino," in Contò and Quacquarelli, *L'Antiquario' Felice Feliciano*, 43–48.

[90] On their support for Hinderbach see Hsia, *Trent 1475*, 123–25, 164 n. 7; Dei Giudici, *Apologia Iudaeorum*, 22–23.

[91] Hinderbach to Zovenzoni, Trent, 1 Oct. 1475: Archivio di Stato, Trent, archivio principesco-vescovile, capsa 69, no. 10, fol. 6v.

son, probably Hinderbach, added comments to a series of notes which seem to have been connected with Pusculo's epic.[92] In Venice support for the cult came from a number of patricians, and from a secretary to the doge.[93]

a. Giovanni Mattia Tiberino

Giovanni Mattia Tiberino (*c.* 1420–*c.* 1500) was born at Chiari near Brescia and studied medicine in Pavia before moving to Trent to practice.[94] His prose account of the death of Simon was written very soon after the arrest and interrogation of the Jews and is dated 4 April 1475. Although his tale is ostensibly in the form of a letter originally sent to inform his Brescian contemporaries, the account was probably elicited by Hinderbach, who certainly praised its style in his letters to Zovenzoni. It is clear that Tiberino had deep religious convictions as well as poetic aspirations. On 2 July 1475 he composed a poem ("Cum tua, sancte Symon, lux sempiterna Tridenti") which demonstrated satisfaction with the recent executions of the Jews, and he produced a number of other poems on the subject including one in the form of a prayer to Simon ("Salve, sancte Symon, Christi pendentis ymago"), which dates to some time in 1478.[95] In that year Tiberino returned to the Bresciano, but he was back in Trent four years later following the death of his wife, his father, and his son Raffaele.[96] On 5 September 1482 Tiberino's *carmen* in praise of the Assumption of the Virgin Mary was pub-

---

[92] Archivio di Stato, Trent, archivio princepesco-vescovile, capsa 69, no. 202. Pusculo noted in his 1481 address to Maximilian that he wanted Hinderbach to read and approve his work: Parma, Biblioteca palatina, MS. Parm. 1583, fol. 56r.

[93] Hinderbach to Zovenzoni, Trent, 1 Oct. 1475: Archivio di Stato, Trent, archivio princepesco-vescovile, capsa 69, no. 10, fol. 6v.

[94] Filippo Maria Visconti, duke of Milan, granted the bishop of Trent feudal rights over Chiari in 1439–1441. Although these were rejected by Brescia and its new governor, Venice, they may help to explain why Tiberino became linked with Trent and with Hinderbach: Carlo Pasero, "Il dominio veneto fino all'incendio della loggia (1426–1575)," in *Storia di Brescia*, vol. 2: *La dominazione veneta (1426–1575)*, prom. and dir. Giovanni Treccani degli Alfieri (Brescia: Morcelliana, 1963), 3–396, here 123 n. 2. In addition, Hinderbach had been on friendly terms with Domenico de' Domenichi, the bishop of Brescia, since they met in Rome in 1466: Daniela Rando, *Dai margini la memoria: Johannes Hinderbach (1418–1486)* (Bologna: Il Mulino, 2003), 203–4. Tiberino was also resident at the archducal court in Innsbruck and dedicated a verse epic on the duke of Burgundy to Sigismund: Antonius Zingerle, *De Carminibus Latinis saeculi XV et XVI ineditis* (Innsbruck: Academicis Wagnerianis, 1880), 125–39.

[95] The dates are indicated below, 75.

[96] See the documents printed in Germano Jacopo Gussago, *Biblioteca Clarense: ovvero notizie istorico-critiche intorno agli scrittori e letterati di Chiari*, 3 vols. (Chiari: Tellaroli, 1820–1824), 1: 83–95, and nn. A biography of Tiberino by Enrico Gaia Bolpagni

lished in Trent together with several prayers and his poem in praise of Lake Iseo (near Brescia). The following year he delivered an elegy in praise of St Francis before Hinderbach in the Franciscan church in Trent.[97]

Like other humanist writers on Jewish matters, Tiberino claimed some expert knowledge of Hebrew rites,[98] and the text of his letter displays some of this basic understanding, albeit heavily reliant on the confessions extorted under torture. Most notable in the text is the emphasis placed on the ritual use of Christian blood by the Jews and their ritual denigration of Christ and other Christian enemies. This emphasis, as has been observed, served Hinderbach's campaign against the Jews in Trent very well, but it also must have reminded Brescians of the danger in their midst, for in the Brescian council regulations against Jews during the preceding thirty years the Jews were often accused of devouring and draining the substance of the poor or sucking the blood of Christians by means of their usurious exactions.[99] Tiberino's blood libel transformed this metaphor into reality.

Tiberino's charge was based on a confused understanding of different Jewish rites, and especially on the belief that Christian blood and curses or insults against Jesus Christ were present in these rites. For example, at the ceremonial circumcision of Jewish children the *mohel*, the rabbi who performed the operation, cleaned the bloody end of the penis with his mouth and spat the blood out into a cup of wine which some women regarded as an aid to conception. Tiberino and the other writers published here probably drew on this rite to describe an assault on the penis of Simon by the "priest" Moses, and it is worth noting that many of the images of Simon of Trent show him with an injured penis or in the process of being circumcised, or even castrated.[100] Furthermore, as some of the writers imperfectly grasped, at *Pesach* (Passover) according to the *Haggadah* the ritual sacrifice of the lamb memorialised the sacrifice of Abraham and signified

---

appears in *Profili biografici di umanisti bresciani*, ed. C. M. Monti and S. Signaroli (Brescia: Edizioni Torre d'Ercole, forthcoming).

[97] Antonio Fappani, "In margine al processo ed al culto del beato Simonino di Trento," *Brixia Sacra*, n.s. 7 (1972): 143–45, at 145 n. 4.

[98] Cf. Y. Deutsch, "Polemical Ethnographies. Descriptions of Yom Kippur in the Writings of Christian Hebraists and Jewish Converts to Christianity in Early Modern Europe," in *Hebraica Veritas?: Christian Hebraists and the Study of Judaism in Early Modern Europe*, ed. A. P. Coudert and J. S. Shoulson (Philadelphia: University of Pennsylvania Press, 2009), 202–33.

[99] Council *provvisioni* in ASC 500, 3 March 1463, fol. 12r; ASC 503, 6 June 1469, fol. 115r; ASC 505, 14 Oct. 1474, fol. 22v; and notably ASC 506, 16 Dec. 1479, fol. 65v.

[100] For example, a Florentine engraving of *c.* 1475–1485 in A. M. Hind, *Early Italian Engraving*, 3 vols. (New York and London: Quaritch, 1938), 3: plate 74. Above, 11–12, figs. 1 and 2.

the promise of the Jews' liberation from their enemies. Tiberino also suggested that the Jews of Trent employed curses in their ritual:

> Gathered all round, therefore, starting from Simon's crown and going down to his soles, they proceeded to pierce him with frequent blows, saying: *Tolle iesse mina elle parechief elle passusen pegmalen.* That is, "Let us butcher this boy just like Jesus, the Christians' God, who is nothing. Thus may our enemies be eternally confounded."

It is likely that these, and other curses recorded by Tiberino, were based on a distortion of the ritual maledictions or plagues intoned against the enemies of Israel at the *seder* feast, and drew on medieval Christian tales of the anti-Christian behavior and words of Jews supposedly encouraged by rabbis and Talmudic authorities.[101]

As already noted, the tales from Trent can be considered part of the humanist contribution to hagiography or sacred biography for which an important model was the *passio*, or narrative of the passion of Christ.[102] Tiberino frequently plays on the analogy between Christ's passion and the fate of Simon. He reminds the reader that God's mother was called Mary, as was Simon's mother. He points out the parallels between the story of Christ's betrayal by the Jews to Pontius Pilate and the events in Trent. In Tiberino's tale the action takes place over three days, like the passion of Christ.[103] Simon's mother Mary acts like the mother of Christ looking for her son among the neighbours (Luke 2: 44–45).[104] Simon is also presented like another Christ: he is imprisoned, tortured, and found in the mire (prefigured in Psalms 69, 88) in his swaddling clothes (Luke 2: 12). The analogy was taken further in the emphasis placed by Tiberino on Simon's silence throughout his ordeal except when he calls for his mother (cf. Matthew 27: 14, John 19: 26). This device not only indicated the youth and innocence of the child but also served to remind Christian readers of the few words uttered by the meek and lamb-like Christ in his passion (Acts 8: 32, cf. Isaiah 53: 7). In contrast, the Jews are depicted as canine, bestial like the enemies of Christ at his passion (Psalm 22: 12–21), and so they "howl", "pour forth loud cries", "shout", "babble", "spew forth", "rasp", and "curse."[105] In an echo of the same passage they part Simon's garments and they pierce his body (Psalm 22: 16–18).

---

[101] Below, 50–53. On medieval suspicions of Jewish blasphemy and the blood imagery of the Passover see Robert Chazan, *The Jews of Medieval Western Christendom, 1000–1500* (Cambridge: Cambridge University Press, 2006), 46, 56, 191–92.

[102] Frazier, *Possible Lives*, chap. 2.

[103] See below, 68–71.

[104] On late-medieval representations of the grieving Mary as a focus for hostility to Jews see Lansing, *Passion and Order*, 149.

[105] See below, 42–43, 48–49, 54–55. On animal imagery in the Good Friday passion psalm, Holy Week liturgy, and passion literature, see Marrow, *Passion Iconography*, 33–43, and 261 n. 120 (on its association with Jews). See also Kenneth R. Stow, *Jewish*

b. Raffaele Zovenzoni

Raffaele Zovenzoni (1434–*c.* 1485) was born in Trieste and studied at Ferrara under the eminent humanist Guarino Guarini Veronese before moving to Capodistria, the capital of Venetian Istria.[106] In 1467 Zovenzoni was appointed chancellor of Trieste, and during his tenure of office the city was marked by Guelph (pro-Venetian) and Ghibelline (pro-imperial) conflict before passing into imperial control. Although he favored Venetian rule and went into exile in Venice, Zovenzoni was crowned poet laureate by Emperor Frederick III in Trent, probably at the behest of his friend Hinderbach whom he had known during his student days in Ferrara.[107]

Zovenzoni naturally responded very willingly to his old friend's request for support in his campaign against the apostolic commissioner sent to investigate the case. Zovenzoni already had some experience of serving a noble patron and of turning a newsworthy event into verse: he wrote verses for the Venetian patrician Jacopo Antonio Marcello, and his *carmen* about the fall of Negroponte to the Turks was printed in Venice in *c.* 1470.[108] In a letter of October 1475 Hinderbach asked Zovenzoni to intervene with the ducal secretaries and other patricians in that city on his behalf, arguing that careful consideration should be given to the matter and that they should not act without hearing Hinderbach's views on the petitions of the papal legate, the *podestà* of Rovereto, and the Paduan doctors.[109] Zovenzoni, who had been a corrector of texts for Venetian printers including Vindelino da Spira and Nicholas Jenson, also offered two poems on the case and ensured their publication in Venice along with Tiberino's account and a letter from Hinderbach.[110] Zovenzoni subsequently visited Trent and dedicated his *Istriade*, a collection of verses in three books, to Hinderbach. The prince-bishop's

---

Dogs: An Image and its Interpreters; Continuity in the Catholic-Jewish Encounter (Stanford: Stanford University Press, 2006); Moshe Lazar, "The Lamb and the Scapegoat: The Dehumanization of the Jews in Medieval Propaganda Imagery'," in *Anti-Semitism in Times of Crisis*, ed. Sander L. Gilman and Steven T. Katz (New York: New York University Press, 1991), 38–80.

[106] The biographical information provided here is derived from Raffaele Zovenzoni, *La vita, i carmi*, ed. Baccio Ziliotto (Trieste: Comune di Trieste, 1950), 13–63.

[107] See his verses of gratitude directed towards Hinderbach in *I carmi*, nos. 3 and 66.

[108] Margaret L. King, *The Death of the Child Valerio Marcello* (Chicago: University of Chicago Press, 1994), 117; Meserve, "News from Negroponte," 466–67, 474.

[109] Hinderbach to Zovenzoni, Trent, 1 Oct. 1475: Archivio di Stato, Trent, archivio principesco-vescovile, capsa 69, no. 10, fols. 5v–7r.

[110] Zovenzoni, *La Vita*, nos. 250, 251.

copy of this work (which Hinderbach passed to Tiberino who admired it) included a portrait of Zovenzoni by the Venetian artist Giovanni Bellini.[111]

Zovenzoni's letters and poems dwell on the Jewish role in the passion of Christ, the details of Simon's torture, the virtue of Hinderbach, and the need for the Jews to be punished. There is every reason to suppose that Zovenzoni wrote with sincere belief in the cult of Simon and some personal animosity towards Jews: he introduces a highly personal note when he describes how his daughter was saved from death by means of a vow to Simon, and in his *Istriade* he included a poem in which he told Hinderbach about a Jew who had snatched away a friendship ring given to him by the prince-bishop.[112]

c. Ubertino Pusculo

Ubertino Pusculo (*c.* 1430–1504) studied Greek at Ferrara under Guarino Guarini Veronese before travelling to Constantinople where he witnessed the events of 1453 and wrote a Latin poem about the city's fall.[113] After being held prisoner for a year by the Turks he returned to Rome by way of Rhodes and Crete, and after a delay of three years he finally reached his native city of Brescia where he gave an oration in its praise.[114] He also composed a verse account in seven books of the siege of Brescia in 1438–1440 by the troops of the Visconti lord of Milan.[115] He opened a school in Brescia and became a key member of the local humanist

---

[111] Archivio di Stato, Milan, Trivulziano 776, published in *La Vita*. See also Jennifer Fletcher, "The Painter and the Poet: Giovanni Bellini's Portrait of Raffaele Zovenzoni Rediscovered," *Apollo: The International Magazine of the Arts*, 134/355 (Sept. 1991): 153–58.

[112] "D. IOANNI INDERBACCO ANTISTITI TRIDENTINO / Rex meus illustri digitum mihi cinxerat auro / aeternum nostrae pignus amicitiae. / Quod Malachar malus hostis inexorabilis acer, / pro dolor, eripuit, carius his occulis": Zovenzoni, *La vita*, no. 91. King, *Death of the Child*, 39, suggests that Zovenzoni may have been the anonymous tutor to Valerio Marcello who recorded in a consolatory work for his grieving father how the child had once been terrified by a Jew.

[113] Pusculo's *Constantinopolis* has been edited and published in *Analekten der mittel- und neugriechischen Literatur*, ed. V. Ellissen (Leipzig: Wigand, 1857). A new edition is reportedly being prepared by M. J. McGann and Estelle Haan of the Queen's University, Belfast. See also M. Philippides, *Mehmed II the Conqueror and the Fall of the Franco-Byzantine Levant to the Ottoman Turks*, MRTS 302 (Tempe: ACMRS, 2007), 51, 161–63.

[114] Ubertino Pusculo, "De laudibus Brixiae oratio," in Guerrini, *Cronache bresciane*, 2: 3–44.

[115] Ottavio Rossi, *Elogi historici de Bresciani illustri* (Brescia: Bartolomeo Fontana, 1620), 235; Leonardo Cozzando, *Libraria Bresciana prima, e seconda parte nuovamente aperta* (Brescia: Gio. Maria Rizzardi, 1694), 200.

networks.[116] In *c.* 1500 the Brescian humanist Daniele Cereto praised him for his knowledge of Greek and Latin.[117] He was recorded among those eligible to be chosen for conciliar membership in Brescia in 1493, and was later buried in the church of San Francesco.[118]

It is likely that on his return to Brescia from Trent in 1478 Tiberino suggested to his friend Pusculo that he write about Simon. A reference to the papal bull of 1478 in Pusculo's text suggests that he may have begun composition of the work at this date and, as already noted, Pusculo seems to have received payments for his work from Hinderbach in 1479 and again in 1480.[119] Tiberino appears to have urged Pusculo to finish his work, and when in 1481 Tiberino returned to Trent he brought a unique copy of Pusculo's verses to the prince-bishop. In a prefatory letter to the poem Pusculo declared that as soon as the prince-bishop had approved the text it should be made known to the public.[120]

One surviving version of the manuscript dating to *c.* 1481–1482 was prefaced by an address to Maximilian, son of the emperor. This address was suggested by Hinderbach after he read the original draft, and it was composed with hints from Tiberino.[121] Maximilian was probably singled out in this way as the local power with most sympathy for the case. The ruler of the neighboring County of Tirol until 1490 was Archduke Sigismund, who had called a halt to the Trent investigations at an early stage. Moreover, Hinderbach's personal relations with Emperor Frederick III, who might have been considered a more exalted addressee, seem to have deteriorated after 1467, and the emperor forbade Hinderbach from

---

[116] Paolo Guerrini, "Un umanista bagnolese prigioniero dei Turchi a Constantinopoli e a Rodi," *Brixia Sacra* 6 (1915): 261–71. I have not seen *Pyladis Brixiani Carmen scholasticum solerti cura impressum; singulisque mendis (ut in annotationibus patet) expurgatum per Ubertinum filium domini Iohannis Petri Pusculi Monteclari habitatoris* (Brescia: Ludovico Britannico, 1553). A biography of Pusculo by Enrico Valseriati appears in Monti and Signaroli, *Profili biografici di umanisti.*

[117] Daniele Cereto, *De foro, et laudibus Brixiae ad Magnificum Ludovicum Martinengum libellus*, ed. B. Zamboni (Brescia: Vescovi, 1778), X. As Pandolfo Nassini recorded in his register of Brescian matters in *c.* 1530: "[Pusculo] fu m[agist]ro de scola al mio tempo homo reputato et da bene, cosa che non se trova più questa stampa stava presso S. Antonio in Bressa, qual m.ro se chiamava mr. Ubertino Pusculo dotto in greco et in latino . . ." Quoted in Lechi, *Le dimore bresciane*, 4: 449.

[118] ASC 514, 12 May 1493, fol. 80r; Virginio Cremona, "L'umanesimo bresciano," in *Storia di Brescia*, 2: 568 (plate of tombstone).

[119] Above, n. 34; below, 204–7.

[120] Pusculo to Hinderbach, Brescia, 29 June 1481: Parma, Biblioteca palatina, MS. Parm. 1583, fol. 55r; below, 120–21.

[121] Pusculo to Maximilian, Parma, Biblioteca palatina, MS. Parm. 1583, fol. 56r. A reference to Maximilian's wife Mary of Burgundy, who died in March 1482, helps to date this address.

obtaining promotion to the cardinalate.[122] Frederick also "intervened forcefully to stop the escalation of persecutions" of Jews at Endingen in 1470, and interfered again in favour of the Jews at Regensburg in 1476. Maximilian likewise intervened to assert imperial authority at a ritual murder trial in Freiburg in 1504, but he seems to have been a strong supporter of the cult of Simon as early as 1479 and subsequently erected a monument in his honor, ordered Simon's coffin opened to visitors, and displayed the relics of Simon in a procession in his honor when he became emperor in 1508. Hinderbach may have admired Maximilian's patronage of humanists and would probably have been been pleased by Maximilian's role in the Reuchlin affair when in 1509 the emperor initially supported a campaign to confiscate Jewish books and examine them for anti-Christian sentiments.[123]

In composing his work Pusculo almost certainly read Tiberino's letter and other works, and he may have consulted Giovanni de Salis who returned to Brescia when his term of office as *podestà* in Trent finished in 1476. Salis was subsequently very active in his campaign against the Jews in Brescia, and is recorded kneeling at the feet of Bernadino da Feltre when he came to preach in the city in 1494.[124] In a letter of July 1480 Salis told Hinderbach about his involvement in the Portobuffolè case and mentioned the miracles associated with Simon that had taken place in the Bresciano. He went on to note that Pusculo had promised to emend and correct a work for Hinderbach.[125] These close links probably explain why Hinderbach and de Salis receive such prominence in Pusculo's epic—much more than in the other works—and in this sense it can be classed as a panegyrical epic.[126]

The subsequent history of Pusculo's work is rather obscure and the passage of the work to print may have been hindered by its length. Two complete manuscript versions survive in libraries in Parma and Vienna, while a manuscript preserved in the state archive in Trent includes material not in the other two manu-

---

[122] On Hinderbach, Sigismund, and Frederick see Hsia, *Trent 1475*, 9, 129. Zovenzoni appealed to Sixtus IV, Frederick III, and Sigismund to act decisively against the Jews, while Tiberino appealed only to Sixtus and Frederick. Pusculo claims that Sigismund was offered gold by the Jews but also inspired by Simon's miracles: below, 192–95.

[123] Hsia, *Trent 1475*, 129; idem, *Myth of Ritual Murder*, 35–36, 77, 103–6. On Maximilian as patron of humanists see James H. Overfield, *Humanism and Scholasticism in Late Medieval Germany* (Princeton: Princeton University Press, 1984), 135–36, 208–11; on the emperor's role in the Reuchlin affair see 248–51.

[124] ASC 514, 30 June 1494, fols. 69v–70r; *Sermoni del beato Bernardino Tomitano da Feltre nella redazione di Fra Bernardino Bulgarino da Brescia Minore Osservante*, ed. P. Carlo Varischi da Milano, 3 vols. (Milan: Renon, 1964), 1: XXXVIII.

[125] "Magister Albertinus [sic] Poscolus habuit opusculum illud et omnia . . . corrigere et emendare pollicitus est": De Salis to Hinderbach, Brescia, 10 July 1480, in Esposito and Quaglioni, *Processi contro gli ebrei*, 448–54 (quotation at 452–53).

[126] See Korenjak, "Latin Poetry."

scripts. The Tridentine notes do not conform either to classical Latin norms of scansion or the accentual rhythms typical of some medieval Latin poetry, but are a very loose mixture of the two. The editorial directions there indicate that the author of the material in the Trent manuscript had the Viennese manuscript in front of him and intended these notes to be incorporated into a version of Pusculo's epic.[127] The passages intended for insertion emphasize the Jews' stinginess and resort to bribery, and also give great weight to miraculous events favouring Christian fortitude and belief. In addition, there are comments alongside these notes in a hand very similar to Hinderbach's, and, given its location in the episcopal files, it seems reasonable to surmise that this manuscript is connected with the work of review and emendation undertaken by Hinderbach when he received Pusculo's unique copy of the verses about Simon in 1481.

The manuscript now in Vienna is a fair copy on vellum with two illuminated initials showing the murder of Simon by Jews and his mutilated body. This version does not include the additions in the Trent manuscript, nor does it include the address to Maximilian, which is in the Parma manuscript. There is a concluding verse with a reference to Sigismund, so it must date to the period before the archduke's death in 1496. The prefatory verse to Emperor Maximilian by Johannes Kurtz von Eberspach was probably added after the completion of the original manuscript, perhaps as much as three decades later.[128] Maximilian visited Kurtz's home town of Augsburg in March 1508, shortly after he became emperor, and it may have been on this occasion that the humanist took the opportunity to present him with a work which would have been of interest to the emperor. In any case, Kurtz was enthusiastic about the poem and had it published in Augsburg in 1511, claiming that it had lain hidden for many years and that he had obtained the manuscript from Christopher Romer of Bolzano who had been given it by the humanist Dr Christian Umhauser.[129]

The scribal circulation of a poem in classicized Latin about a sensational case of ritual murder is hardly surprising, and it seems to have moved straightforwardly enough along a north-south route between Trent and Munich via Bolzano and Innsbruck. The publication in Augsburg may be explained by the fact

---

[127] "In folio octavo proxime sequenti eiusdem libri Secundi in tertio versus ibi: 'Egerit et siquid sibi conscia noverit uxor'.": Archivio di Stato, Trent, archivio princepesco-vescovile, capsa 69, no. 202, fol. 3r. This corresponds to the correct line on the eighth folio of the second book in Vienna, Österreichische Nationalbibliothek, Codex Vindobonensis Palatinus, series nova 12,822, fol. 25r.

[128] Vienna, Österreichische Nationalbibliothek, Codex Vindobonensis Palatinus, series nova 12,822. The verse at fol. 1r is in a different, rather untidy, hand and is not illuminated or decorated.

[129] See Appendix 2; Frieder Schanze, "Kurtz, Johann," in *Die deutsche Literatur des Mittelalters: Verfasserlexikon*, ed. Kurt Ruh et al., 2nd ed. (Berlin and New York: de Gruyter, 1985), 5: cols. 463–68.

that the city was the leading center for printing in the empire, although it seems as if the printer did not understand some of the abbreviations used in the manuscript from which he was working, and in most instances where there is a difference between the Vienna manuscript and the Augsburg edition the former is better. In any case, the Augsburg publishers were probably aware of the anti-Jewish feeling at the heart of the Reuchlin affair which erupted in the empire and spread to the Universities of Paris and Louvain between 1507 and 1520. In 1510 an imperial commission recommended the confiscation of Jewish books suspected of containing anti-Christian sentiments, while several universities submitted anti-Jewish opinions to Maximilian. In contrast, Johannes Reuchlin reminded Maximilian that Jews had the same rights as Christians thanks to their position as subjects of the emperor, and he argued that the Talmud and the Cabala (based on mystical Hebrew texts), were worthy of study. Pusculo presented his work as a warning to Christians to avoid all contact with Jews, and it is not difficult to imagine how an edition of his account of the murder at Trent printed in the week preceding the commemoration of the passion of Christ in 1511 might have provided ammunition for the opponents of Reuchlin.[130]

In Book 1 of his work on the Trent case Pusculo attacks the "savage race" of the Jews and contrasts them with the innocence of the martyred child Simon. The Jews, he says, had been chosen by God to receive his laws but they were guilty of bringing about the death of Christ. That crime, which had led to divine punishment, was compounded by Jewish obstinacy in the face of the revealed truth of God, which they continued to deny. The exiled Jews subsequently insinuated themselves into society by practicing usury or, as in the case of Tobias, acting as doctors who could pass freely through Christian society. By contrast, Simon is presented by Pusculo as a young innocent with a simple vocabulary (the often repeated cry of "Mama") and humble background with whom the reader is meant to sympathise. More than this, by denouncing the Jewish conspiracy in Trent and throughout Europe, and by describing in great detail the torture of Simon, Pusculo seems intent on dispelling any doubts about the case against the Jews, bolstering Simon's credentials as a martyr, and supporting Hinderbach's campaign of persecution and expulsion.

In the second book of his verse epic Pusculo describes the struggle between "justice and gold" which followed the death of Simon. On the one hand, the Jews turn to gold in order to bribe others to remove the corpse of Simon, to gain access to the authorities, or to pervert the course of justice. However, the *podestà* Giovanni de Salis is presented as a careful investigator of the affair, alert to clues, immune to bribery, and dogged in his pursuit of the truth to which he seems guided

---

[130] Overfield, *Humanism and Scholasticism*, chap. 7, emphasizes the anti-Jewish feelings in this matter. See Erika Rummel, *The Case Against Johann Reuchlin: Religious and Social Controversy in Sixteenth-Century Germany* (Toronto: University of Toronto Press, 2002).

by divine inspiration. He acts with Hinderbach to bring about justice: the Jews' crimes are revealed in a series of confessions and punishment is swiftly executed. Meanwhile, the justice of Simon's cause as martyr is underlined by his mother's laments, the miracles associated with him, the attack by young boys on the papal envoy who is accused of corruption, and the climactic voluntary conversion of one of the Jewish women who is then consigned to the bonfire.

Pusculo's work, as noted above, can be considered an epic in the Vergilian mould with many allusions to the *Aeneid* and a number of similar characteristics, including the hexameter form, artfully constructed speeches, descriptions of the town, and historical notes. As Martin Korenjak has pointed out, the tale of the Jews' hatred for the Christians echoes the account of the enmity between Carthage and Rome in the Vergilian description of the love of Dido and Aeneas, while their rage and fury may be compared with the wrath of Juno. However, it should be noted that some classical allusions in the text may equally be related to scriptural passages, and Korenjak has concluded that the work may also be regarded as a Christian epic, indeed the very first martyr epic in neo-Latin literature, with the pagan Muse displaced explicitly by God and the Virgin as the source of inspiration. [131]

d. Giovanni Calfurnio

Giovanni Perlanza dei Ruffinoni (*c.* 1433–1503), usually but obscurely called 'Calfurnio', was born in the Bergamasco but often referred to himself as Brescian, or was claimed as such by Brescian writers since he completed some of his studies in the city before taking up the post of professor of rhetoric in Padua in 1486. [132] Calfurnio, who has been described as "[a]n honest plodder rather than a front-runner" among the humanists involved with the world of print, seems to have attached himself to Antonio Moretto, a Brescian publisher in Venice. [133] Between 1478 and 1481 Calfurnio edited works published in Venice, Treviso, and Vicenza. [134]

---

[131] Korenjak, "Latin Poetry." For allusions by Tiberino and Pusculo which are both classical and scriptural see below, 43 n. 3, 141 nn. 1, 2.

[132] Capriolo, *Chronica,* fol. LXXXr; Cremona, "L'umanesimo bresciano," 546–51; below, 84–85.

[133] Lowry, *Nicholas Jenson,* 127.

[134] John Monfasani, "Calfurnio's Identification of Pseudepigrapha of Ognibene, Fenestella, and Trebizond, and his Attack on Renaissance Commentaries," *Renaissance Quarterly* 41 (1988): 32–43.

Calfurnio's *Mors et apotheosis Simonis infantis novi martyris* was published in Trent in *c.* 1481 and dedicated to the Venetian patrician Francesco Tron.[135] In 1476 Tron "cum multis aliis nobilibus Venetis" was cited as a supporter of the cult of Simon in Venice by the Franciscan preacher Michele Carcano in a letter to Hinderbach.[136] Tron was Venetian ambassador to the prince-bishop of Trent in 1480.[137] According to Calfurnio, Tron had urged him to put his account of Simon's death down on paper. Calfurnio duly composed his work in Venice and finished it by the time Tron had completed his tour of duty in Trent and had taken up a post at Riva del Garda. Calfurnio praised Tron extravagantly, and the patrician may even have ensured that the work, which was sent to him at Riva del Garda, was printed at Trent by Giovanni Leonardo Longo. Calfurnio's account of Simon's death is clearly based on the text of Tiberino, and, while more self-consciously humanist in style than Tiberino's rather more plain or pious compositions, it adds few details and largely serves to flatter Hinderbach, Tron, and his brother with extravagant praise of their learning, virtues, and achievements.

VII. Conclusion

News of Simon of Trent's murder was noted by Italians in their diaries and chronicles, reworked in verse and prose, and represented in churches and in prints as the martyred innocent flanked by the instruments of his torture and death: cloak, needles and pincers. The cult received support from the emperor's son, the prince-bishop, some Venetian patricians, Brescian nobles and citizens, and from humanists, and it aroused strong popular devotion in parts of northern Italy. Even if it was not "on everyone's lips" as Hinderbach hoped,[138] nevertheless the humanist authors of the narrative of Jewish perfidy and infanticide drew on established stereotypes and social attitudes and reached out to a larger audience via the new medium of print and with the impressive language of classical Latin. In doing so, Tiberino, Calfurnio, Zovenzoni, Pusculo, and others helped to turn it into one of the most notorious cases of ritual child murder in European history.

---

[135] The poem was also printed, together with a poem in praise of Hinderbach, in Catullus, *Carmina*, ed. Giovanni Calfurnio (Vicenza: Giovanni da Reno and Dionysius Bertochus, 1481), sigs. y r-[y 3 v].

[136] Carcano to Hinderbach, Trent, 6 Nov. 1476, in Paolo Sevesi, "Beato Michele Carcano, O.F.M. Obs., 1427–84 (documenti inediti)," *Archivum Franciscanum Historicum* 33 (1940): 366–408, here 396.

[137] Archivio di Stato, Venice, Senato deliberazioni secreta, reg. 29, fols. 126r–v, 127r.

[138] Calfurnio notes: "There are also people who, only just returned from the Muses' spring, seem to condemn my poem in this respect: that it is more fitting to employ one's talent in trivialities." Below, 98–99.

Section I

SECTION I

[p. 1] Raphael Zovenzonius M[agistro] Gabriel Sal[utem].

Imprime tu, Gabriel, nostri nova gloria saecli,
    Iudaei horrendum quod peperere nefas!
Imprime millenis, precor, o precor, imprime chartis,
    omnis ut, heu, possit noscere[1] posteritas!

Ioannes Hinderbach, divina pietate antistes Tridentinus, suo Raphaeli Zovenzonio Tergestino poetae Augu[sti] laureato salutem plurimam.

Venit ad nos frater Nicolaus Cruciger tuus visitandi gratia, non tam suo proprio quam tuo nomine; necnon visendi innocentis pueri ab impiis noxiisque Hebraeis hoc paschali tempore in civitate nostra, heu, nequiter occisi, inquirendaeque veritatis causa, tam de eius nece quam miraculorum quae indies crebro apud eius tumbam fiunt, et ab omnibus perspicue videri possunt et lustrari, prout et ipse vidit et audivit. At tibi ceterisque fidelibus referre poterit. Facti vero seriem — quo ordine hoc facinus a perfidis Iudaeis patratum sit — Ioannes Mathias physicus noster Clarensis admodum claro atque eleganti stilo, nuper a suis patriotis, qui magna frequentia huius rei causa huc venerant, rogatus ut ad suos scriberet, prae-[p. 2] toribus civitatis Brixiae epistolam misit, cuius copiam tibi edi iussimus;

---

[1] *correxi*: noscete *P*

SECTION I

[p. 1] Raffaele Zovenzoni greets Master Gabriele [di Pietro].[1]

> Print it—you, Gabriele, new glory of our age—print the horrible outrage
>   that the Jews have committed!
> Print it, I beg you, O I beg you, print it on a thousand sheets, so that all
>   posterity, alas, can learn about it!

Johannes Hinderbach, by God's goodness bishop of Trent, warmly greets his friend Raffaele Zovenzoni of Trieste, laureate of the emperor.[2]

Your friend, Brother Niccolò Cruciger, has been to visit me, not so much on his own behalf as on yours; and also to see the innocent boy who, alas, has been foully slain by impious and villainous Hebrews in our city at this Eastertide, and to inquire into the truth about his death, as well as the truth of the miracles which frequently occur each day at his tomb, and which can be clearly seen and observed by all, as he himself has also seen and heard. But he will be able to report this to you and the rest of the faithful. However, my physician Giovanni Mattia [Tiberino] of Chiari having recently been asked by his compatriots (who had come here in large numbers because of this affair) to write to his own people about the sequence of events—in what stages this crime was committed by the faithless Jews[3]—[p. 2] has sent the city of Brescia's magistrates a very lucidly and

---

[1] All the texts in this section up to and including Zovenzoni's poem "Surgite pontifices:" ("Arise, you bishops") are in *P* and are paginated accordingly.

The meter of this opening exhortation, as with several of the shorter poems in all three sections, is the elegiac couplet (a dactylic hexameter followed by a pentameter), as perfected by the Roman classical poets Catullus and Ovid.

[2] Zovenzoni was crowned poet laureate by Emperor Frederick III in Trent, probably at the behest of his friend Hinderbach whom he knew in Ferrara as a student. Biographical details are in Raffaele Zovenzoni, *La vita, i carmi*, ed. Baccio Ziliotto (Trieste: Comune di Trieste, 1950), 13–63.

[3] The adjective *perfidus*, and the cognate noun *perfidia*, are sometimes applied to the Jews by several of the writers represented in the present book, probably because of a medieval prayer in the Church's Good Friday liturgy which appeared in the Tridentine Mass: "Oremus et pro perfidis Judaeis: ut Deus et Dominus noster auferat velamen de cordibus eorum; ut et ipsi agnoscant Jesum Christum, Dominum nostrum." Though *perfidus* was here translated as 'perfidious' until recent times, after World War II the translation

et per praefatum fratrem Nicolaum ad te deferri debere credebamus. Sed hic, taedio fortasse expectationis et morae affectus, hinc iam discesserat. In qua nihil confictum credito, sed omnia prout rei veritas se habet descripta fore firmiter teneto, ceterisque veluti verissimum referto.

Tu autem, pro tua singulari erga nos et fidei Christi devotione, hanc rem veluti impiissimam a Iudaeis ipsis vere perpetratam tuis carminibus poemateque execrare, et hunc novellum martyrem nostrum, prout meretur, verbis tuis adornato, ut omnibus Christicolis pateat, et per ora cunctorum haec res palam fiat et praedicetur—ad laudem Omnipotentis Dei et fidei nostrae Christianae exaltationem, huiusque novelli martyris et urbis nostrae glorificationem, atque horum nostrorum temporum, quas[1] Deus nobis tribuit inter alia eius munera, gratiarum maiorem commendationem. Et quicquid in hanc rem scripseris ad nos quam primum transmittito. Aderunt prope diem Ascensionis Dominicae cives Tridentini aput vos, et praecipue Stephanus noster, per quem hanc mittimus, qui ea ad nos referet.

De Iudaeis vero [p. 3] iamdudum sup[p]licium quod merentur sumptum esset, nisi essent falsi Christiani aurum illorum magis quam mortem aut poenam quam merentur sitientes, qui apud illustrissimum Principem Ducem Austriae—ex cuius sententia et arbitrio nostrum pendere necesse est—quibusdam falsis suggestionibus pollicitisve maximis effecerunt, ut post elicitam et extortam a Iudaeis veritatem aliquanto supersederi in hac re fecerit, donec de re ipsa clarius fuerit informatus; et hoc idem etiam apud clementissimum Imperatorem agitari formidamus. Non deficit tamen ultrix Dei manus: quae unum ex procuratoribus eorundem in oppido Reveredi vallis Langarinae divino quodam iustissimo ignis et

---

[1] *correxi*: quam *P*

elegantly phrased letter, the full text of which I have ordered to be shown to you; and I believed that the aforesaid Brother Niccolò was the right person to bring it to you. But he, perhaps affected by the weariness of waiting and delay, had already left here. Please believe that nothing in this letter is made up, but rest assured that you will find everything described in exact accordance with the truth, and report it to the others as absolutely true.

Bearing in mind, however, your remarkable devotion towards us and to faith in Christ, I ask that in your lyrical poetry you curse this as an utterly impious act, truly perpetrated by the Jews themselves, and that in your words you honor this new little martyr of ours as he deserves, so that this affair may be revealed to all Christ-worshipers and, by being on everyone's lips, may be publicly known and proclaimed—to the praise of almighty God and the heightening of our Christian faith, and to the glorification of this new little martyr and of our city, and a greater appreciation of the blessings, present to us here and now, which God has granted us amongst his other gifts! And please send on to me as soon as possible whatever you write on this matter. Very soon, on Ascension Day, some of Trent's citizens will be with you, and in particular my friend Stephen, by whom I am sending this letter, and who will bring those words of yours back to me.

From the Jews, however, [p. 3] the penalty they deserve would long since have been exacted, had there not been false Christians thirsting more for those people's gold than for the death or punishment they deserve, and who by certain false suggestions or grand promises have had such influence with the most illustrious archduke of Austria—on whose opinion and authority my own authority inevitably hangs—that, now when the truth has been coaxed and forced out of the Jews, he has brought about a temporary moratorium in this matter, until he has been more clearly informed about the actual facts; and I fear that this same idea is also being bandied about at the court of the most merciful emperor. Yet God's avenging hand does not fail: it has miraculously struck one of the same people's proctors[1] with a sort of divine and perfectly just judgment of fire and boiling water in the town of Rovereto in the Langarine valley, so that he was al-

---

'faithless' was accepted as more accurate, since the word refers not to the Jews' supposed perfidy but to their lack of faith in Jesus as the Christ, and since Vatican II (1962–1965) and the encyclical *Nostra aetate* (1965) all such derogatory references to the Jews have disappeared from the liturgy: see Jean-Claude Guillebaud, *Re-Founding the World: A Western Testament*, trans. W. Donald Wilson (New York: Algora Publishing, 2001), 286. Throughout the present book we have consistently translated *perfidus* as 'faithless', and *perfidia* as 'faithlessness'.

[1] See *A Miracle*, below, 59. For the importance of representation by proctors (*procuratores*) in late medieval Europe, see Robert Brentano, *Two Churches: England and Italy in the Thirteenth Century* (Princeton: Princeton University Press, 1968), 22–28 and 35–48: "Proctors received grants of land and loans; they appeared for the parties in law suits, and sought privileges from governments" (26–27).

aquae ferventis iudicio miraculose percussit, ut totus paene vivus crematus et exustus sit, et a Christianis domibus repulsus inter Iudaeos, quorum erat procurator, miser eiulansque lectulo voce penitus amissa decumbat, et suum reatum defleat—ultimumque, ut creditur, spiritum sit emissurus. Speramus tamen brevi cessare abrogarique hanc Principis Austriae intercessionem sive voluntatem, ex falsa sinistraque aliquorum perversorum suggestione provenientem, ipsumque et omnes de veritate huius rei luce meridiana clariore infor-[p. 4] mari.

Nec plura. Vale, mi Raphael, et, si quo potes modo, veni, vide et mirare hoc sanctum venerandumque corpusculum, quod Dei gratia adhuc integrum illaesumque servatur, omnibusque patet huc adventantibus—quorum tantus ex omni parte Italiae Germaniaeque nostrae quotidie confluit numerus, ut Ecclesia Sancti Petri, in qua tenetur, admodum angusta sit et illos continere non possit, neque etiam cap[p]ella ubi repositum est signa illic relicta servare. Videbis enim mirabilia Dei, quae in hoc puerulo operatur, et impiam Iudaeorum hanc gentem, et a Christi gratia penitus prophanam, meritas pro tanto facinore luere poenas; hortosque virentes nostros, at moenia arcem, vivosque de vivo marmore profluere fontes. Ex Arce nostra Boni Consilii Tridentina, iam fere tota circumcirca innovata, pridie calen[das] Maias.

M.CCCC.LXXV.

[p. 5] Ioannes Mathias Tyberinus Clarensis, artium et medicinae doctor, Raphaeli Zovenzonio, p[oetae] cla[rissimo] sal[utem].[1]

Rem maximam, qualem a passione Domini ad haec usque tempora nulla unquam aetas audivit, ad te scribo, Raphael Zovenzoni,[2] quam[3] nuper his diebus elapsis Dominus noster Iesus Christus, humano benigne misertus generi, tanto tamque horribili scelere stomachatus, tandem produxit in lucem, ut Catholica fides nostra, si qua in parte debilis est, fiat tanquam turris fortitudinis, et antiqua Iudaeorum rabies toto ex orbe Christiano deleatur, et de terra viventium eorum

---

[1] S. Simonis martyris *for* Ioannes . . . Salutem *B* Joannes Mathias Tiberinus, liberalium artium et medicinae Doctor, magnificis Rectoribus, Senatui populoque Brixiano salutem *for* Ioannes . . . Salutem *A*

[2] ad vos scribo, Magnifici Rectores civesque praeclarissimi *for* ad te . . . Zovenzoni *BA*

[3] et quam *for* quam *B*

most completely burned and fried alive, and now, after being driven away from Christian homes into the company of the Jews, whose proctor he was, he lies sick on his bed moaning pitifully, his voice completely lost, and laments his own guilt—and, as is believed, is about to breathe his last. We hope, however, that this veto or wish of the prince of Austria, proceeding as it does from the false and immoral suggestion of certain misguided people, will soon cease and be revoked, and that he himself and everyone else will be informed of the truth of this matter, which is clearer than the midday sun. [p. 4]

No more now. Farewell, my dear Raffaele, and, if at all possible, do come, see and marvel at this holy and venerable little body, which by the grace of God is still preserved whole and unimpaired, and is on view for all those coming here—so many of whom stream in each day from all over Italy and my native Germany that St Peter's Church, where it is kept, is far too small to contain them, nor even is the chapel where the body has been laid big enough to house the tokens left there. For you will see God's wonders, which he works in the person of this small boy, and see that this race of Jews, impious and utterly cut off from Christ's grace, is paying the penalty they deserve for so great a crime; you will also see my verdant gardens, the citadel near the city walls, and see living waters cascading down living marble. Sent from my castle of Buonconsiglio in Trent, now almost totally restored on all sides, April 30th.

1475

[p. 5] Giovanni Mattia Tiberino of Chiari, doctor of arts and medicine, greets Raffaele Zovenzoni, renowned poet.[1]

I am writing to you, Raffaele Zovenzoni, about a most important event such as no era—from the Lord's passion up to these times—has ever heard of, one which recently in these past days our Lord Jesus Christ, kindly pitying the human race and enraged by so great and so heinous a crime, has at last brought forth into the light, so that our Catholic faith, if it is weak in any respect, may become—so to speak—a tower of strength, and so that the ancient, savage race of the Jews may be eliminated from the whole Christian world, and remembrance

---

[1] This letter of Tiberino (together with the attached verses titled "A Miracle") exists in other versions apart from that of *P*, which alone contains all the first three documents included in this section. We have therefore taken *P* as our basic text, but show in the text-notes where (for grammatical or contextual reasons) we have preferred variant readings found in two other versions (identified as *A* and *B*). For full details of all three versions see our introductory note on texts.

penitus memoria pereat. Audite, qui regitis populos, inauditum scelus, et pasto-
rum more fidelium vestris populis invigilate! Expergiscantur habitantes terram
et videant quales in sinu proprio viperas nutriant![1] Crudeles Iudaei non solum
Christianorum res rabiosa usurarum fame consumunt, sed in capita nostra per-
niciemque coniurati, filiorum nostrorum vivo sanguine depascuntur,[2] quos atroci
in synagogis suis affligunt sup[p]licio et instar Christi crudeli funere iugulant.

Nuper in civitate Tridentina, quae versus Aquilonem Italiam a Germa-
nia Laviso[3] flumine interlabente disterminat—ea in regione quae ab Athesis
ponte [p. 6] recedens versus castellum a laeva protenditur—tres Iudaeorum
familiae considebant,[4] quorum capita fuere Tobias, Angelus[5] et Samuel; apud
quem senex quidam barbatus[6] Moyses nomine, quem venturi Messiae tempus et horam prophetico spiritu scire decantabant. Hi ea in hebdomade[7] quam
nos Christiani Sanctam appellamus, die Martis xii[8] calendas Aprilis anno ab
Incarnati Verbi septuagesimo quinto supra millenum quatercentenum, con-
venerunt in domum[9] Samuelis, ubi synagoga et eorum templum est,[10] spec-
tandi gratia viventem vitulum, qui ad eos ea luce de Levigi pago delatus erat.
Et dum inter se plurima vario sermone conferrent, Angelus hanc rabido fudit

---

[1] nutriant *A* nutriunt *PB*
[2] pascuntur *A*
[3] Lavisio *A*
[4] considebant *A* consedebant *PB*
[5] Angelus, tobias *B*
[6] barbatus quidam *B*
[7] epdemoda *B* hebdomado *A*
[8] duodecimo *A*
[9] in domo *B*
[10] est *A om. PB*

of them utterly vanish from the land of the living.[1] Listen, you rulers of peoples, to the unheard-of crime, and watch over your peoples as faithful shepherds should! Let earth's denizens awake and see what snakes they are nurturing in their own bosom![2] The cruel Jews not only eat up Christians' property in their frenzied craving for interest payments but, conspiring against our lives and for our destruction, they feast on the living blood of our sons,[3] afflicting them with terrible punishment in their synagogues and cruelly slaughtering them in place of Christ.

Recently in the city of Trent, which separates northern Italy from Germany, with the River Adige flowing between them—in the area which, leading from the Athesis Bridge, [p. 6] extends towards the fortress on the left bank—there dwelt three families of Jews headed by Tobias, Engel, and Samuel; with the last was a certain bearded old man named Moses who, so they babbled,[4] knew by prophetic inspiration the time and hour of the Messiah who was to come. These men, during what we Christians call Holy Week, on the twenty-first of March in the one thousand four hundred and seventy-fifth year of the Word Incarnate, met in Samuel's house, the place of their synagogue and temple, to look at a live calf which had been brought to them that morning from the Levico district.[5] And while they were exchanging various remarks on many topics, Engel poured forth these words from his frenzied breast: "On this Day of Preparation we have plenty of flesh and fish. We lack only one thing." Samuel answered: "What are you

---

[1] Cf. Job 18: 17: "His remembrance shall perish from the earth, and he shall have no name in the street."

[2] Cf. Erasmus, *Adagia* 4.20.40 ("colubrum in sinu fovere").

[3] The eucharistic overtones of this description are clear. See Caroline Walker Bynum, *Wonderful Blood*, 168–72. Bynum notes that "theology, devotion, and practice in the fifteenth century simply assume that blood itself . . . is alive. Some kind of traditional idea . . . that blood is life seems to fuse with the idea that *Blut Christi* is miraculous" (cf. Leviticus 17: 11, 14). She also notes that descriptions of Christ's blood in devotional writings of the period "are not only evocations of his suffering love" but "are also references to baptism, penance, and eucharist," and that the characteristics of blood so vividly portrayed in such writings—its liquidness and redness—"convey a sense that *sanguis Christi* is the true continuing—because living—presence of Christ here on earth" (168, 171). For the use of the expression 'living blood' in classical literature, see Ovid, *Metamorphoses* 5. 436–437, where the nymph Cyane's blood is replaced by water ("denique pro vivo vitiatas sanguine venas / lympha subit . . ."), and Statius, *Thebaid* 8. 760–761, where Athena sees Tydeus gnawing Melanippus' severed head ("atque illum effracti perfusum tabe cerebri / aspicit et vivo scelerantem sanguine fauces").

[4] The first of several emotive verbs used by Tiberino, *decantare* (literally "to sing off") usually implies parrot-like repetition. Note the juxtaposition of the names Tobias and 'Angel', as in the Book of Tobit. On Moses, who lived in the household of Samuel, see Appendix 2.

[5] Levico was a town near Trent.

de pectore vocem: "In isto Parasceve et carnes et pisces abunde nobis sunt. Unum tantum nobis deest." Respondit Samuel: "Et quid te[1] deficit?" Tunc, coniectis oculis adinvicem, taciti omnes intellexerunt quod de immolando Christiano infante[2] loqueretur,[3] quem in contemptum[4] Domini nostri Iesu Christi mactant atrociter, et exhausto sanguine vescentes in azimis[5] suis a foetore, quo graviter olent,[6] Christiano se cruore praeservant. Huncque suum appellant Iobel,[7] id est, Iubilaeum. Sed annuebant cautius eloquendum fore propter servos, qui ob instans Parasceven[8] diversis impediti ministeriis, nunc huc nunc illuc[9] discurrebant.

Postero autem [p. 7] die,[10] cum omnes in synagoga convenissent, consultabant quonam[11] in loco possent illum aptius occidere. Tobias et Angelus in domibus suis, earum ob angustiam, fieri recusabant, propterea quod exiguo in loco difficile esset a pueris tam vastum facinus abscondere. Sed propter rerum omnium commoditatem et amplitudinem loci melius apud Samuelem fore asseverabant. At ubi sic decrevissent, disputabant quo possent ingenio masculum infantem surripere; dumque inter se diversa opinione contenderent, Samuel ad se Lazarum servum suum[12] iussit accedere. Coram quo statim cum astitisset, "Lazare," inquit, "si tibi praestat animus Christianum puerum furari et nobis illum tradere, centum ilico te donabimus Philippeis." Ad quem[13] responsum paucis ita reddidit ille: "Res haec, Patres venerandi,[14] maximi discriminis est: eam ego penitus tentare recuso." Et confestim exiens de templo, collectis sarcinulis suis ad alias terras commigravit.

Die autem Iovis omnes in synagoga congregati ad Tobiam dixerunt: "Animadvertimus neminem plus[15] votis nostris posse satisfacere quam te;[16] versaris enim quotidie cum Christicolis, et paene omnes tibi familiares sunt. Facile potes unum intercipere, quia nemo, cum civitatem obambulas, in te advertit.

---

1 tibi *BA*

2 infante *BA om. P*

3 loqueretur *A* loquebatur *PB*

4 in contemptu *A*

5 vestentes in armis *B*

6 quo redolent *for* quo graviter olent *B*

7 Jobel *A* ioel *PB*

8 parasceuem *B* Parasceve *A*

9 misteriis, nunc hac, nunc illac *B*

10 Postera autem *for* Postero autem die *B*

11 quoniam *A*

12 suum *BA om. P*

13 ad quae *A*

14 venerandi *om. B*

15 mage *B*

16 te *A* tu *PB*

without?" Then, glancing at each other, all silently realized that he was speaking about the sacrifice of a Christian infant, whom, in contempt of our Lord Jesus Christ, they brutally slay and, devouring his drained-off blood in their unleavened loaves, use Christian gore[1] to keep themselves free from the powerful stench they exude. And they call this gore their "Joel", that is, "Jubilee."[2] But they agreed that they would have to talk quite carefully because of the servants who, involved in various jobs for the impending Day of Preparation,[3] were running about hither and thither.

Next [p. 7] day, however, when they had all met in the synagogue, they discussed where they could best kill him. Tobias and Engel refused to let it be done in their homes due to lack of room, since in a confined area it would be hard to conceal so huge a crime from their children. On grounds of general suitability and generous space, however, they declared a preference for Samuel's house. But having taken this decision, they started discussing by what clever trick they could kidnap a male infant; and while they were arguing their different points of view, Samuel told his servant Lazarus to come to him. When he promptly came and stood before him, "Lazarus," he said, "if you have the nerve to steal a Christian boy and hand him over to us, we will instantly give you a reward of a hundred ducats." Lazarus curtly replied: "This, respected fathers, is a very dangerous business; I utterly refuse to attempt it." And, leaving the temple forthwith, he collected his belongings and went to live abroad.

On Thursday, however, having all gathered in the synagogue, they said to Tobias: "We notice that no one can satisfy our wishes better than you; every day you have dealings with Christ-worshipers, and nearly all are well-known to you. You can easily catch a boy, for no one notices you when you walk about the city. We shall certainly ensure [p. 8] that you always get plenty of good things from us." Tobias declined, and pointed out that on many counts it was a hazardous

---

[1] For the medieval distinction between *sanguis* (inside blood) and *cruor* (outside blood), see Bynum, *Wonderful Blood*, 17–19, and the two main sources she draws on: Isidore of Seville, *Isidori Hispalensis episcopi etymologiarum sive originum libri XX*, ed. W. M. Lindsay, 2 vols. (Oxford: Clarendon Press, 1911), 2: bk. 11, chap. 1, paras. 122–23; and Vincent of Beauvais, *Vincentius Bellovacensis Speculum quadruplex: sive Speculum maius: naturale, doctrinale, morale, historiale*, 4 vols. (Douai: B. Bellei, 1624), *Naturale*, bk. 28, chap. 27, vol. 1, col. 2010, and bk. 26, chap. 68, vol. 1, col. 1880. For an English version of the passage from Isidore see *The Etymologies of Isidore of Seville*, trans. and ed. Stephen A. Barney, W. J. Lewis, J. A. Beach, and Oliver Berghof (Cambridge: Cambridge University Press, 2006), 239. In order to preserve this distinction, throughout the present volume *sanguis* is translated as 'blood', and *cruor* as 'gore'.

[2] 'Jubilee', in fact, as described in Leviticus 25: 8–17, denoted that special year, occurring every fifty years, when Jewish slaves regained their freedom and land reverted to its former owners.

[3] That is, Friday, the day spent in preparing for celebration of the Sabbath, which lasted from sunset on Friday until sunset on Saturday.

Dabimus operam profecto [p. 8] ut tibi multa bona a nobis semper accedant." Negat Tobias, et periculum in negocio multis assignat rationibus. At illi suis hunc execrationibus[1] astringunt, et nisi pareat eum perpetuo interdicent synagoga. Tobias ergo, videns omnes in eum conspirasse, et praemium sibi iam fore propositum, auri caeca cupidine captus, "Ag[g]rediar," inquit, "Patres, libenter provinciam hanc, verum ut nostis pauper sum ego, et ad commode vivendum ars mea non sufficit. Sunt et plures mihi filioli; eos et me vobis unice commendo." Responderunt omnes: "Affer puerum huc. Nulla enim unquam erga te nos arguet ingratitudo." Tunc, ad Samuelem conversus, proditor inquit: "Nulla clave postes[2] tui concludantur, ut si mihi quisquam opportune contigerit, intro possim illum leviter impellere." Et transactis vesperis egressus coepit totam viciniam solus obambulare. Transiensque per viam quam Fossatum vulgus appellat, sese usque ad plateam celeriter transtulit. At ubi commode repperit neminem, flexit iter propere, simul et vestigia retro observata legit.

Postea[3] quam locum illum attigit quem Fossatum vocant[4] incolae, insignem puerum ante fores patris super ligno sedentem conspexit,[5] nomine SIMONEM, qui nondum viginti novem menses[6] natus adeo formosus erat in cunctis, ut in eo non comprehenderetur quod iure reprehendi [p. 9] posset. Et accedens lustrat neminem in puerum advertere; porrigit digitum Tobias blandus infanti. Speciosus puer, benignus ut erat et facilis, candida manu capit molliter indicem. Procedit sequiturque puer non passibus aequis. Cumque genitoris sedem[7] pertransisset, proditor rabida dextra pulcherrimam manum praehensat infantis; et nunc illum trahit, et nunc mollia terga pulsans genibus impellit. Tunc respiciens puer coepit cum lachrymis pios extollere vagitus, et dulce matris nomen invocare.[8] Exanimatus ilico proditor denarium extraxit argenteum, et porrigens infanti illum blando sermone compescuit. Postea quam ad extremum viae pervenit carnifex, omnia rite collustrans, cerdonem a sinistris respicit consuentem. Ibi exanimatus ilico gressum continuit, donec aliorsum tandem lumina flecteret artifex.[9] Tunc occasionem nactus celeri gradu viam pertransiens, in domum Samuelis intrusit infantem.

Hic Samuel, veluti tygris expectans ad sanguinem, corripiens puerum ocyus in suum thalamum sustulit. Praetereo hic quanta tunc dra[c]ones illi sunt

---

[1] coniurationibus *B*
[2] fores *B*
[3] Hic postea *for* Postea *B*
[4] vocitant *A*
[5] conspexit *A* inspexit *PB*
[6] attigerat *add. B*
[7] aedem *A*
[8] invocare nomen *A*
[9] donec in aduersum artifex tandem lumina flecteret *B*

assignment. Yet they coerced him with their curses, and said that unless he obeyed they would permanently bar him from the synagogue. So Tobias, seeing that they had all plotted against him, and that he would now be offered a reward, smitten as he was by blind greed for gold,[1] said: "I will gladly take on this special task, fathers, but as you know I am poor, and my skill is not enough to give me a comfortable living. I also have many small sons; them and myself I especially commend to you." They all answered: "Bring a boy here. Never shall we be accused of any ingratitude towards you." Then, turning to Samuel, the betrayer said: "Have your door left unlocked, so that if any boy comes my way at the right moment, I can easily push him inside." And going out after vespers had finished, he began to pace about the whole neighborhood by himself. And crossing by what people call Ditch Street, he quickly reached the square. But when, unluckily, he found no one, he hastily changed course, at the same time carefully retracing his steps.[2]

After he reached the place the inhabitants call the Ditch, he caught sight of a fine boy sitting on a plank in front of his father's front door, SIMON by name. Not yet twenty-nine months old,[3] he was so handsome in every way that one could not rightly find fault with any of his features. [p. 9] And Tobias, approaching him, observed that no one was watching the boy; he held out a coaxing finger to him. The pretty boy, kindly and compliant as he was, tenderly grasped Tobias's forefinger with his fair hand. On Tobias went, and the boy followed with shorter steps.[4] And when he had gone past the boy's father's home, the betrayer grabbed the infant's beautiful hand with his own rabid right hand; and now he dragged him, now, thumping his tender back, he pushed him onto his knees. Then the boy, looking back, began tearfully to utter pious cries and call out the sweet name of his "mama". Alarmed, the betrayer instantly drew out a silver coin and, holding it out to the infant, silenced him with coaxing talk. After the murderer reached the end of the street, duly glancing all round, he saw, behind him on the left, a cobbler mending shoes. There, alarmed, he stopped dead, waiting until the craftsman finally turned his gaze elsewhere. Then, when he got the chance, passing right along the street at a swift pace, he thrust the infant into Samuel's house.

Here Samuel, like a tiger eager for blood,[5] snatching the boy, hastily took him up to his bedroom. I do not mention here how great was the joy those dragons

---

[1] Cf. Lucretius, *De rerum natura*, 3. 59: "denique avarities et honorum caeca cupido . . .".

[2] Cf. Vergil, *Aeneid* 9. 392–93: "simul et vestigia retro / observata legit."

[3] If, as Tiberino says later, Simon's birth-date was 26 November 1472, he was now not quite twenty-eight months old.

[4] Cf. Vergil, *Aeneid* 2. 724: "sequiturque patrem non passibus aequis."

[5] For the comparison of an angry warrior with a predatory tiger, see Vergil, *Aeneid* 9. 728–730 (Turnus), and Ovid, *Metamorphoses* 5. 164–166 (Perseus).

affecti laetitia. Ululabant[1] siccis faucibus super Christianum sanguinem. Et ne puer peregrino loco deterritus clamores effunderet, alii porrigebant uvas, alii poma, alii res alias quibus ut plurimum infantes delectantur, donec silente puero [p. 10] dies se cum nocte coniungeret. Interea genetrix eius Maria, puerum ut vidit abesse, nec solito more apud vicinos illum offenderet, percusso pectore una cum coniuge Andrea totam per civitatem explorabat infantem. Pueri autem omnes, e quorum labris saepe Spiritus sanctus eloquitur,[2] illum apud Iudaeos inquirendum fore asserebant; futurum enim ut eum rapuissent Iudaei et in Christianae fidei opprobrium in cruce suspenderent. Et nisi de medio nox repente diem abstulisset, ad Iudaeos vertissent iter; unde collapsis tenebris impulsi, flentes amare, domum sese receperunt.

Tempus erat quo prima quies humana reficit pectora, atque quiescebant voces hominumque canumque. Tunc crudelis Moyses, una cum reliquis atrocissimis Iudaeis, benignum illum deportantes infantem, ingressi sunt vestibulum, quod cum primis synagogae foribus adiungitur.[3] Ibique super bancho iuxta caminum considens,[4] puerum suis[5] super genibus excepit. Et[6] circumfusi omnes vestem[7] ei[8] ad umb[i]licum et cubitos usque verso ordine detraxerunt,[9]

---

[1] enim quemadmodum lupi rapaces *add. A*

[2] loquitur *A*

[3] quod ante cum synagoga coniungitur *for* quod. . .adiungitur *B*

[4] residens *A*

[5] suis *BA om. P*

[6] Porro *A*

[7] tunicam *B*

[8] ei *A* sibi *PB*

[9] ut brachiis impeditis mouere se facile non posset *add. B*

felt then. Dry-throated, they howled[1] over Christian blood. And so that the boy, scared as he was by the strange place, might not make a noise, some held out grapes, others apples, others again other things which infants most enjoy, wait-ing—with the boy now quiet—[p. 10] until day merged into night. Meanwhile his mother Maria, broken-hearted when she realized the boy was missing and could not, as was usual, find him among the neighbors,[2] went all over the city with her husband Andreas in search of the infant. But all the children—out of whose lips the Holy Spirit often speaks[3]—kept declaring that they would have to look for him among the Jews, for it would turn out that the Jews had seized him and, to insult the Christian faith, were hanging him on a cross. And had not night suddenly removed daylight from the scene, they would have bent their steps towards the Jews; hence, hampered by the onset of darkness, weeping bit-terly, they went back home.

It was the time when earliest rest refreshes human breasts, and the voices of people and dogs were quiet.[4] Then cruel Moses, together with the other utterly brutal Jews, carrying the kindly infant down, entered the entrance-hall which adjoins the front doors of the synagogue. And there, sitting down on a bench next to the fire, he took the boy up on his lap; and all of them, crowding around, pulled his clothes inside out down to his waist and elbows,[5] and picking up his

---

[1] As pointed out by R. Po-chia Hsia, *Trent 1475: Stories of a Ritual Murder Trial* (New Haven: Yale University Press, 1992), 54, the verb here (*ululare*) is both onomato-poeic and "barbaric". The phrase added here in *A* ("like rapacious wolves") reinforces this. Cf. Vergil, *Aeneid* 9. 63–64, where Turnus is likened to a dry-throated wolf hungry for the blood of lambs: "collecta fatigat edendi / ex longo rabies et siccae sanguine fauces." The equation of Jews (and other enemies of Christ) with dogs was found in the liturgy of Holy Week. The fourth-century writer John Chrysostom identified the Jews with the re-jected dogs mentioned in Matthew 15: 26: K. Stow, *Popes, Church, and Jews in the Middle Ages: Confrontation and Response* (Aldershot and Burlington, VT: Ashgate, 2007), I. 9; VI. 259.

[2] Perhaps influenced by Luke 2: 44–45, where Jesus' parents, after visiting Jerusa-lem with their son (also at the time of Passover), similarly fail to find him amongst rela-tions and acquaintances.

[3] Cf. Matthew 21: 16 (quoting Psalm 8: 2 = Vulgate Ps. 8: 3): "Quia ex ore infantium et lactantium perfecisti laudem."

[4] The resemblance of the first clause to Vergil, *Aeneid* 2. 268–269 is mentioned by Hsia, *Trent 1475*, 154 n. 12 (citing Diego Quaglioni). For the second clause another Vergilian parallel comes to mind, *Aeneid* 4. 522–528, especially since there (as here) the peacefulness of night is immediately contrasted with torment: Dido's in Vergil, Simon's in Tiberino.

[5] The additional clause added here by the writer of *B* ("so that with his arms entan-gled he could not easily move") makes it clear that the clothing of Simon is meant, not that of his captors: hence our replacement of *sibi* (as in *B* and *P*, referring to the subject of the sentence, the Jews) with *ei* (as in *A*, referring to Simon) in the present clause. This

colligentesque fluentem tunicam[1] succinxerunt lateri, ita ut a femore usque ad talos detractis caligis nudaretur. Et apprehendens sudarium Samuel, quod sibi[2] pendebat a balteo, colloque circumvolvens comprimebat [p. 11] puerum, ne vagitus effunderet. Alii vero manus pedesque continebant. Tunc evaginato Moyses cultro,[3] summum virgae perforavit infantis, correptaque forcipe coepit maxillam dextram iuxta mentum dilaniare,[4] et particulam[5] carnis abscissam[6] in parato ibi cratere[7] reposuit. Colligebant astantes sacrum sanguinem, et alterno ordine forcipe porrecta quilibet sibi frustulum vivae carnis excidebat.[8] Sic fecerunt omnes primi, donec vulnus ovi rotunditatem multum excederet. Et si quando cedente[9] laqueo puer gutture[10] perstrepebat, admotis crebro manibus ad os illum[11] crudeliter suffocabant.

Hoc Moyses ita[12] peracto, dextram tibiam confestim[13] elevavit infantis, eamque suis[14] super genibus statuens, aggreditur exteriorem partem, quae inter cau[d]illam et cruris musculum[15] interiacet, similiter eodem ferro convellere, et capta forcipe vicissim carnem vivam vivo cum sanguine lacerabat.[16] Postmodum saevissimus senex ille, tanti sceleris caput, semimortuum erigens infantem, petiit Samuelem a sinistris pueri secum considere, et uterque, sanctissima illius brac[c]hia[17] instar crucifixi violenter[18] extendentes, hortabantur reliquos ut sacrum illud corpus[19] duris acubus infoderent. Collecti ergo omnes circum, incipientes a vertice usque ad plantas illum densis [p. 12] ictibus perforabant, dicentes: "Tolle iesse mina elle parechief[20] elle passusen pegmalen."[21] Quod est: "Sicut

---

[1] palium *B*

[2] sibi *BA* eius *P*

[3] gladio *B*

[4] dilaniare *BA* dillaniare *P*

[5] particulam *A* particula *PB*

[6] abscissam *A* abscissa *B* abscisa *P*

[7] in parato ibi cratere *A* parato ibi in cratere *PB*

[8] excindebat *A*

[9] cedente *BA* sedentem *P*

[10] gutture *BA* gutturem *P*

[11] illud *A*

[12] crudeliter *add. A*

[13] confestim *om. B*

[14] suis *om. B*

[15] masculum *B*

[16] lacerabant *BA*

[17] brachia illius *B*

[18] crudeliter *B*

[19] infantis *add. B*

[20] parachief *B* parichief *A*

[21] pasuen pecinalem *B*

flowing tunic gathered it up to the side, so as to make him bare from thigh to ankles when his boots were removed. Samuel, taking a handkerchief which hung from his belt and winding it round the boy's neck, tried to stop [p. 11] him from wailing aloud. Others, however, held down his hands and feet. Then Moses, unsheathing a knife, pierced the tip of the infant's penis, and, seizing pincers, began to tear apart his right jaw next to the chin, and placed the severed piece of flesh in a bowl that was there ready. His assistants started to gather the sacred blood and, as the pincers were held out to them in succession, anyone who so wished proceeded to cut out for himself a little bit of living flesh. All the main participants did this, until the wound was as round as an egg but much bigger; and if ever the boy started making a noise in his throat as the gag slackened, by frequent application of their hands to his mouth they would cruelly smother him.

After all this, Moses speedily lifted the infant's right shin and, placing it on his lap, set about similarly ripping open with the same knife the outer portion of flesh lying between the tiny penis and the leg muscle, and, taking up the pincers again, proceeded to rend the living flesh with its living blood. Presently the utterly savage old man, ringleader of this great crime, raising up the half-dead infant, asked Samuel to sit down with him on the boy's left, and both of them, violently stretching out his most holy arms in place of the crucified [Christ's], began to urge the rest to dig into that sacred body with hard needles. Gathered all round, therefore, starting from Simon's crown and going down to his soles, they proceeded to pierce him with frequent [p. 12] blows, saying: *Tolle iesse mina elle parechief elle passusen pegmalen.*[1] That is, "Let us

---

tallies with Pusculo's account (sig. aviv), whereas Calfurnio (sig. a3v) applies a similar description to the Jews' clothing. A trivial discrepancy perhaps, but it does point to some confusion in the tale. For the focus on Simon's clothing, cf. Ps. 22: 16–18 (= Vulgate Ps. 21: 17–19).

[1] Cf. Isaiah 1: 6, foreshadowing the passion. The words are a version of the phrase 'Talui, Ieshu ha-min', or 'Jesus the heretic hanged'. On the belief that Jewish prayers contained insults against Christ and the Virgin see Joshua Trachtenberg, *The Devil and the Jews: The Medieval Conception of the Jew and its Relation to Modern Antisemitism* (New Haven: Yale University Press, 1943), 182–83. On ancient and medieval sources for the idea that Jews tortured Christian children in imitation of Christ see Gavin I. Langmuir, "Thomas of Monmouth: Detector of Ritual Murder," in idem, *Toward a Definition of Antisemitism* (Berkeley and Los Angeles: University of California Press, 1990), chap. 9.

Iesum Deum Christianorum, qui nihil est, trucidemus[1] istum.[2] Sic inimici nostri confundantur in aeternum." Iam plus quam per horam miserandus puer terribili duraverat in sup[p]licio, et interdicto[3] spiritu collapsis viribus deficiebat. Attollens graves oculos in caelum, superos advocare videbatur in testes, et inclinato capite sanctum Domino reddidit spiritum:

> "purpureus veluti cum flos succisus aratro
> languescit moriens, lapsoque papavera collo
> demisere caput, pluvia cum forte gravantur."

Tunc Moyses et omnes reliqui, oculos et palmas elevantes in caelum, egere gratias Deo, quod de Christianis vindictam simul et sacrificium obtulissent. Relictoque illic corpore, cum plausu et clamore maximo summa per tecta discurrentes, ineffabilem laetitiam se percepisse demonstraverunt. Et descendentes ad coenam, servis praecepit Samuel[4] ut sub cadis vinariis illud occulerent. Timebant enim proclamationes antistitis, et crebrescentem in eos magis atque magis[5] famam, ne furore populi capti et caesi ad torturam subito traherentur.

Altera die, quae[6] Passionem Domini cunctis in Christo credentibus ad memoriam revocat, restrictis labentibus in urbem fluviis, parentes [p. 13] infantis una cum cohorte praetoria ubicumque quaerentes non invenerunt eum. Die autem Sabbati convenientes Iudaei[7] in synagoga, cunctis cernentibus cadaver super almomor extenderunt. Est enim almomor mensa quaedam ante altare, ubi psalmos, antyphonas hymnosque decantant. Perfectisque orationibus suis, rursus eodem in loco reposuerunt corpus. Tertia vero die, quae[8] sanctum Pascha Christi fidelibus attulerat, ut praesenserunt Iudaei omnium paene mentes in eos fore[9] suspensas, inito consilio libratisque plurimorum opinionibus, dixerunt: "Proiiciamus corpus istud vestitum in flumen, quod nostra domo subterfluit, et euntes ad pontificem dicamus quoniam illud in domum nostram aqua deduxit, et crate ferrea[10] retentum non potuit una cum flumine delabi.[11] Talibus enim visis,[12] credet

---

[1] trucidavimus *A*

[2] istum *om. A*

[3] vitali *add. A*

[4] Et relinquentes illic corpus, seruis preceperunt *for* Tunc Moyses et omnes . . . praecepit Samuel *B*

[5] magis magisque *A*

[6] Altero die, qui *A*

[7] Judaei *A om. PB*

[8] Tertio vero die, qui *A*

[9] esse *A*

[10] rethe fereo *B*

[11] dilabi *B*

[12] visis *A* usis *P* usi *B*

butcher this boy just like Jesus, the Christians' God, who is nothing. Thus may our enemies be eternally confounded." Already the pitiable boy had lasted out for more than an hour in terrible punishment and, with breath denied and strength lost, was fading away. Lifting heavy eyes to heaven, he seemed to be summoning the powers above as witnesses, and bending down his head he gave up his holy spirit to the Lord:[1]

> "as when a purple flower, felled by the plow,
> wilts dying, and as poppies, necks collapsed,
> bend drooping heads, when weighted down by rain."[2]

Then Moses and all the rest, raising eyes and hands to heaven, gave thanks to God because they had offered up to him vengeance on the Christians and a sacrifice as well. And having left the body there, as with loud clapping and shouting they ran about along the rooftops, they showed themselves gripped by joy unspeakable. When they came down for the evening meal, Samuel ordered the servants to hide the body under the wine-jars. For they were afraid of the bishop's proclamations and the gradually increasing rumors against them, in case the people's rage might cause them to be arrested, flogged, and suddenly dragged off to torture.

On the second day, which for all who believe in Christ calls back to remembrance the Lord's passion, after the streams flowing into the city had been dammed, the infant's parents, [p. 13] together with the *podestà*'s squad, failed to find him despite a thorough search. But the Jews, assembling in the synagogue on the Sabbath, stretched out the corpse on the almemor in full view of everyone. (The almemor is a sort of table in front of the altar where they babble[3] psalms, antiphons, and hymns.) After finishing their prayers they put the body back again in the same place. On the third day, however, which had ushered in Christ's Holy Easter for the faithful, the Jews—anticipating that nearly everyone's thoughts would be anxiously directed at them—held a meeting, gauged most people's views, and said: "Let us throw out this body, fully clothed, into the river that flows under our house, and then go to the bishop and say that the water brought it down to our house, and that, blocked by an iron mesh, it could not float downstream. When such things are considered no one will believe that

---

[1] Cf. John 19: 30, referring to the death of Jesus on the cross: "Et inclinato capite tradidit spiritum."

[2] Vergil, *Aeneid* 9. 435–437, describing the death of Euryalus. Tiberino's only alteration of the standard text is in the second line, where *lapsoque* replaces *lassove*.

[3] Again the verb used is *decantare*. See above, 43 n. 4.

nemo[1] Iudaeos puerum extinxisse." Placuit omnibus sententia; et ascendens ad antistitem[2] proditor rerum seriem eo quo fuerat institutus[3] ordine pandidit.[4]

Tunc gavisus pontifex Ioannem de Salis praetorem et Iacobum de Sporo praefectum[5] suae Tridentinae civitatis illuc[6] ubi iacebat puer secum iussit accedere. Et descendentes statim invenerunt cadaver in aqua, pannis involutum; quo protinus extracto eiusque vulneribus diligenter annotatis, illud in basilica[7] Sancti Petri collocaverunt, ubi maxima populorum languentiumque confluente [p. 14] frequentia multis maximisque indies miraculis fulget.

Ecce, Christiane, Iesum inter latrones rursus[8] crucifixum! Ecce quid facerent Iudaei si inter Christi fideles haberent imperium! Gloriosus Simon, Virgo, Martyr et Innocens, vix ablactatus et cuius lingua nondum humanum solvebat[9] eloquium, in contemptum nostrae fidei a Iudaeis est extensus in cruce! Audi, qui tam crudele hominum genus tuis in urbibus pateris! Iudaei aeterno statuto decreverunt, ut divinae Eucharistiae beataeque Mariae semper Virgini quotidie maledicatur, pol[l]uta omnia verba per[10] peccatum asserentes praeter[11] illa quae in contemptum Romanae Ecclesiae vergere dignoscuntur. Item in Keser[12] Theusesim,[13] id est,[14] in tertio libro Talmut — hunc enim codicem praeferunt Iudaei libris Moysi et prophetarum, et ut magis credatur Talmut fabulis[15] addunt[16] fabulas, dicentes quod Deus studeat Talmut[17] — ibi perpetua lege sancitur, ut ter singulis diebus in oratione, quam efficaciorem cunctis precibus existimant, omnes Christi fideles devoveantur.[18] Hanc autem[19] orationem stantes[20] iunctis pedibus, ad nullam rem mundi intentionem agentes, evomunt, viri in Hebraeo,[21] mulieres ea

---

[1] nemo credet *A*
[2] Pontificem *A*
[3] instructus *A*
[4] pandit *A*
[5] Capitaneum *B*
[6] illic *A*
[7] in sacello *B*
[8] rursum *B*
[9] sonabat *A*
[10] *supplevi*: per
[11] propter *B*
[12] chieser *B for* Sefer?
[13] Theusesim *om. B*
[14] in Keser Theusesim, id est *om. A*
[15] fabulae *A*
[16] addit *B*
[17] *correxi*: Tamult *P*
[18] devoveantur *A* deuouentur *PB*
[19] etiam *A*
[20] et *add. B*
[21] Hebraice *A*

Jews killed the boy." All of them approved of this suggestion; and the betrayer, going up to the bishop, unfolded the sequence of events exactly as he had been instructed.

The bishop, gladdened by this, then ordered Giovanni de Salis, the *podestà*, and Jakob von Sporo, the captain of his city of Trent, to come with him to the spot where the boy lay. And going down, straightway they found the corpse in the water, wrapped in swaddling-clothes;[1] and immediately drawing it out and carefully noting its wounds [Fig. 1], they placed it in St Peter's Basilica, where—as a huge throng of people and invalids streams in—[p. 14] it shines forth every day with many mighty miracles.

Behold, Christian, Jesus crucified between thieves[2] again! Behold what the Jews would be doing if they held sway among Christ's faithful![3] Glorious Simon, virgin, martyr and innocent, only just weaned, his tongue not yet uttering human speech, has been stretched out on a cross by the Jews in contempt of our faith! Listen, you who suffer so cruel a race of people in your cities! By an everlasting statute the Jews have decreed that the divine Eucharist and the Blessed ever-Virgin Mary are to be cursed every day, sinfully alleging that all words are polluted except those perceived to imply contempt of the Roman Church. Likewise in the Keser Theusesim[4]—that is, in the third book of the Talmud, for they prefer this tome to the books of Moses and the prophets and, to make the Talmud more believable, they pile stories on stories, saying that God studies the Talmud[5]—there it is ordained by a perpetual law that three times each day, in a prayer which they deem more effective than all others, all Christ's faithful are to be execrated. And they spew forth[6] this prayer, standing with feet close together, taking no notice of anything worldly, the men speaking in Hebrew,

---

[1] Cf. Luke 2: 12, where an angel tells the shepherds how to identify the Christ-child: "Invenietis infantem pannis involutum."

[2] Matthew 27: 38, Mark 15: 27.

[3] Not "Behold the Jews did this so as to have power over Christians." Hsia, *Trent 1475*, 55.

[4] "Keser" (both here and later) is possibly a confused spelling of the Hebrew word *Sefer* ("Book"): the first consonant is a rather strange form of K, and the second could be due to misreading 'f' as 's' (older form). "Theusesim", on the other hand, does not correspond with the name of any part of the Talmud, the third of whose six divisions (*sedarim*, 'orders') is called *Nashim* ('Women'); nor does the Talmud contain any such material as Tiberino purports to quote from it.

[5] Cf. Jacob Neusner, *Invitation to the Talmud* (New York: Harper and Row, 1973), 28: "This [i.e., the view conveyed in the Talmud] is an extraordinary conviction, expressed to begin with in the mythic picture of God's studying Torah along with Moses and the heavenly academy, of the rabbi's imitating God through his learning of the law."

[6] Like *ululare*, a powerfully emotive word (*euomere*); cf. Cicero (referring to Mark Antony), *Philippics*, 5. 20: "in me . . . orationem ex ore impurissimo evomuit."

lingua quam a primis annis didicerunt; solus Levita eam alta voce decantat, aliis omnibus respondentibus "Amen."

Verba orationis sic sonant: [p. 15] "Conversis non sit spes, et omnes repente dispergantur; in matribus[1] minorentur parvuli; ac amplius non resurgant! Et omnes inimici tuae gentis, Israhel, destruantur, et regnum nequitiae Christianorum eradicetur et confundatur! Fac, Domine, fac impleas quod petimus in diebus nostris velociter, quia tu es Deus benedictus, fugans inimicos et destruens impios." Et in Keser[2] Naasim, id est[3] in secundo Talmut, affirmant quod Dominus noster Iesus Christus[4] maxima in inferno tormenta patiatur. Non est mirum, Christiani, si nos bello, fame, siti, grandine, pruina Christus affligat—si nos populum suum precioso sanguine suo redemptum[5] semper ad deteriora labi sustineat—cum patiamur[6] inter nos regnare inimicos eius! Non est aliud[7] quam sacrosancta fide despecta eius[8] perpetuis hostibus adhaerere.

Natus est Simon, de quo agimus,[9] die Veneris sexto calendas Decembris, anno a partu Virginis salutifero septuagesimo secundo supra millenum quatercentenum, ex Maria et Andrea[10] parentibus pauperrimis, divo Ioanne Inderbach, quarto pontifice et domino Tridentino, imperante feliciter. Ob quam rem Iudaei omnes a maiore usque ad minorem in carceribus cathenisque [p. 16] conclusi sunt, non inde recessuri prius quam debitas poenas luant.

Vale, Raphael Tergestine, Musarum decus. Tridenti secundo nonas Aprilis,[11] MCCCCLXXV.[12]

---

[1] in matricibus *A*

[2] chieser *B for* Sefer?

[3] in Keser Naasim, id est *om. A*

[4] Salvator noster *add. A*

[5] sanguine suo redemptum *B* suo sanguine redemptum *A* sanguine redemptum *P*

[6] patiamur *A* patimini *PB*

[7] Quid quaeso, hoc est aliud *for* Non est aliud *A*

[8] eius *A* suis *PB*

[9] Simon, de quo agimus *add. A*

[10] ex Andrea et Maria *BA*

[11] Vale . . . nonas Aprilis *om. B* Valete. Tridenti Nonas Aprilis *A*

[12] MCCCCLXXV *add. A*

the women in the language they have learned from their earliest years; a single Levite babbles[1] it in a high voice, while all the others answer "Amen."

The words of the prayer sound like this: [p. 15] "May there be no hope for converts, and may they all be suddenly scattered; may the young ones shrivel up within their mothers; and may they rise up again no more! And may all your race's enemies, Israel, be destroyed, and may the Christians' reign of wickedness be rooted out and confounded! Grant this, O Lord, grant that you fulfill our petition speedily in our lifetime, for you are the blessed God, putting your foes to flight and destroying the impious."[2] And in the Keser Naasim, that is, in the second book of the Talmud, they maintain that our Lord Jesus Christ suffers mighty torments in Hell.[3] No wonder, Christians, if Christ should afflict us with war, hunger, thirst, hail, and frost—if he should accept that we, his own people, redeemed by his own precious blood, are always sinking towards a worse state—since we suffer his enemies to rule amongst us! What we are doing is simply clinging on to his perpetual enemies, disdaining the inviolable faith.

Simon, the subject of our letter, was born on Friday the twenty sixth of November in the one thousand four hundred and seventy-second year since [Christ's] saving Virgin-birth, of very poor parents, Maria and Andrea, while godly Johannes Hinderbach, fourth bishop and lord of Trent, happily held sway. Because of this event all the Jews, from the older down to the younger, have been chained up in dungeons, with no hope of coming out until they pay the due penalties.

Farewell, Raffaele [Zovenzoni] of Trieste, ornament of the Muses. Trent, April 4th, 1475.

---

[1] A third and final pejorative use of the verb *decantare*, this time describing chant rather than speech.

[2] This is a much embroidered version of the Twelfth Benediction (added as a supplement to the original Eighteen Benedictions, which therefore total nineteen in the present Jewish prayer book), which reads: "And for slanderers, let there be no hope, and let all wickedness perish as in a moment; let all thine enemies be speedily cut off, and the dominion of arrogance do thou uproot and crush, cast down and humble speedily in our days. Blessed art thou, O Lord, who breakest the enemies and humblest the arrogant": *The Authorised Daily Prayer Book*, ed. Joseph H. Hertz (New York: Bloch, 1948), 143–45. As Hertz comments: "[This petition] is directed against Jewish sectaries (*Minim*) in the generation after the Destruction of the Second Temple. They wrought division and havoc in the religious camp of Israel. Especially detestable were their fratricidal activities in the political field. They played the informers for the Roman authorities, and brought many of their brethren to a painful death. The wording of this Benediction has undergone manifold modifications. In its present form it has a universal and timeless application. The statement that in this prayer Jews of today utter an imprecation against those of another Faith, is a baseless calumny."

[3] For "Keser", see above, 55 n. 4. Again, the alleged statement appears nowhere in the Talmud, which admittedly has a name like *Naasim* for one of its 'orders', but that order is the third, not the second.

Miraculum.[1]

Sayth[2] Hebraeorum[3] causam protector adortus[4]
   dum sedet infelix, hic sibi somnus adest.
Hunc[5] locus impatiens miserum deturbat in ignes;[6]
   auxilium quaerens, carpit aena manu.
Tempora confestim ferventibus obruit undis,   5
   et cute consumpta lumine coctus[7] eget.
Terra Rovereti, miracula maxima lustrans,
   hanc sedem merito dat tibi, sancte Simon.[8]

Divo Ioanni Inderbacchio, antistiti Tridentino, Raphael Zovenzonius poeta dat dedicat.

Surgite, pontifices, tuque, o sanctissime Caesar;
vosque, duces regesque, precor, populique patresque
qui Christum colitis: Christum, qui sanguine lavit
erroris quicquid[9] nostri admisere parentes!
Stringite fulmineos enses; trucidate nefandum   5
Iudaicum nomen, totaque expellite terra!

At Iudaea fuit Virgo, quam Spiritus unam
Sanctus obumbravit, nostri illa puerpera Christi.
Iudaeusque fuit Moses sanctique prophetae; [p. 17]
et solis sacrum descendit ab aethere manna   10
Iudaeis, pelagi quibus incedentibus undae
cesserunt, dira merso Pharaone procella.
Quis Deus omnipotens flammarum aliquando columnam
misit, ut in tenebris luceret, et insuper hostis
confecit, Iudaea, tuos. Quid grata rependis?   15
Audire est operae precium? Prius obruis omnis
qui tibi vera canunt saxo, perimisque machaera.

---

   [1] Miraculum *om. B*
   [2] Sayt *B* Sait *A*
   [3] Hebraeorum *BA* Iudaeorum *P*
   [4] adhortus *B* adorsus *A*
   [5] Hunc *A* Huic *PB*
   [6] ignem *A*
   [7] caecus *A*
   [8] puer *B* Puer. Miracula magna mirandaque signa, quae Deus circa beatum hunc
puerum operatur, quia indies in confusionem Judaeorum magis crebrescunt, post debitas
eorum poenas solutas alio libello conscribentur. *A*
   [9] quicquam *T*

A Miracle.

While Sayth[1] the Hebrews' guardian, having undertaken their cause, is sitting disconsolate, this dream appears to him. A place that cannot endure him casts this wretch down into the flames; seeking help, with his hand he grasps the bronze cooking-pots. Straightway he plunges head-first into the seething waves, and now, burnt up, with his skin destroyed, he has no sight. The land of Rovereto, observing mighty miracles, for your merits gives you this abode, holy Simon.

To godly Johannes Hinderbach, bishop of Trent, the poet Raffaele Zovenzoni presents and dedicates this.[2]

Arise, you bishops, and you, most holy emperor; and I implore you, leaders and kings, peoples and fathers who worship Christ: Christ who washed away with his blood whatever wrongdoing our ancestors committed! Unsheathe your flashing swords; slaughter the nefarious nation of the Jews, and drive it out of the whole earth!

Yet the Virgin was Jewish, that child-bearer of our Christ whom alone the Holy Spirit overshadowed.[3] Jewish, too, was Moses, and so were the holy prophets; [p. 17] and the sacred manna came down from the sky to the Jews alone, for whom, as they marched on, the waters of the sea receded, when Pharaoh was overwhelmed by a disastrous squall. For them almighty God sometimes sent a column of flames, so that it might shine in the darkness, and he also destroyed your enemies, Judaea. With what gratitude did you repay him?[4] Is it worth hearing? First you stoned to death and put to the sword all those who prophesied the truth to you.

---

[1] Conrad Sayt (or Schayth) acted as the Hebrews' guardian in Rovereto where he suffered an injury after falling from his chair into a fire: Wolfgang Treue, *Der Trienter Judenprozess: Voraussetzungen, Abläufe, Auswirkungen, (1475–1588)* (Hannover: Hahnsche Buchhandlung, 1996), 95.

[2] The text of this poem is also found in the edition of Tiberino's poems printed in Trent by Leonardo Trivisano in September 1482. A few of the variant readings found there (denoted by the letter *T* in the textual notes) are better than those of our Venetian main source (denoted by the letter *P*).

The meter of Zovenzoni's poem, following the elegiac distichs of *Miraculum*, is the dactylic hexameter, the standard classical Latin meter for narrative and didactic poetry, Vergil's *Aeneid* and Ovid's *Metamorphoses* being the best-known examples.

[3] Cf. Luke 1:35: "Spiritus sanctus superveniet in te, et virtus Altissimi obumbrabit tibi."

[4] This passage recalls the *Improperia* or 'Reproaches' of the Good Friday Liturgy.

Adde quod ipse tua voluit de Virgine nasci
quem tu expectabas Messiam, perfida. Quid tum?
Signa facit, morbos curat, multumque cadaver   20
suscitat. Invidia rapis hunc, tristique columna
devinctum caedis loro, illudisque silenti,
et spuis in faciem; barbam vellisque capillum.
Nec satis hóc: crucibus mundi Dominumque Deumque
affigis.[1] Triduo, ut praedixerat, ille resurgit,   25
et tecum est; tandem cunctis cernentibus, ecce,
tollitur in caelum, necdum, vesana, peracti
poenitet, heu, sceleris; te pascit, te iuvat error,
quod velum ante oculos[2] Dirae posuere Sorores,
ne solem videas, circundata morte perenni.[3]   30

Praeterita ut sileam, quod nuper in urbe Tridenti
ausa nefas! Puerum lactantem perdita blando
invitas digito, donec tua tecta subintrat.
Angelus hic Samuelque vapher crudusque Tobias [p. 18]
et Moses—cui fas soli novisse futura—   35
ilicet arripiunt puerum, clauduntque gementis
oscula, per tenerum intendunt[4] diademate collum.
Crudelis Moses pueri praeputia ferro
demetit; hinc rapta stridentem forcipe malam
execat; excipiunt posito cratere[5] cruorem.   40
Inde aliud coxae frustum[6] convellitur, et sic
pascitur haec rabies oculis ardentibus. Inde
in cruce distendunt infantem, et quisque gravatum
pungit acu. Ille oculos in caelum sustulit, unde
spiritus aetheras felix effulsit ad arces.   45

Interea sacer antistes scitarier urbem
imperat infantem, sonti[7] et crudele minatur
sup[p]licium. O summi miranda potentia Christi,
qui nihil occultum voluit! Proiectus in undis,

---

[1] affigi *T*
[2] occulos *T*
[3] perhenni *T*
[4] intendunt *T* incendunt *P*
[5] crathere *T*
[6] frustrum *T*
[7] *correxi*: raptori *PT*

Add this, that the very one whom you, faithless people, awaited as Messiah chose to be born of a Virgin of yours. What then? He performed signs, healed the sick, raised many a corpse. Spitefully you seized him, tied him to a grim column and flogged him, and you mocked him when he stayed silent, and you spat in his face; you pulled out his beard and hair. Nor was this enough: you nailed to a cross the Lord and God of the universe. Three days later he rose again as he had predicted, and was with you; at last, in full view of everyone, behold, he was taken up into heaven, and even yet, you crazy people, you did not, alas, repent of the crime you had committed; your folly fed you and pleased you, because the Dread Sisters[1] had placed a veil before your eyes so that—wrapped in everlasting death as you were—you might not see the sun.[2]

To say nothing of past events, what an outrage you have recently dared to commit in the city of Trent! With a coaxing finger you treacherously allured a nursing boy, until he came under your roof. Here Engel, cunning Samuel, fierce Tobias, [p. 18] and Moses—he who alone was allowed to know the future—straightway seized the boy, closed his mouth when he wailed, and stretched a headband across his tender neck. Cruel Moses cut off the boy's foreskin with a knife; next, seizing pincers, he tore out the screaming boy's cheek; the others collected the gore in a bowl placed there. Another piece was then wrenched out of his hip, and thus was this frenzy fed by their gloating eyes. Then they stretched the infant out on a cross and, weighed down as he was, each of them pierced him with a needle. He lifted his eyes to heaven, whence his blessed spirit blazed forth[3] towards the citadels of the sky.

Meanwhile the holy bishop commanded that the city find out about the infant, and threatened cruel punishment for the criminal. O wondrous power of supreme Christ, who wanted nothing hidden![4] Thrown into the waves, behold,

---

[1] In classical mythology, the three Fates or Parcae (Clotho, Lachesis, and Atropos), supposed to control everyone's birth, life, and death.

[2] In Christian tradition, Christ is "the Sun of righteousness" (Malachi 4: 2).

[3] The verb *effulgere* is appropriate for heavenly bodies such as comets: cf. Tacitus, *Annals* 14. 22: "sidus cometes effulsit."

[4] Cf. Mark 4: 22, Luke 8: 17.

ecce, Simon sanctus puer est monstrante[1] repertus 50
Iudaeo. Qui mox Petri fuit aede repostus
martyr, et hic claudis, surdis caecisque medetur.
At vos carnifices meus Inderbacchus in Arcem
Consilii princeps trahit includitque cathenis;
afficietque suis, mihi credite, corpora poenis! 55
Impius ast animas manet Orcus, et impia Ditis[2]
Tartara, qui[3] Scariot, qui[4] te quoque, maxime, punit,
Herodes, qui rex puerili sanguine cultros
foedasti, ut gemitus Rachel et Rama dederunt. [p. 19]

Hoc genus ulterius, vos o qui sceptra tenetis, 60
hoc genus in terris — genus hoc, precor[5] — esse sinetis?
Sixte pater, prohibe — prohibe, Federice[6] — cruorem
qui nostrum sitiunt nostris simul urbibus esse
amplius! Imperii dux Sygismunde Latini,
nunc animos ostende tuos, tu porrige flammas 65
in quibus Hebraeum scelus exuratur,[7] et insons
sanguis apud superos te praedicet! O mea laurus,
praesidiumque meum, pater Inderbacche Ioannes,
perge! Vetat nemo quin perdas perfida verpos
corpora, quin rapidis cinerem des spargere ventis. 70
Hoc iubet ipse Deus; iubet hoc tua sancta potestas
iustitiae pietasque, fides et candida virtus,
quae te caelicolis[8] est donatura catervis.

Vale, pacis ac iustitiae pater.

---

[1] mostrante *T*
[2] ditis *T* dictis *P*
[3] *correxi*: quae *PT*
[4] *correxi*: quae *PT*
[5] praecor *T*
[6] friderice *T*
[7] exurat *T*
[8] colicolis *T*

the holy boy Simon was found, for a Jew showed the way. Soon the martyr was placed in St Peter's church, and here he cures the lame, the deaf, and the blind. But as for you murderers, my friend prince Hinderbach has dragged you into the castle of Buonconsiglio and chained you up; and, believe me, he will subject your bodies to his chosen punishments! But impious Orcus awaits your souls, and so does the impious underworld of Dis,[1] who punishes [Judas] Iscariot and also punishes you, mighty Herod, king who smirched your knives with boys' blood, when Rachel and Ramah wailed aloud.[2] [p. 19]

O you who hold kingly scepters, will you allow this race — *this* race, I pray — to exist any longer on the earth? Sixtus our father, forbid — you, Frederick, forbid — those people who thirst for our gore to live with us in our cities any longer![3] Sigismund, archduke of the Latin Empire, show your mettle *now*, spread forth flames to incinerate the Hebrew crime, and innocent blood will then proclaim you among the powers above! O my triumph and my stronghold, father Johannes Hinderbach, go forth! No one orders you *not* to destroy those faithless circumcised bodies, *not* to give their ashes to the whisking winds to scatter. This is what God himself enjoins; this is what your holy power of justice enjoins, and so do your piety, your faith, and your shining virtue, which will surely bestow you on the companies of heaven's denizens.

Farewell, father of peace and justice.[4]

---

[1] In classical mythology, Orcus was traditionally god of the underworld, otherwise known as Dis.

[2] A reference to Matthew 2: 18, which in turn refers to Jeremiah 31: 15.

[3] References to Pope Sixtus IV and Emperor Frederick III: see Appendix 2.

[4] This envoi does not occur here in *T* but follows an additional poem which appears as the final item of this section.

[sig. Ar] Iohannis Matthiae Tiberini Clarensis in beatum
Symonem novum sanctissimae Passionis Christi lumen et
martirem epigram[m]a.

Sum puer ille Symon, quem nuper in urbe Tridenti
   gens Iudaea Sacra torsit in Epdomade.
Accipe inauditum[1] facinus dictuque nephandum;
   audi, qui rabidos tam colis usque canes![2]
Paschatis ante diem[3] lux tercia, vespere facto,   5
   et Martis dictus nomine mensis erat.
Ante fores patris puerili more sedebam;
   non aderat genitor, non mea cara parens.
Non advertenti mihi proditor, ecce, Tobias
   astitit, et torvo lumine cuncta notat.   10
Ut nullum vidit, blanda me voce moratur;
   non ego[4] fabar adhuc[5]—vix ego natus eram.
Nondum terdenos menses mea viderat aetas;
   ista meae vitae parvula summa fuit.
Corripior, me fertque statim Samuelis ad aedes.   15
   Impia Iudaeum[6] gens simul illic[7] erant,
concilium[8] hor[r]endum, trucesque in lumine vultus;
   non homines—colubri,[9] diraque monstra magis!
Nox ruit; hinc[10] gemini Salgmon,[11] Samuelque, Tobias,
   Vitalis, Moses, Israhel atque Mohar   20
ante synagogam laeti mea pectora nudant.
   Convellit carnem forcipe quisque mihi
et, ne clamarem, Samuel mihi[12] guttura stringit;[13]
   ille mihi plantas, continet ille manus. [sig. Av]
Sanguine collecto de me crudeliter, addunt   25
   impia Iudaei verbera. "Verba, minas

---

  [1] inauditum O in auditum T
  [2] quisquis iudaeos sustinet accipiat O
  [3] ante diem pasche O
  [4] ego O ergo T
  [5] adhuc O ad huc T
  [6] iudeum O iudei T
  [7] illic O ille T
  [8] consilium O
  [9] viperae O
  [10] hinc O hic T
  [11] salgmon T Salmon O
  [12] mea O
  [13] velat O

[sig. Ar] An epigram of Giovanni Mattia Tiberino of Chiari on blessed Simon, new light and martyr of Christ's most holy Passion.[1]

I am the boy Simon whom recently, in the city of Trent, the Jewish race tortured in Holy Week. Listen to the unheard-of and unspeakable outrage; hear, you who forever pay court to such ravening dogs!

It was the third day before Easter when evening had set in, and the month was the one named after Mars. I was sitting in front of my father's front door, as any boy might; my father was not there, nor was my dear mother. Without my noticing, Tobias the betrayer suddenly came and stood by me, and with fierce eye noted everything. Seeing no one about, he detained me with flattering talk; I still could not speak—I had hardly been born. I had not yet lived to see thirty months; that was the tiny sum of my life-span. I was seized, and he took me straight to Samuel's house. The impious Jewish race was there too, a terrifying assembly, and they had pitiless looks in their eyes; they were not men—rather, snakes and fearsome monsters!

Night hurried on; next, the two Seligmans, Samuel, Tobias, Vital, Moses, Israel, and Mayer joyfully laid bare my chest in front of the synagogue. Each tore out my flesh with pincers and, to stop me shouting, Samuel throttled me; one of them held down my feet, another my hands. [sig. Av] After cruelly gathering blood from me, the Jews impiously punched me as well. "Listen

---

[1] This text and those that follow in this section are all based on *T*, whose signature numbers are therefore inserted. The present poem, however, also appears in *O*, whose variants are duly noted, and are sometimes preferred. Like *Miraculum* above, and like all but one of Tiberino's other poems in this section, it is written in elegiac distichs.

accipias, suspense Deus![1] Fecere sic olim
  maiores nostri funera rite tibi.
Sic confundantur caelo terraque marique
  Christicolae et nostrae gens inimica tribus!"   30
Iamque propinquabat mihi mors, iam luce carebant
  lumina, iam gelidum funere corpus erat.[2]
Erigor;[3] hinc dextrum Moses, Samuelque sinistrum
  in cruce pandentes brac[c]hia nostra trahunt.
Tunc omnes crebris acubus mea pectora pungunt;   35
  dant multo Iesum, me quoque convicio.[4]
Sic cecidi; molles[5] caput inter concidit ulnas,
  ad superos vita et[6] libera fecit iter.
Ut perii, plaudunt omnes superosque salutant,
  quod de Christicolis ulcio facta sibi est.   40
Ad cenam properant rebus sic deinde peractis,
  deque meo in mensa sanguine quisque bibit,
de nostro mandunt mixtasque cruore placentas[7]
  in Iesu Christi dedecus, iniuriam.[8]
Inclytus Hinderbach, praesul, princepsque Iohannes   45
  sceptra Tridentini qui regit alta soli,
Hebraeos postquam mihi funera summa dedisse
  praesensit, de me nocte dieque dolet.
Colligit extinctum corpus, mandatque reponi;[9]
  Iudaeos merita morte perire[10] iubet. [sig. A2r]   50
Adsis, Sixte, precor,[11] fidei ratis anchora nostrae:
  pontifici nostro porrige praesidium!
Hic pugil est constans;[12] hic est pius ille sacerdos,
  cuius vota Patri complacuere Deo.[13]
Sume sacrum scutum et[14] gladium triplicemque coronam; 55

---

[1] iesu *O*
[2] fugerat pectora nostra calor *O*
[3] erigor *O* errigor *T*
[4] afficiunt vitio meque piumque ihesum *O*
[5] molles *O* moles *T*
[6] *supplevi*: et
[7] confectas mandunt azimas de sanguine nostro *O*
[8] in christi solum dedecus omne ihesu *O*
[9] sepulchro *O*
[10] *correxi*: ferire *OT*
[11] precor *O* praecor *T*
[12] constans *O* conflans *T*
[13] cuius vota mea complacuere ihesu *O*
[14] sume scutum et sacrum *O*

to our words and threats, God who was hanged! Thus did our ancestors duly kill you long ago. Thus may the Christ-worshipers and the race that hates our tribe be confounded in heaven and earth and sea!"

And now my demise drew near, now my eyes were bereft of light,[1] now my body was ice-cold in death. I was lifted up; next they pulled my arms out on a cross, Moses extending my right arm and Samuel my left. Then they all pricked my chest with needles, thick and fast; they subjected Jesus and me to much abuse. So I collapsed; my head fell down between my soft forearms, and my life, set free, went off to join those above. When I died, they all clapped and hailed those above,[2] because they themselves had taken revenge on the Christ-worshipers. Then, having thus finished their business, they hurried to their meal, and each drank some of my blood at the table, and they chewed cakes mingled with my gore as an insult and injury to Jesus Christ.

When renowned Johannes Hinderbach, bishop and prince, who directs the sovereign governance of Trent's domain, suspected that the Hebrews had finally consigned me to death, he grieved for me night and day. He gathered up my lifeless body and commanded that it be laid to rest; he ordered the Jews to suffer the death they deserved. [sig. A2r] Help us, Sixtus, I pray, anchor of our ship of faith: give support to our bishop! He is a doughty champion; he is the devoted priest whose prayers have found favor with God the Father. Take up your sacred shield and sword and your triple crown;

---

[1] Cf. Vergil, *Georgics* 4. 255–256: "tum corpora luce carentum / exportant tectis . . ."

[2] Cf. Ovid, *Metamorphoses* 15. 730–31: "obvia turba ruit . . . /. . . laetoque deum clamore salutant."

tolle induratos, Papa beate, canes![1]
Adsint et reges; adsis, fortissime Caesar,
    adsis cum populis principibusque tuis!
Dede neci Hebraeos qui res preciosaque[2] rerum
    Christicolum rabidi nocte dieque vorant,   60
Christicolum fuso tantum qui sanguine gaudent,
    qui mandunt tepida et[3] membra[4] cruenta virum!
Vale, dive pontifex, spes nostra.[5]

Divo Iohanni Hinderbach, quarto pontifici ac domino Tridentino, Iohannes Matthias s[alutem] p[lurimam] d[icit].

Eiusdem.

Cum tua, sancte Symon, lux sempiterna Tridenti,
    in mentem nostram Passio dira subit,
tunc mihi recolitur sanctissima Passio Christi,
    et fluit ex oculis languida gutta meis.
Christus divino atque humano semine fulsit;   5
    est satus Italico theutonicoque Symon.
Virgo Maria, Dei genetrix, sanctissima semper
    et pueri mater dicta Maria fuit.
Concilium de morte Dei gens fecit[6] Hebraea;
    de pueri fato consuluere canes. [sig. A2v]   10
Venditus est Christus florente vir integer aevo,
    et sub lacte Symon venditus iste fuit.
Ad sedes rabidi Christum traxere Pilati;
    barbatum hic Mosen ducitur ante canem.
Innumerabilibus Christum laesere[7] flagellis,   15
    et sacrum spinis implicuere caput;
infantis teneram laceravit forcipe carnem,
    et caput et pectus gens fera fodit acu.
In cruce mutavit vitam cum funere Christus;
    in cruce distentus concidit iste puer.   20
Caeso Iudaei certant illudere Christo;

---

[1] tolle induratum papa beate caput *O*
[2] preciosaque *O* praeciosaque *T*
[3] *supplevi*: et
[4] membra *O* menbra *T*
[5] Vale dive Pontifex spes nostra o*m. O*
[6] *correxi*: faecit *T*
[7] *correxi*: caedere *T*

get rid of the obstinate dogs, blessed Holy Father! May kings also help us; may you, mighty emperor, help us, together with your peoples and princes! Deliver to their doom the Hebrews who savagely devour Christ-worshipers' property and precious goods day and night, who are so glad when Christ-worshipers' blood is shed, who chew men's warm and gory limbs!

Farewell, godly bishop, our hope.

To godly Johannes Hinderbach, fourth bishop and lord of Trent, Giovanni Mattia [Tiberino] addresses warmest greetings.

By the same author.

Whenever your dread passion comes into my mind, holy Simon, Trent's everlasting light, then do I recall Christ's most holy passion, and a tear slowly trickles from my eyes. Christ shone forth from divine and human seed; the seed from which Simon sprang was Italian and German. The most holy perpetual Virgin, God's mother, was called Mary, and so was Mary, the boy's mother.

The Hebrew race held a council to plan God's death; the dogs consulted to plan the boy's fate. [sig. A2v] Christ was sold[1] as a healthy man in the prime of life, and this Simon was sold[2] as a nursing child. The ravening dogs dragged Christ to Pilate's palace; this boy was brought before the bearded dog Moses. They wounded Christ with countless lashes, and entwined his sacred head with thorns; the savage race tore the infant's tender flesh with pincers, and stabbed his head and chest with needles. On a cross Christ exchanged life for death; stretched out on a cross this boy collapsed. When Christ was flogged the Jews vied in mocking him; this boy was likewise mocked and cursed.

---

[1] For the thirty pieces of silver paid to the traitor Judas Iscariot (Matthew 26: 14–16).

[2] That is, sold to the Jews of Trent by Tobias for gold, as described in Tiberino's letter to Zovenzoni.

hic fuit illusus et maledictus item.
Hebraei fuso laetantur sanguine Christi;
   haec gens de pueri sanguine laeta bibit.
Tertia lux Domino devicta morte refulsit;   25
   tertia lux pueri pandit ubique necem.
Apparuit multis surgens a funere Christus;
   inventus multis consulit[1] iste puer.
Non quae concessit miracula maxima dicam,
   nec referam leto[2] quot levat iste viros.   30
Corrupto emicuit Dominus custode sepulchri;
   iudice corrupto non latet, ecce, Symon!
Lucentis caeli Christus superastitit arce;
   hic novus aeterna miles in arce sedet.
Rex Titus ob crimen gentem delevit Hebraeam,   35
   aequavitque solo moenia, templa, domos. [sig. A3r]
Lustravere Titi Capitolia celsa triumphum;
   Baccha ibi Caesareas cinxit honore comas.
Iohannes, princeps et praesul in urbe Tridenti,
   nemine iustitia nec pietate[3] minor,   40
Iudaeos—tandem flagranti in crimine captos—
   de medio merita tollere morte iubet.
Caetera turba canum Romae devicta fatiscit;
   omnia pro domino iura fuere meo.
Non potuere doli nec Hebraea tributa nec aurum   45
   vulgatum facinus quin sit in orbe suum.

---

[1] *correxi*: contulit *T*
[2] *correxi*: laeto *T*
[3] *correxi*: piatate *T*

The Hebrews rejoiced when Christ's blood was shed; this same race joyfully drank some of the boy's blood. The third day shone out on the Lord when he conquered death; the third day spread abroad news of the boy's murder. Rising from death, Christ appeared to many; this boy, once found, shows care for many. I shall not speak of the mighty miracles which [Christ] granted, nor report how many men this boy releases from death. The guard of the tomb was bribed but the Lord shone forth;[1] "Mr Judge" [dei Giudici][2] was bribed but, behold, Simon does not lie hidden! Christ took his place high above in heaven's shining citadel; this new soldier also sits in the eternal citadel. The ruler Titus destroyed the Hebrew race because of their crime, and razed their walls, temple, and homes to the ground.[3] [sig. A3r] The Capitoline hill watched Titus's triumph;[4] there a Bacchante[5] encircled Caesar's locks with a crown of honor. Johannes, prince and bishop in the city of Trent, second to none in justice or piety, gives orders for the Jews — at last caught red-handed — to be removed from our midst by the death they deserve.

The rest of the pack of dogs languishes, defeated, in Rome; all the laws have been in my lord's favor. No Hebrew wiles, tribute-money, or gold have been able to stop their misdeed becoming common knowledge in the world. Under the

---

[1] See Matthew 27: 62–66, and 28: 11–15: in the first passage, leading Jews persuade Pilate to set a military guard before Jesus' tomb in order to prevent the removal of his body by the disciples; in the second, the soldiers of the guard, shocked by their encounter with the risen Christ, report it to the Jews and are bribed by them to say that the disciples had in fact removed the body while they themselves were asleep.

[2] The envoy sent by the pope to judge the legality of Hinderbach's trial and execution of the Jews of Trent was Giovanni Battista dei Giudici, and in Italian *giudice* means "judge." See Appendix 2. As to his motives, see Pusculo's description of him below, 200–1: "obviously a Hebrew defender posing as an envoy! Gold had blinkered him, and had also made him deaf: his heart had been hardened by gold."

[3] Titus joined his father Vespasian in 67 AD in his mission to suppress the Jewish revolt, and after capturing Jerusalem in 70 was hailed as *imperator* by his troops; he did not become emperor until 79.

[4] In a Roman triumph the victorious general proceeded to the temple of Jupiter Optimus Maximus on the Capitoline hill.

[5] A female votary of Bacchus.

Capta est Iudaea sub rhinoceronte potenti,
    atque suum terrae[1] crimen ubique patet.
Alma duos huius lustravit Roma triumphos,
    unde suum duplici velat[2] honore caput.   50
"Gloria in excelsis et pax ubicunque per orbem!"
    rhinoceron victor intonat ante Deum.
Rhinoceron, fidei lux ardentissima nostrae,
    sacra Deo victor debita vota refert.
Quae vox pontificis laudes deprom[p]serit huius,   55
    aut ubi sunt[3] tanto praemia digna viro?
Donec lenta trahent septem sua plaustra Triones,
    et referet clarum praevia stella diem,
virtutes laudesque suae per saecula vivent—
    nomen perpetuo vivet in orbe suum!   60

Eiusdem deprecatio.

Salve, sancte Symon, Christi pendentis ymago [sig. A3v]
    in cruce, fulgentis lucida stella poli!
Salve, sancte Symon, caelestibus addite divis,
    in nece postque necem plurima passe puer!
Cum tibi Iudaei lacerarent forcipe carnem,   5
    in cruce cumque tua brac[c]hia tenta forent,
tanquam pullus ovis coram tondente silebas,
    deque tuis oculis lachrima nulla fluit.
Quippe tibi laqueo tam mollia colla premebant,
    fod[i]ebantque tuum nobile corpus acu.   10
Hoc tu martyrio fulgentia sydera caeli
    scandis, et Hebraeum pandis ubique scelus.
Non potuere canes rabidi pervertere tantum
    quod tua Christicolis fata sepulta forent!

---

[1] *correxi*: triste *T*
[2] *correxi*: vellat *T*
[3] *correxi*: aut sunt ubi *T*

powerful rhinoceros[1] Jewry has been taken captive,[2] and all over the earth its crime lies exposed. Gracious Rome has watched Hinderbach's two triumphs; because of them she covers his head with a double crown of honor. "Glory in the highest and peace throughout the whole world!" thunders the victorious rhinoceros before God. The victorious rhinoceros, brightest light of our faith, renders to God the sacred vows that are due.

What voice could utter the praises of this bishop, or where are there rewards worthy of so great a man? For as long as the seven Bears[3] draw their slow-moving wagon, and the herald-star[4] brings back broad daylight, throughout the ages shall his virtues and praises live — for all time shall his name live in the world!

A prayer by the same author.

Hail, holy Simon, image of Christ hanging [sig. A3v] on the cross, bright star of the gleaming sky! Hail, holy Simon, ranked now with the gods of heaven, boy who suffered so many things in death and after death! Though the Jews were tearing your flesh with pincers, and though your arms were stretched on a cross, you were silent like a young lamb before its shearer,[5] and no tear trickled from your eyes. They were, we know, tightening a noose round your soft neck, and stabbing your noble body with needles. Through this your martyrdom you now ascend to heaven's gleaming stars, and make the Hebrews' crime known everywhere. The ravening dogs were unable to twist the truth so much that your fate

---

[1] For Isidore of Seville the rhinoceros, the monoceros, and the unicorn were one and the same animal — so much so that he applies to it the legend that the unicorn could be captured only by a virgin who cradled its head in her lap. See his *Etymologiarum . . . libri*, ed. Lindsay, 2: bk. 12, chap. 2, paras. 12–13; English translation in Barney et al., *The Etymologies*, 252. The legend occurs in the much earlier, but equally popular, medieval collection *Physiologus* which appeared in Greek between the second and fourth centuries, and in Latin between the fourth and sixth centuries, followed by: "The unicorn has one horn because the Savior said, 'I and the Father are one' [John 10: 30]. 'For he has raised up a horn of salvation for us in the house of his servant David' [Luke 1: 69]. Coming down from heaven, he came into the womb of the Virgin Mary. 'He was loved like the son of the unicorns' [cf. Psalm 22: 21 – Vulgate Ps. 21: 22] as David said in the psalm": *Physiologus*, trans. Michael J. Curley (Austin: University of Texas Press, 1979), 51. Tiberino is therefore using this traditional identification of the rhinoceros with the unicorn, and of the unicorn with Christ, in order to make an unusually colorful reference to Christ as Hinderbach's powerful supporter in heaven.

[2] Coins commemorating Titus's taking of Jerusalem bear the legend IUDAEA CAPTA.

[3] The seven stars comprising the constellations Great and Little Bear.

[4] The planet Venus.

[5] Cf. Isaiah 53: 7: "et quasi agnus coram tondente se obmutescet, et non aperiet os suum"; quoted in Acts 8: 32.

Non potuere canes tot clam depromere nummos   15
    occultum facinus quod sit in orbe tuum!
Ceu de sole iubar de te miracula fulgent,
    atque tuam sentit languidus orbis opem.
Tu nunc e caelo vindictam sanguinis hausti
    sumis,[1] et offensas ultus es usque tuas;   20
proque tua in terris pugnavit morte Iohannes,
    regna Tridentini qui regit alta soli.
Tertia fluxit hyemps, et tertia labitur aestas,
    quod cum Iudaeis bella Iohannes agit.
Iustitia e caelo tandem delapsa per auras   25
    sancta Tridentini praesulis acta probat.
Te probat extinctum nostri sub ymagine Christi, [sig. A4r]
    te quoque inter sanctos approbat esse choros;
et genus Hebraeum, quo non crudelius[2] ullum,
    usque—et ab antiquo—comprobat esse nequam.   30
Salve, sancte Symon, martyr sanctissime; salve,
    o salve, aeterna laude canende puer!
Tu nunc, ante Deum victor, ceu stella coruscas;
    tu crucis in caelo signifer ante Deum.
Nemo preces ad te fundit devotus inanes,   35
    quod suspensa tibi plurima vota docent.
Praesulis ergo tui semper memor esto Iohannis,
    proque salute sua nocte dieque roga!
Protege et ante Deum cives populumque Tridenti,
    atque tui vatis—si licet—esto memor!   40

Eiusdem deprecatio.

Sum memor, alme Symon, cum te Iudaea necasset
    atra tribus, primum me retulisse canes.
Templa tridentino domino subeunte Iohanne,
    hanc illi vocem nostra Thalia dedit:
"Heri[3] cum puero mulier dignissima vidit   5
    Iudaeum blandis ora movere sonis."
Huic dicto sapiens praesul meus addidit aures,
    praetorique iubet quaerere rite scelus.
Extemplo[4] in latebris gentis compertus Hebraeae,

---

    [1] *correxi*: summis *T*
    [2] *correxi*: crudaelius *T*
    [3] *correxi*: haeri *T*
    [4] *correxi*: ex templo *T*

would lie buried and hidden from Christ-worshipers! The dogs were unable to secretly produce sufficient cash for world-wide concealment of the outrage against
you! Miracles gleam from you like radiance from the sun, and the weary world
feels your power. From heaven you are now taking revenge for the draining of
your blood, and you are still avenging the offenses against you; and on earth Johannes [Hinderbach,] ruler of the lofty realm that is Trent's domain, has fought
to establish your [martyr's] death.

A third winter has slipped by, and a third summer is now passing, as Johannes
pursues his war with the Jews. Justice, having finally flown down through the air
from heaven,[1] confirms the holy acts of Trent's bishop. It confirms that you were
killed in the image of Christ our God, [sig.A4r] and assents to your inclusion in
the companies of saints; and it acknowledges that the Hebrew race, which is second to none in cruelty, is still — as it has been from of old — wicked.

Hail, holy Simon, most holy martyr; hail, O hail, boy whose praise should
be sung eternally! Victorious now before God, you twinkle like a star; you are the
cross's standard-bearer[2] before God in heaven. No devotee pours forth prayers
to you in vain, as is shown by a host of votive offerings hung up for you.[3] Be ever
mindful, then, of your bishop Johannes, and pray night and day for his health!
And, before God, protect the citizens and people of Trent, and be mindful — if
you may — of your poet!

A prayer by the same author.

I remember, gracious Simon, that when the deadly Jewish tribe had slain you,
I myself first reported the dogs. As Johannes, Lord of Trent, was entering his
church, my Muse[4] passed on to him this remark: "Yesterday a most worthy
woman noticed a Jew speaking in flattering tones to a boy." My wise bishop
listened to these words, and ordered the *podestà* to make due inquiry into the
crime. Immediately you were discovered in the Hebrew race's hiding-place,

---

[1] Cf. Vergil, *Aeneid* 11. 595; Ovid, *Metamorphoses* 3. 101, *Ars amatoria* 1. 43; Silus
Italicus, *Punica* 2. 542.

[2] The word *signifer* can also mean "bearing the constellations".

[3] Hung up in Simon's shrine, that is.

[4] Traditionally Thalia was the Muse not only of comedy (as in Martial, *Epigrams* 7.
17. 4) but also of lyric poetry (as in Horace, *Odes* 4. 6. 25).

detegis illata et[1] vulnera[2] multa tibi.   10
Et nova languenti saeclo miracula monstras,
   quilibet unde tuam sentit egrotus opem. [sig. A4v]
Si merui, tunc cum veniet lux ultima nobis
   de caelo, martyr, porrige, sancte, manum!
   Amen.

Iohannis Matthiae Tyberini liricum carmen ad beati Symonis Tridentini com[m]endationem feliciter incipit.

Sacrosancta fides Christi
sub imperio Papae Sixti
   tanquam sol resplenduit.
Est detectus Iudaeorum
fons rabiei, fons malorum   5
in populos Christianorum,
   martyrizato Symone.
Sanctum Symonem negabant
clam necesse, et litigabant,
falsos testes quaeritabant   10
   in Romana Curia.
Papa tunc sex cardinales,
sanctitate et fama[3] aequales —
ut decet — elegit[4] tales
   hanc audire causulam.[5]   15
Se Iudaei cum tributis
et cautelis cum astutis
opponebant, sed versutis
   inimica est veritas.
Iustus praesul tunc Iohannes   20
Tridentinus Hebraeos canes
per processus non inanes
   confudit, obtinuit.

---

[1] *supplevi*: et
[2] *correxi*: ulnera *T*
[3] *correxi*: famma *T*
[4] *correxi*: ellegit *T*
[5] *correxi*: causam *T*

and you revealed the many wounds inflicted on you. And you are showing forth to a weary age fresh miracles, through which any invalid feels your power. [sig. A4v] If I have deserved it, stretch out your hand to me from heaven, holy martyr, when my last day comes!

Amen.

A lyric poem of Giovanni Mattia Tiberino in commendation of blessed Simon of Trent begins auspiciously.[1]

The inviolable Christian faith shone out like the sun under the rule of Pope Sixtus.

A fount of Jewish frenzy, a fount of evils done to Christian peoples, was revealed when Simon was martyred.

They secretly denied that Simon must be made a saint, and went to law, earnestly seeking false witnesses in the Roman Curia.

The Pope then — rightly   chose six cardinals, equal in holiness and repute, to hear this petty lawsuit.

By dint of tribute-funds and shrewd precautions the Jews put up a fight, but truth is hostile to schemers!

Then just Johannes, bishop of Trent, through purposeful procedures routed the Hebrew dogs, and prevailed.

---

[1] Uniquely in the present volume, this poem is written in a medieval meter: twelve stanzas, each of which (except the first) consists of three accentual trochaic dimeters acatalectic followed by one catalectic, rhyming *aaab*; the first stanza has only two acatalectic lines followed by one catalectic, rhyming *aab*.

Papae misit Sanctitati
restitutos sanitati;   25
plus quam mille deprecati
    Symonis auxilium.
Veritate Papa inventa—
quod Iudaei per tormenta
in cruce membra distenta   30
    consumpsissent pueri—
approbat Dei adiutorio
sanctum Symonem in consistorio,[1]
tanto laudans in auditorio
    Tridentinum praesulem.   35
In cathalogo sanctorum
hunc scripsit, qui iuxta t[h]ronum
Christi stat, Symon, flos florum,
    virgo, martir et innocens.
Ecce, Symon, crucifixus   40
instar Christi et acu transfixus,
ante t[h]ronum Dei fixus, [sig. A5r]
    pro devotis rogitat!
Sancte puer, caeli stella,
pro nobis Deum compella,   45
ut in Paradisi[2] cella
    nos collocet in saecula!
    Amen.

[sig. A7r] **Divo Iohanni Hinderbacchio, antistiti Tridentino dignissimo, salutem.**

[sig. A8r] **Eiusdem Iohannis Matthye carmen.**

Corticibus prisci numeros scripsere poetae,
    lactea cum nondum[3] carta reperta foret. [sig. A8v]
Aurea tunc habuit Saturnia saecula mundus,
    et tunc Pierios duxit Apol[l]o choros.
At nunc, exculto rerum tot munere mundo,   5
    cum Phoebo Musae conticuere novem.
Crevit avaritiae tantum sitis, aestus et ardor,

---

[1] *correxi*: concistorio *T*
[2] *correxi*: pardisi *T*
[3] *correxi*: nundum *T*

He sent to his Holiness the Pope those restored to health; more than a thousand had prayed for Simon's help.

When the Pope found out the truth — that the Jews had stretched the boy's limbs out on a cross and worn him down by torture — he, with God's help, in the consistory approved Simon as a saint, praising Trent's bishop at this great assembly.

He enrolled in the list of saints this boy who stands next to Christ's throne, Simon, flower of flowers, virgin, martyr, and innocent.

Behold, Simon crucified and pierced with steel[1] in place of Christ, set before God's throne, [sig. A5r] earnestly prays for his devotees!

Holy boy, star of heaven, speak to God on our behalf, so that he may place us in the inner chamber[2] of Paradise for ever!

Amen.[3]

[sig. A7r] To godly Iohannes Hinderbach, most worthy bishop of Trent, greetings.[4]

[sig. A8r] A poem of the same Giovanni Mattia [Tiberino.]

Ancient poets wrote their lines on strips of bark, since milk-white paper was not yet invented. [sig. A8v] That was when the world enjoyed Saturn's golden age,[5] and when Apollo led forth the Muses' chorus.[6] But now, with the world enriched by so many bounties, the nine Muses, and Apollo too, have fallen silent. Avaricious thirst, passion, and desire have grown so great,

---

[1] Though *acus* usually means "needle", here it seems to refer also to the spear (=*lancea* in the Vulgate) with which Christ's side was pierced after his death: see John 19: 34.

[2] The word *cella* in religious contexts denotes a principal or subsidiary chamber of a temple.

[3] The next poem in this document, addressed to Hinderbach as "Gloria pontificum", extends from sig. A5r to the end of sig. A6v, but is here omitted as not strictly relevant to the case of Simon.

[4] The text and translation of the following poem, Zovenzoni's "Surgite pontifices" ("Arise, you bishops"), which extends from sig. A7r to sig. A8r, have been placed earlier in this section, where the two available versions are collated.

[5] With this reference to the legendary golden age when Saturn reigned, cf. Vergil, *Eclogues* 4. 6: "iam redit et Virgo, redit et Saturnia regna." See also below, 85 n. 2.

[6] For Apollo as 'Leader of the Muses', see Vergil, *Eclogues* 6. 66: "utque viro Phoebi chorus adsurrexerit omnis." The Muses are sometimes called 'Pierides' as (in classical mythology) the nine daughters of Pierus, a king of Emathia, and 'Pierius' is the corresponding adjective.

vatibus ut toto[1] nullus in orbe locus.
Solus in hoc Latio, princeps sanctissime, restas,
    affers qui miseris vatibus auxilium.   10
Tu solus pleno diffundis munera cornu;
    tu curam aeterni solus honoris habes.
Haec igitur digno suadent ut carmine semper
    ipse tuum, princeps, nomen ad astra feram!
    Vale, pacis ac iusticiae pater.

---

[1] *correxi*: toro *T*

that there is no place in the whole world for poets. In Italy today, most holy prince, you stand alone, bringing help to wretched poets. You alone dispense bounties from a full horn;[1] you alone have a concern for eternal honor. These thoughts, then, urge me always to exalt your name, prince, to the stars in fitting verses of my own!

Farewell, father of peace and justice.[2]

---

[1] An allusion to the magical horn of Plenty (*cornu Copiae*), supposed to satisfy all its owner's desires. Cf. Horace, *Carmen Saeculare* 59–60: "apparetque beata pleno copia cornu."

[2] The following long poem by Tiberino in praise of the Assumption of the Blessed Virgin Mary—omitted in this edition—extends from sig. A8v to sig. A10v, and is in turn followed by a tetrastich which identifies the printer as Leonardo Trivisano, priest-in-charge of "the Church of the Mother of Christ." The place and date of printing are given as Trent, 5 September 1482.

Section II

SECTION II

[sig. ar] **Calphurnii poetae Brix[iensis] mors et apotheosis Simonis infantis novi martiris, ad Iohannem Inderbacchium, pontificem Tridentinum et dominum praestantissimum.**

Vir sacer et nostro princeps memorabilis aevo,
cui praeclara dedit virtus moderamina iusti
imperii, et populos rexisse ex ordine plures,
et fidei vixisse decus venerabile—quod non
conticeat praesens nec postera deleat aetas!—   5
en, ego primitias vates tibi defero. Fas sit
te nugas cepisse meas, quae pectore parvo
insurgunt! Sat erit magnum voluisse laborem
suscipere atque animum magno sub pondere vinci.
Non mea Musa tamen laudes aequare canendo   10
contendat, nec si faveat mihi doctus Apollo.
Quis tibi par, magni moveat nisi plectra Maronis
M[a]eonidaeque sacri? Nam te, quem nostra minorem
non tulerit priscis aetas, celebrare laboret
antiquum quisquis vates imitatur acumen.   15
Quid primum memorem? Superos Astr[a]ea reliquit
te regnante iterum terris victura libenter;
nam te non fugiunt clari praecepta Solonis,
debita qui meritis persolvas praemia, poenis
afficias sontes iusto moderamine rerum.   20
Quis pauper queritur leges et iura resolvi?
Ad[i]ice quod vatum M[a]ecoenas solus haberi
nunc possis, in quo studiorum summa relicta est,
et spes tota sedet Latiis exclusa tyrannis;
qui non Pieridum, sed numina grandis acervi   25
nummorum observant. Heu, mendicare poetae
cogimur, et raris iuvat impal[l]escere chartis!
Nunc ubi prisca aetas? Doctis non praemia dantur
vatibus, utque olim cum totus paruit orbis,
Roma, tibi! Haut magnos carmen sortitur honores.   30
       Sed revocas quantum potes, Inderbacchie, Musas, [sig. av]
nec pateris torpere viros, praecordia quorum
numen Apollineum doctus spirantia cernis.
Quis tibi collatus princeps non cesserit, et te

SECTION II

[sig. ar] **An account by [Giovanni] Calfurnio, poet of Brescia, of the death and apotheosis of the new infant martyr Simon, addressed to Johannes Hinderbach, bishop and most distinguished lord of Trent.**[1]

Remarkable priest and prince of our time, to whom outstanding virtue has given the reins of just dominion, guidance of many peoples in succession, and veneration as a living ornament of the faith—one which the present age should not ignore, nor a future age forget!—here am I, a poet bringing you my first-fruits. May you be right in accepting my trifles, the products of a puny intellect! It will suffice that I wanted to take on a great task and am mentally crushed by its great weight. Yet my poetic Muse would not strive to make its praises equal to the theme, not even if learned Apollo should smile on me. Who would be a match for you, unless he wielded the plectrum of great Vergil and divine Homer? For *any* poet who emulates ancient insight would struggle to celebrate you, whom our age has called not inferior to the men of old. What should I first record? Astraea[2] has left the powers above to live freely on earth again in your reign; for the precepts of famous Solon do not escape you, who by just control of affairs duly reward the deserving and punish the guilty.[3] What poor man complains that laws and rights are nullified? Add to this that you alone can now be considered a 'Maecenas of poets',[4] one in whom the sum total of scholarship survives and all its hope resides, banished by Latin tyrants; *they* worship the divine powers, not of the Muses,[5] but of a huge pile of money. Alas, we poets are forced to beg, and our joy lies in growing pale over rare folios![6] Where now is antiquity? Rewards are not given to learned poets, and as they were given long ago when all the world obeyed you, Rome! Small indeed are the honors poetry obtains.

But you, Hinderbach, with all your might call back the Muses, [sig. av] nor do you suffer laziness in those whose hearts you, learned man, perceive as

---

[1] All the texts in this section are in *L*, whose signature numbers are therefore inserted throughout. Like Zovenzoni's 'Surgite, pontifices' in Section I, and Pusculo's *Simonis* in Section III, Calfurnio's long opening poem, recounting the tale of Simon, employs the meter most appropriate for serious Latin poetry—the dactylic hexameter.

[2] The goddess of justice whose return marks a new golden age: Vergil, *Eclogues* 4. 6: "iam redit et Virgo, redit et Saturnia regna." See also above, 79 n. 5, 75 n. 1.

[3] Cf. Priscian, *Panegyricus*, 251. Solon (fl. *c.* 594 BC) was an Athenian lawgiver who sought to resolve conflicts within Athenian society.

[4] Maecenas (died 8 BC) was a wealthy Roman statesman and trusted counselor of the emperor Augustus, and his name became proverbial as a munificent patron of poets.

[5] For 'Pierides' as an alternative title for the Muses, see above, 79 n. 6.

[6] Cf. Persius, *Satires* 5. 62: "at te nocturnis iuvat impallescere chartis."

inferior quo non decedat iudice victus?   35
Nulli nota magis tibi quam Parnasia[1] rupes,
teque magis nemo vera pietate colendus;[2]
quo tibi quae paret Pyliam gens laeta senectam,
Cum[a]eique annos te vivere pulveris optat.
Non formidaris, miro sed honore verendus   40
occurris; te nulla potest flexisse voluptas.
Integer et constans, ullo non tangeris auri
ardore, atque[3] oculis potuit non gemma coruscans
perplacuisse tuis; quo divus et aethere lapsus
crederis, et tecum pax summa enata videtur.   45
Comis es, et summa semper gravitate probandus.
Effigiem imperii Xenophon quam rectius olim
finxisset iusti, si tunc te fata tulissent!
Sponte sua claros nulloque monente Penates
intrasset; Clario vel se sine numine veri   50
aeterno optasset tibi iungi foedere amoris.
Commoda respectas hominum, nec cuncta reponis
utilitate tua. Magno non aere premuntur
qui tua iura colunt; nusquam quoque visa moveri
seditio; patuere aures atque atria semper   55
omnibus, et faciles aditus das saepe querelis.
Nil[4] nisi quod possit iustum decernis haberi,
utque[5] feras falso nullius gratia tangit
iuditium: proh, quanta tuae constantia mentis!
Desinat Alcinoum tellus Phaeacia tantum   60
efferre, et prisco iam non memorentur ab aevo
plurima quae docti fingunt mendatia vates!
Sed licet haec fuerint, veroque minora ferantur,

---

[1] *correxi*: pernasia *L*
[2] *correxi*: collendus *L*.
[3] *correxi*: ad que *L*
[4] *correxi*: Et *L*
[5] *correxi*: ut ve *L*

breathing out Apollo's divine power. What prince, ranged against you, would not yield, and what judge would not make him withdraw defeated as your inferior? No one knows craggy Mount Parnassus[1] better than you, and no one should be cherished for true piety more than you; hence your happy subject people pray that you will live to enjoy a ripe old age as if at Pylos,[2] and longevity as if on Cumae's ashy soil.[3] You are not dreaded, but present yourself as one to be revered with wondrous honor; no love of pleasure can ever sway *you*! Upright and resolute, you are not touched by any lust for gold, and no sparkling gem has ever been able to gratify your gaze; hence you are believed divine and heaven-sent, and perfect peace seems to have sprung forth with you. You are affable, and always to be commended for your perfect dignity. How much more accurate a picture of just dominion would Xenophon[4] have painted long ago, if the Fates had produced you then! Of his own accord and without anyone's advice he would have entered your famous home; he would have wished to be joined with you in an everlasting bond of true love even without Apollo's divine influence.[5] You have regard for people's interests and do not make everything depend on your own advantage. Those who cherish your laws are not coerced by large sums of money; nowhere, either, has discord been seen to stir; your ear and your palace have always been open to all, and you often give easy access to complaints. You decree nothing but what can be considered just, and no one's favor influences you to pronounce a crooked verdict: ah, how resolute you are! Let the land of Phaeacia[6] stop proclaiming Alcinous so great a man, and let the frequent falsehoods invented by learned poets *not* be recalled now from a bygone age! But even if such things as these did occur, and even if the truth is still greater than the things reported,[7]

---

[1] In ancient times sacred to Dionysus, Apollo, and the Muses, with the Castalian Spring and Delphi on its slopes.

[2] In Greek mythology Nestor was the wise old king of Pylos during the Trojan War.

[3] Cumae was close to Puteoli (now Pozzuoli, Italy), which was renowned for its volcanic ash. In classical mythology the Sibyl of Cumae refused Apollo's offer of eternal life if she accepted his love, and was punished with an eternity of growing old.

[4] In other words, Hinderbach might well have replaced Cyrus the Great (560/59–530 BC), king of Persia, whom Xenophon saw as a paragon of kingship and immortalized in his *Cyropaedia*.

[5] 'Clarius' is used as an epithet of Apollo because in classical mythology Claros was a town in Ionia sacred to him: see Ovid, *Metamorphoses* 1. 516. Xenophon's touching faith in traditional Greek religion is shown in *Anabasis* 3. 1. 4–7: on Socrates' advice he goes to Delphi, asks Apollo how to ensure that his journey with Cyrus is the best and safest possible, and duly reports back to Socrates, who then rebukes him for not first asking the oracle whether he should join the expedition or not.

[6] Where, according to Homer (*Odyssey* 6), Odysseus was entertained by the king, Alcinous.

[7] Literally, 'even if things less than the truth are reported.'

non tibi par, namque ille vagum suscepit Ulyssem,
tu cunctos misera qui paupertate premuntur. [sig. aiir]   65
    Hospitioque foves rerum quos cernis egenos.
Attica[1] si quondam dominum te terra tulisset,
non Sardium[2] aut Croesi claro memoranda Soloni
regia visa foret, Cilicum quo venit ad agros
tempore. Non Veneris Cyprum, ostia[3] Nili   70
lustrasset; doctas potius coluisset Athenas.
Vivat Pell[a]ei Cinicus contemptor alumni!
Tecum erit, atque volet tectis habitare sub isdem,[4]
et regere imperium discet te hortante magistro.
Quid loquar ut cunctis tua sit prudentia rebus,   75
qui memor exacti quae mox ventura trahantur
prospicis, et summa quod adest ratione gubernas?
Cur totiens iac[t]et sapientes Graecia septem
si tu conspiceris? Taceat Milesia tellus,
nec ferat in caelum praeconia magna Thaletis;   80
non Lesbos, nec terra mihi Salaminos alumnum
amplius ostentet, non Spart[a]e aut Lyndia tellus,
quaeque Bianta tulit; sileat[5] simul alta Corynthos!
    Quis tantas animi dotes non carmine donet
aut, si non possit, tantum miretur, ut illas   85
crediderit non posse homini contingere soli?
Tu fidei exemplum nostrae memorabile, et idem
rel[l]igionis honor; quo praemonstrante pudorem
Curia suscipiat mores Romana severos!
Quid magis est cultum templis ubi sacra frequentas,[6]   90
aut ubi plura hominum vota exolvuntur ad aras?
Non sub rege Numa coluit sic Romula plebes
divinos ritus, quamvis is valle sub ima

---

[1] *correxi*: Actica *L*.
[2] *correxi*: Sardae *L*
[3] *correxi*: hostia *L*
[4] *correxi*: hisdem *L*
[5] *correxi*: scileat *L*
[6] *correxi*: frequentes *L*

Alcinous is no match for you, since *he* played host to wandering Ulysses, but *you* do so to all those weighed down by wretched poverty.

[sig. aiir] By your hospitality you also foster those you see in need of material things. If the territory of Attica[1] had borne you as its lord in the past, the palace of Sardis, or Croesus,[2] would not have seemed remarkable to renowned Solon[3] when he came to the country of the Cilicians. He would not have traversed Venus's Cyprus[4] or the mouths of the Nile; rather he would have cherished learned Athens. Farewell to the Cynic[5] who despised his protégé from Pella! Alexander will be with *you*, and he will want to dwell under the same roof, and he will learn how to rule an empire with *you* as his encouraging teacher. Why should I tell how your prudence is seen in everything, since, while mindful of the past, you foresee what events are destined soon to occur, and govern the present with sovereign reason? Why should Greece so often boast of its Seven Sages[6] if you are before our eyes? Let the land of Miletus be quiet, and cease loudly praising Thales to the skies; let Lesbos, and the territory of Salamis,[7] no more parade their respective sons before me, nor the land of Sparta or of Lindos, or the land that produced Bias; let lofty Corinth be silent too!

Who would not reward such great mental gifts with poetry or, if that were beyond him, would not so marvel at them as to believe they cannot be granted to one person alone? You are a notable exemplar of our faith, and also a credit to religion; following your model of self-restraint, let the Roman Curia adopt strict habits! What church is better attended than those where you officiate at services, or where are more people's vows fully discharged at altars? Not even under King Numa did Romulus' folk observe sacred rites like this, although he pretended

---

[1] The district of central Greece whose capital was Athens.

[2] Sardis was the capital of Lydia, whose king (*c.* 560–546 BC) was the famously rich Croesus.

[3] The Athenian legislator is reputed to have visited Croesus while travelling overseas for ten years after his reforms (see Herodotus, *Histories* 1. 29–33), but if he died *c.* 560/559 BC this is unlikely.

[4] In ancient times Cyprus was renowned for the worship of Venus: see Horace, *Odes* 1. 30. 2.

[5] Diogenes (*c.* 412/403 *c.* 324/321 BC), founder of the Cynic sect at Athens. According to Plutarch (*Life of Alexander* 14), when asked by Alexander the Great if he lacked anything he replied: "Stand a little less between me and the sun." Pella (the capital of Macedonia under Philip II) was Alexander's birthplace.

[6] First explicitly listed by Plato (*Protagoras* 343a) as Thales of Miletus, Pittacus of Mytilene (chief city of Lesbos), Bias of Priene, Solon of Athens, Cleobulus of Lindos (on Rhodes), Myson of Chen (replacing Periander, tyrant of Corinth and so not acceptable to later ages), and Chilon of Sparta.

[7] Athens with its *alumnus* Solon having already been mentioned in this section, Calfurnio omits it from his list of the Seven Sages' homes, and alludes instead to Salamis with its ancient king Ajax, the next greatest Greek warrior at Troy after Achilles.

fingeret esse deam, cum qua congressus utrinque
nocturni fierent. Tu divus et integer, almam   95
virtutem ostendens, sola es pietate verendus.
    At quis M[a]eonio satis explicet ore colendas
iustitiae vires, poenas aut crimine tanto
enumeret dignas, quas gens Iudaea coacta est [sig. aiiv]
persolvisse tibi—et merito? Nam perfida nuper   100
ausa nefas, quantum non saecula prisca tulerunt,
aut nostro factum nusquam memoratur in aevo.
Vos, o mortales, vero qui pectore C[h]ristum
excolitis, placeat vestro cur sanguine pasci
Iudaeam gentem? Cui mos—ut barbara quondam   105
natio consuevit, Latia dum lege repressa est—
stat mactare aliquem, diro dehinc pane repleri,
noster ubi admixtus sanguis, quo corpus odorem
deponat taetrum. Quid si dominentur et in nos
imperium teneant? Scelus est non perdere gentem   110
atque e vita hominum non extrusisse nefandam!
    Namque dies aderat nobis, qua sacra quotannis
atque resurgentis Domini sol[l]emnia fiunt,
et lux Martis erat. Subito Samuelis ad aedes
Iudaei properant, quibus ii posuere sacellum,   115
scilicet ut solito spectarent more iuvencum,
qui Levigi fuerat nuper devectus ab agris.
Inter se vario sed dum sermone volutant
plurima, tunc[1] falsi qui nominis Angelus esset
incipit effari: "Nobis ut cuncta supersunt   120
ad sol[l]emne sacrum festaeque ad fercula cenae,
deficere his unum doleo." Nec plura locutus.
Cetera turba atrox vocem percepit, in illum
lumina coniectans: caedem quod posceret atram
sanguinis humani. Sic foede[2] victima tristis   125
ludibrio[3] C[h]risti et facinus, proh,[4] grande paratur!
Delegere locum: foedi placuere Penates,
illi ubi constiterant. Post haec contentio surgit,
qua ratione queant infantem abducere qui mas
esset; at in variis donec sententia verbis   130

---

   [1] *correxi*: tuuc *L*
   [2] *correxi*: foedere *L*
   [3] *correxi*: Ludibriro *L*
   [4] *correxi*: proth *L*

there was a goddess deep down in a valley with whom meetings of two kinds took place at night.[1] You, godly and upright, displaying gracious virtue, for your piety alone deserve respect.

But who could fitly describe the powers of justice, worthy of adornment by Homer's voice, or list the penalties, merited for so great a crime, which the Jewish race has been forced [sig. aiiv] to pay you in full—and deservedly so? For recently the faithless race has dared a wicked deed which exceeds anything antiquity produced, nor is it recorded to have happened anywhere in our own age.[2] You mortals who in trueness of heart honor Christ, why would you be pleased that the Jewish race feeds on your blood? They have an established practice—it became a habit when, long ago, the barbarous tribe was restrained by Roman law—to sacrifice somebody, and then to fill themselves with gruesome bread containing our mingled blood, so as to get rid of their foul body-odor. What if they were our lords and held rule over us? Failure to destroy their wicked race and eject it from human society is a crime!

For that day was with us when each year the sacred ceremonies of the Lord's resurrection take place, and it was a morning in March. Promptly the Jews hurried to Samuel's house, where they had placed their shrine, no doubt to look—as was their tradition—at a young bullock recently brought from the fields of Levico. But just as they were tossing about various remarks on many topics, the one misnamed Engel [Angel] blurted out: "While we have plenty of everything we need for the sacred ceremony and for the dishes of our festive supper, I am sorry that there is one thing lacking." And he said no more. The rest of the brutal mob, glancing at him, understood his words: that he demanded the grisly shedding of human blood. So, foully, a sad victim and, alas, a mighty misdeed were prepared in mockery of Christ! They chose the place: the foul home where they had assembled found favor. Afterwards a dispute arose as to how they could abduct a male infant; but while amid various arguments they tried to reach a decision, straightway Samuel spoke in coaxing tones to his servant:

---

[1] Numa Pompilius, legendary second king of Rome (traditionally 715–673 BC), was the reputed organiser of its official religion. The word *utrinque* (literally, 'on both sides', here translated 'of two kinds') refers to two passages of Livy (*Ab Urbe Condita* 1. 19. 5 and 1. 21. 3): in the first, Numa's wish to imbue a rough people with fear of the gods is said to have led him to 'invent' nocturnal meetings between himself and his wife (and counselor), the water goddess Egeria; in the second, he is said to have declared a certain grove sacred to the Muses because they went there to converse with his wife.

[2] This seems to show a surprising ignorance of previous ritual-murder allegations against Jews in English, French, and German lands.

quaeritur, extemplo[1] blanda sic voce locutus
est servo[2] Samuel: "Age, Lazare, nostra voluptas,
C[h]risticolam infantem nobis, en, sur[r]ipe! Centum [sig. a3r]
aureoli[3] precium." Verum is discrimine tanto[4]
abnuit, et pavida stupefactus mente Tridenti   135
sarcinulis lectis sedes et tecta refugit.
Hinc Tobiae mandata oneris provintia, nostrae
usus erat multum qui consuetudine gentis.
Horrendum hic posita subiit mercede periclum
egrediturque foras, passuque incedit inerti[5]   140
cuncta oculis lustrans, solusque perambulat urbem,
si quis forte infans cara sine matre vagetur,
nec comitatus eat. Sed Sors sit ut improba semper
hinc dignosce, homini praesto quae occur[r]it, agendum
est quotiens dirum facinus:[6] genitoris ad aedes,   145
ecce, marem aspexit nullo observante sedentem,
qui Phoebi nondum[7] ternos expleverat orbes;
cuius erat pulchra visum nihil indole maius.
Huic placide arridens digitum porrexit, et intra
perduxit miseros blando sermone[8] Penates.   150
      Gaudia quis fando, quis promat carmine vates
quae gens dira tulit? Siccis nam faucibus illum
non secus aspexit, tigris velut orbe repertam
Hircano lacerat praedam catulisque relinquit.
Illico concursu trepido petiere sacellum,   155
implentes totas diris ululatibus aedes,
nec potuere moras optati ferre cruoris.
Interea genitor Maria cum matre vagatur
Andreas maestis perlustrans planctibus urbem,
exploratque gemens si fors vestigia nati   160
occurrant. Aditus omnes et compita lustrat;
astitit hos circum puerilis turba frequenti
concursu, et natum divino ex ore monebat
esse apud [H]ebraeos, quo mactaretur ad aras.

---

[1] *correxi*: ex templo *L*
[2] *correxi*: servum *L*
[3] *correxi*: aurcoli *L*
[4] *correxi*: tauto *L*
[5] *correxi*: incerti *L*
[6] *correxi*: faciuus *L*
[7] *correxi*: nundum *L*
[8] *correxi*: sermnne *L*

"Come now, Lazarus, my joy, go and snatch an infant Christ-worshiper for us! A hundred [sig. a3r] ducats is the price." But he refused, so great was the risk, and, stunned and terror-struck, after gathering up his chattels fled from the homes and habitations of Trent. Hence the burdensome task was entrusted to Tobias, who had been on very friendly terms with our people. He, after establishing the fee, took on the terrible, hazardous assignment and went out, proceeded at a sluggish pace as he scanned everything, and walked alone through the city, in case he chanced upon a stray infant without its dear mother and without an escort. But observe from this how perverse Fortune always is, presenting herself on the spot to someone whenever a dreadful crime is to be committed: behold, he saw a boy, sitting near his father's house with no one minding him, who had not yet completed three of the sun's circling years; his beautiful nature seemed second to none. With a gentle smile Tobias stretched out a finger to him, and with coaxing talk took him all the way into the wretched [Jewish] home.

Who could express in speech, what poet in verse, the joy the dreadful tribe felt? For, dry-throated,[1] they looked at him in the same way as a tiger that tears the prey it has found in Hyrcanian country[2] and leaves it for its cubs. Anxiously assembling there and then, they rushed to the shrine, filling the whole house with dreadful howls,[3] and they could not endure any delay of the gore they craved. Meanwhile the boy's father Andreas, accompanied by Maria his mother, wandered about, gloomily sighing as he scoured the city, and tearfully searched in the hope that some traces of the child might emerge. He scanned all the doorways and cross-roads; around the former stood a large throng of boys, and from their godly lips they gave warning that the child was with the Hebrews, to be sacrificed at their altars. And since people's minds were on edge, the Jews would have been attacked, and in a moment, had not late evening ushered in the night,

---

[1] For a reference to the 'dry-throated' wolf see above, 49 n. 1.

[2] Hyrcania, on the south-east side of the Caspian Sea, was a land of vast forests: see Lucan, *Civil War* 3. 268. For the 'tiger' simile see above, 47 n. 5.

[3] Cf. Ovid, *Metamorphoses* 3. 178–180, where Diana's nymphs, surprised by Actaeon's arrival, fill the grove with their outcry: "viso sua pectora nymphae / percussere viro subitisque ululatibus omne / implevere nemus . . ." See above, 48–49.

Cumque hominum suspensa foret mens, factus in illos   165
impetus, ac subito, ni sera crepuscula noctem
traxissent, totae[1] flagrassent ignibus aedes. [sig. a3v]
Sed rediere domum iam merso sole parentes,
fata expectantes lucis peiora futurae.
     Et iam tempus erat noctis quo cuncta quiescunt.   170
Vestibulum ingreditur templi ventura furore
qui falso Moses senio vergente canebat,
excipit et genibus puerum, qui victima tristis
deprensus stat ut agna lupi cum dentibus haesit.
Cetera turba ferox vestes succincta cucur[r]it,   175
fibula quas lateri vinxit, manicisque reductis
nudavit foedos media plus parte lacertos,
et crura ad suras. Duris cruciatibus olim
sic, C[h]riste, occumbis — pateris cur, optime Rector,
tanta in te fieri genus hoc quin fulmine perdas?   180
Heu, quis non gemitus fundet, cui fata legentur
haec dura infantis? Samuel properavit et illi
quod zonae evinctum perstrinxit guttura velo,
ille manus, sacrum caput hic atque ora repressit,
edere ne tristes vagitus posset. At ense   185
quam primum Moses praeputia summa nefando
perforat, et malae frustum convellere dextrae
forcipe festinans nitido cratere reponit.
Colligitur sanguis; tenero de corpore partem
quisque secat, donec visum est excedere vulnus   190
orbem ovi; manibus pueri saepe oscula claudunt
si strepere auditur.[2] Culpae saevissimus auctor,
ecce, iterum Moses dextro de crure trementem
execat et vivo lacerat cum sanguine pulpam.
Hic una et Samuel distendunt brac[c]hia, duram   195
inque crucem tollunt; laceratum corpus acuta
quisquis pungit acu, ne pars sincera supersit.
Praetereo in C[h]ristum tot verba obscena, tot inter
vulnera contemptus, dira nam voce precantur:
"Sic hostes nostri pereant, sic perdite C[h]ristum!"   200
     Has inter poenas tanta et ludibria fessos [sig. a4r]
erigit ille oculos, suspectat sidera, testes
implorat superos. Laceri iam corporis artus
deficiunt humerisque caput declive recumbit,

---

   [1] *correxi*: totas *L*
   [2] *correxi*: aditur *L*

all their houses would have been set afire and aflame. [sig. a3v] But Simon's parents returned home at sunset, expecting worse events on the morrow.

And now it was the time of night when all things are at rest.[1] Moses, who in his declining old age with feigned ecstasy prophesied the future, entered the hallway of the temple and took up the boy on his lap, while he, a sad victim, stayed caught like a ewe lamb held in a wolf's fangs.[2] The rest of the brutal gang ran along with garments gathered up, fastened to their sides with a pin, and rolling back their sleeves bared more than half of their filthy upper arms, and their legs as far as the calves.[3] Just so, Christ, did you long ago succumb to harsh tortures—why, supreme Ruler, do you suffer such evils to be done to you without destroying this race by a lightning-strike? Alas, who will not groan aloud when the infant's harsh fate is recounted to him? Samuel moved quickly to clamp round his neck a cloth he had tied to his belt; someone held down his hands, another his sacred head and face, to forestall his plaintive howls. But in a flash Moses pierced the tip of Simon's foreskin with his abominable knife and, hastening to tear off a piece of his right cheek with pincers, placed it in a gleaming bowl. The blood was gathered; each man cut off part of the tender body, until the wound appeared as round as an egg but bigger; often they shut the boy's mouth with their hands if his screams were audible. Behold, again the utterly savage author of the crime, Moses, cut out and tore quivering flesh from Simon's right leg with its living blood. He and Samuel together stretched his arms apart and lifted him onto a harsh cross; whoever so wished pricked his torn body with a sharp needle, lest any part survive unimpaired. I pass over *so* many blasphemies against Christ, *so* many mockeries amid the blows, for in a dreadful voice they prayed: "So may our foes perish, so destroy Christ!"[4]

Amid these torments and such great mockeries, [sig. a4r] Simon raised weary eyes, looked up at the stars, and called the powers above to witness. Now his torn body's limbs were failing, his drooping head sank down on his shoulders, his tongue lolled, his beauty died, and his spirit departed. After the blessed boy

---

[1] Like Tiberino (see above, 49 n. 4), Calfurnio emulates Vergil, adopting some of the vocabulary and the alliterativeness of *Aeneid* 2. 268–269 ("Tempus erat quo prima quies mortalibus aegris / incipit . . .") in this line.

[2] Cf. Ovid, *Metamorphoses* 6. 527–528, likening Philomela to a lamb as she cowers in terror before her wolf-like attacker, Tereus: "illa tremit, velut agna pavens, quae saucia cani / ore excussa lupi nondum sibi tuta videtur."

[3] Compare the details given at this point by Pusculo and Tiberino. Here it is the Jews' clothing which is pulled down, whereas in Pusculo's account a similar description is applied to Simon—and in Tiberino's account either interpretation is possible, depending on which version of the text is followed. See above, 49–51 n. 5, and below, 139 n. 1.

[4] This is an abbreviated version of the insulting prayer supposedly uttered by the Jews and given more fully by Tiberino and by Pusculo. See above, 50–53, 54–57, and below, 138–39.

lingua cadit, moritur facies, et spiritus exit.   205
Qui postquam aethereos felix volitavit ad axes,
ecce iterum quanto[1] plausu et clamore per aedes
insultant, aut hos tenuit quam magna voluptas!
Nanque super celsi transcurrunt culmina tecti,
oraque vel geminas tollunt ad sidera palmas,   210
atque Deo innumeras referunt pro crimine grates,
quod sacrum obtulerint sol[l]emne infante perempto.
Protinus ad lautae descendunt fercula cenae,
oc[c]ultumque cados subter posuere cadaver,
quod pius antistes totam lustrarier urbem   215
iussisset. Sceleris magna hos formido tenebat,
quod iam suspecti populo atque parentibus essent.
      Septima lux aderat. Mensa posuere cadaver
et sacros cecinere hymnos; quis rite peractis,
occultant iterum trepidi, nec gaudia ponunt.   220
Ecce, diem Titan fidis mortalibus almam
extulerat iubare exorto qua, Christe, resurgis!
Quaeritur ex variis melior sententia verbis
quicquid agant, cum iam crimen[2] vix posse viderent
ulterius condi, suspectique omnibus essent.   225
Hoc unum placuit, corpus cum veste recinctum
flumine submergi subter quod labitur aedes,
mitti ad pontificem,[3] ductum qui perferat undis
infantem extinctum sed non potuisse relabi,
exceptum ferri claustris. It nuntius; illi   230
haec mandata refert. Subito Inderbacchius heros
assurgit magna comitum stipante caterva,
corporeque invento pueri perspecta notavit
vulnera. Sensit enim fraudem, iussitque catenis
Iudaeos taetro praecludi carcere vinctos. [sig. a4v]   235
Qui meritas passi poenas, nanque igne cremari
hos voluit, populi tractos ante ora per urbem.
At sacer ille Simon Petri stat in aede repostus
integer, et nullo vitiatur tempore corpus;
plurima quod divo fundit miracula nutu.   240
Lumina restituit caecis rectumque roganti
dat claudo incessum, surdique audita loquuntur.

---

   [1] *correxi*: quamto *L*
   [2] *correxi:* crimine *L*
   [3] *correxi*: pontifficem *L*

had flown up to the heavenly regions, behold again how loudly the Jews clapped and shouted as they danced through their houses, or how great a delight gripped them! For they ran across the high rooftops, and raised their eyes or both their hands to the stars,[1] and rendered countless thanks to God for the crime, which they offered him as a sacred rite when they killed the child. Straightway they went downstairs to the dishes of a splendid supper, and hid the corpse under wine-jars, since the pious bishop had ordered the whole city to be scoured. Great dread of their villainy gripped them, since they were now suspected by the people and by the boy's parents.

The seventh morning had come. They placed the corpse on a table and sang sacred hymns; having duly performed these, they again anxiously hid it, but did not lay aside their joy. Behold, the Sun-god[2] had at first light brought forth the day, full of grace for faithful people, when you, Christ, rose again! From various suggestions they sought the best decision on their next steps, since they now saw that the crime could hardly be hidden any longer, and they were universally suspected. This view alone found favor, that the body be dressed up again and sunk in the river which flowed under the house, and that someone be sent to the bishop to inform him that the dead infant had been carried there by the waves but, halted by an iron barrier, had been unable to float back. The messenger went; he delivered this report to the bishop. Promptly the hero Hinderbach set out surrounded by a great crowd of attendants;[3] and after finding the boy's body inspected and noted its wounds. For he smelled foul play, and ordered the Jews to be locked up, chained, in a vile prison. [sig. a4v] They suffered condign punishment, for he sentenced them to be to be burnt alive after being dragged through the city in full view of the people. But the holy child Simon, laid to rest in St Peter's Church, stays unblemished,[4] and his body is not marred by any passage of time; with divine approval it pours forth a host of miracles. It restores sight to the blind, to a lame supplicant it gives an upright gait, and the deaf speak audible words.

---

[1] Cf. Vergil, *Aeneid* 1. 93–94: "ingemit, et duplicis tendens ad sidera palmas / talia voce refert . . . ."

[2] 'Titan' in Latin, as (in classical mythology) son of the Titan Hyperion.

[3] Cf. Vergil, *Aeneid* 1. 497, describing Dido's stately progress through Carthage: "incessit magna iuvenum stipante caterva."

[4] For details of other cases where preservation of a body after death was cited as miraculous, see Pierre Delooz, "Towards a Sociological Study of Canonized Sainthood in the Catholic Church," in *Saints and their Cults: Studies in Religious Sociology, Folklore and History*, ed. Stephen Wilson (Cambridge: Cambridge University Press, 1983), 189–216, here 210. According to Caroline W. Bynum, during the late Middle Ages "the incorruptibility of a corpse came increasingly to be seen as a sign of sanctity": *Wonderful Blood*, 147.

I nunc et dubita Christum, gens perfida, votis
excoluisse piis, potuit quae signa dedisse
certa magis fidei! Non credis; crimina causam   245
dant ut non videas, nec possint ista probari.
Sunt quoque Pieridum qui, vix a fonte reversi,
hac in parte meum carmen damnare videntur:
quod magis ingenium deceat consumere nugis.
Sed sat erit, sacer antistes, si nostra probabis   250
Franciscusque, Tronae celeber[r]ima gloria gentis,
finibus extremis qui nunc dat iura Tridenti
et mihi M[a]ecoenas omni virtute probandus,
quique tuas vero laudes narraverit ore.
Impulit haec chartis mandarem; suscipe vultu   255
tu modo percaro,[1] donec maiora dabuntur.
        Finis.

Elegia Calphurnii poetae Brix[iensis] ad Franciscum Tronum, patricium Venetum clarissimum et M[a]ecoenatem suum.

Ibis ad extremos fines, Francisce, Tridenti;
        ibis, ego in Veneta dum moror urbe tuus,
huc, ubi vera tenet ripae[2] cognomina tellus,
        crebraque Baenaci personat unda lacus.
Heu, qualis pietas, animi quam rara modesti   5
        simplicitas, quis honor nobilitatis abit!
Felices illi qui te rectore fruentur,
        quaeque unus[3] dederis iura tenere ferent!
Dignus eras maiore gradu qui dantur honorum,
        spectetur virtus si tua nota magis. [sig. a5r]   10
Plurima sed demunt anni suffragia: nondum[4]
        triginta excedis (si magis, adde duos).
Quaeque tamen senibus tractantur[5] pondera rerum,
        quam bene sunt ductu saepe[6] peracta tuo!
Bis Iulea tui senserunt oppida vires   15
        consilii, et populus tutus ab hoste fuit.

---

1   *correxi*: peecato *L*
2   *correxi*: rippae *L*
3   *correxi*: uno *L*
4   *correxi*: nundum *L*
5   *correxi*: tranctantur *L*
6   *correxi*: ducta sepae *L*

Go now, faithless race, and hesitate to honor Christ with pious prayers, you who could have provided surer signs of faith! You do not believe; your crimes supply the reason why you do not see, nor could they be approved. There are also people who, only just returned from the Muses' spring,[1] seem to condemn my poem in this respect: that it is more fitting to employ one's talent in trivialities.[2] But it will suffice, holy bishop, if you approve my efforts, you and Francesco, far-famed glory of the Tron family,[3] the man who now governs Trent's furthest territories and is for me a Maecenas to be commended for every virtue, and the man who with the voice of truth has sung your praises. He urged me to commit this account to paper; acknowledge it now with your beloved countenance, until greater things are given you.

The End.

An elegy by Calfurnio, poet of Brescia, to Francesco Tron, most illustrious patrician of Venice and his own Maecenas.

You will be going to Trent's furthest territories, Francesco; while I, your friend, stay in the city of Venice, you will be going to where the land holds the lake-shore's true name,[4] and where Lake Garda's splashing waves make constant music. Ah, what piety, what rare guilelessness of a modest mind, what grace of noble feeling departs with you! Happy are those who will enjoy your rule and patiently keep the laws that you alone will give them. You deserved a higher rank of the honors that are granted, if your known virtue were more carefully examined. [sig. a5r] But your age deprives you of a great many votes: you are not yet over thirty (if older, add two years more). And yet how well the weighty affairs handled by old men have often been conducted under your leadership! Twice the Julian towns[5] have felt the strength of your advice, and their people have been kept safe from the enemy.

---

[1] In classical mythology the spring of the Muses was on Mt Helicon.

[2] Calfurnio clearly feels that his own subject-matter is far more important than that of the *studia humanitatis*, that is, the seven liberal arts comprising the preliminary trivium (grammar, rhetoric, and logic) and the advanced quadrivium (arithmetic, geometry, astronomy, and music).

[3] For details of the Venetian patrician Francesco Tron see Introduction and Appendix 2.

[4] That is, to Riva del Garda (literally, 'the lake-shore of Garda'), where Tron was *podestà* at this time.

[5] Presumably a reference to Tron's service in the Friuli (now the Friuli Venezia-Giulia region).

Adde Opiterginos[1] cives, quos rexeris olim
    paene puer: de quo grandius omen erat,
aut[2] famae maioris opus? Iamque urbis honores
    praetereo Venetae: quis neget astra poli?   20
Quaeque magistratus iuveni dat iura senatus
    poscere si libuit, nulla repulsa data est.
Haec tibi sorte dari potuit tunc dicere nemo,
    tanta erat ad partes ordine turba[3] tuas.
Quo bene qui[4] sentit summis te laudibus effert;   25
    si quisquam indoluit, perdidit inde fidem.
His morum accedit gravitas, constancia mentis,
    quodque unus[5] possis esse Catone prior,
cum tibi sit semper mens[6] sobria pectore sano,
    fortius et posses qui mala cuncta pati.   30
Si magnus fato Caesar revocetur ab umbris,
    et redeat toto victor ab hoste ferox,
non animum perdes, nec te servire putabis;
    libertas pereat—pectore liber eris!
Spernis opes et quod toto sit in orbe caducum,   35
    et rude quae vulgus semper habenda putat.
Nanque facis magni solos virtutis honores;
    quod partum est claris artibus omne iuvat.
Quid referam ut studiis mens sit tua dedita Phoebi,
    et Musas[7] magni quam Ciceronis ames?   40
Sic a te docto colitur studiosa iuventus,
    ut semper praestes, si petat ullus opem.
Ut sis M[a]ecoenas Augustum saecula praestent,
    a quo praedives grandia regna petas! [sig. a5v]
Tu tamen es gravior: luxu non tangeris ullo,   45
    utque illum non te coccina rara iuvant.
Carmine quo referam quam sit concordia fratris
    victoris tecum, quis sociatus amor?
Quis non te aut illum Pol[l]ucem et Castora credat?
    Turba tibi fratrum sit, Proculeius eris?   50

---

    [1] *correxi*: oppitergiues *L*
    [2] *correxi*: Ct *L*
    [3] *correxi*: turbe *L*
    [4] *supplevi*: qui
    [5] *correxi*: uno *L*
    [6] *correxi*: meus *L*
    [7] *correxi*: inusas *L*

Add the citizens of Oderzo,[1] whom once you ruled when almost a boy: of whom was there ever a mightier omen, or whose work was ever of greater fame? And I now pass over the honors given by the city of Venice: who would deny the stars of heaven? And if as a young man you wished to demand the magistrate's rights which the senate gives, you were never rebuffed. No one was then able to say that these things were given you by chance, so great was the multitude successively ranged on your side. Hence every right-thinking person honors you with highest praise; if anyone has been pained by this, he has therefore lost faith.

To these qualities are added seriousness of character, firmness of mind, and the fact that you alone could excel Cato,[2] since you always have a sober mind in a sound breast,[3] and could suffer all evils more bravely than he. Should great Caesar be recalled by fate from the underworld, and should he return from all his foes an arrogant victor, you will not lose heart, nor will you think you are his slave;[4] let freedom perish—in your breast you will be free! You spurn riches and anything in the whole world that is fleeting, and things that the vulgar herd thinks one always *should* have. For you value highly only virtue's honors; everything produced by the illustrious arts[5] delights you. Why should I relate how your mind is devoted to the pursuits of Apollo,[6] and how much you love the inspirations of great Cicero? Scholarly young people are so cherished by you, learned as you are, that if anyone asks for help you always give it. So that you may be a Maecenas, may our times provide an Augustus[7] from whom you, with your great wealth, may request mighty kingdoms! [sig. a5v] You, however, are more serious: you are not touched by any extravagance, and rare scarlet fabrics[8] do not delight you as they delighted him.

How am I to tell in verse what harmony you enjoy with your victorious brother, what mutual love? Who would not believe that you and he were Pollux and Castor?[9] Suppose you had a multitude of brothers—will you [still] be

---

[1] A Venetian town in the Trevisan marches, near the border of Friulian territory.

[2] The fervent republican politician M. Porcius Cato 'of Utica' (95–46 BC), who sided with Pompey against Julius Caesar and fled into Africa after Caesar's victory at Pharsalus (48 BC), then becoming governor of the city of Utica.

[3] Cf. Juvenal, *Satires* 10. 356: "orandum est ut sit mens sana in corpore sano."

[4] After the republican defeat at Thapsus in 46 BC, Cato committed suicide rather than accept pardon from Caesar.

[5] That is, the liberal arts of the *studia humanitatis*. See above, 99 n. 2.

[6] For Apollo as 'Leader of the Muses', see 79 n. 6.

[7] On Maecenas and Augustus, see above, 85 n. 4.

[8] Venetian senators wore red robes. For the association of 'scarlet' (*coccum*, an insect dye) with wealth, see Horace, *Satires* 2. 6. 100–103.

[9] Twin sons of Tyndareos and Leda, and brothers of Helen, regarded almost as a single deity at Rome, where their temple occupied a prominent place in the Forum.

Non poterat natura ullos effingere, qui sic
    moribus atque pares simplicitate forent:
hic animo et forma praestans et mente fidelis;
    te nemo in verbis verior esse queat.
Utque tui mores gravitasque ut digna Catone!   55
    Nil nisi Socraticum decidit[1] ore tibi.
Id quod turpe fugis, scopulos ut navita sol[l]ers;
    si quis amat vitium, non placet inde tibi.
Quod cum maiorum sola virtute probetur
    sanguis, erit cuivis clarior usque Tronus,   60
qui traxisse polo cognomina clara videtur,
    quem superis dignum iam facis esse magis.
Sic il[l]ustre dedit victa Carthagine nomen
    Scipio, sic dictus nobilitasse domum;
cui par esse potes, Poenum si demis et arces   65
    devictas: nostro tempore bella iacent.
Hunc vero[2] superas, victorem Zama[3] quod illum
    oderit: omnis amat te, colit, atque favet.
Tu iuvenis praegressus avos, quae[4] tarda senectus
    non aliis dederit nomina magna tenes.   70
Quod si fata[5] dabunt te, ut spero, vivere canum,
    quantus eris, quanto dignus honore senes!
Vade bonis avibus; festinas; vade; tuique
    Calphurnii infixum pectore nomen habe!
Me cito, si dabitur, forsan tua ripa videbit,[6]
    te ut nostrum possim visere dulce decus.
    Vale.

Ad librum.

I, liber, extemplo[7] pro me quo, parve, iuberis; [sig. a6r]
    si quaeris quid agas, accipe ius[s]a brevi.
Discedens Veneta properabis ab urbe Tridentum;
    sed prius est ripae terra petenda tibi,
cui dat iura Tronae Franciscus gloria gentis.   5

---

[1] *correxi*: detulit *L*
[2] *correxi*: vno *L*
[3] *correxi*: rama *L*
[4] *correxi*: quam *L*
[5] *correxi*: facta *L*
[6] *correxi*: uidedit *L*
[7] *correxi*: ex templo *L*

a Proculeius?[1] Nature could not have fashioned any men who were so equal in character and guilelessness: he is outstanding in mind and body, and loyal in purpose; no one could speak more truly than you. And how worthy of Cato[2] is your character, how worthy your seriousness! Nothing that is not of Socratic depth falls from your lips. You steer clear of what is base, as a skilled sailor steers clear of rocks; if anyone loves vice, he therefore displeases you. But since blood is judged solely by ancestral virtue, a Tron's blood will always be more illustrious for anyone who is seen to have drawn his illustrious surname from heaven, one whom you are already making more worthy to join the powers above. Thus did Scipio pass on a glorious name after he conquered Carthage, thus was he said to have ennobled his house;[3] you can be his equal, if you take away the words 'Punic' and 'conquered citadels': in our time warfare is in abeyance. Yet you surpass him, for Zama[4] hates him, its conqueror: by contrast, everyone loves, cultivates, and smiles on you. Having as a youth outstripped your ancestors, you hold great titles such as creeping old age has not given to others. But if, as I hope, the fates grant that you live until you are silver-haired, how great you will be, what great honor you will deserve as an old man! Go on your way attended by good omens; hasten; go on your way; and keep Calfurnio's name implanted in your breast! Your lake-shore will perhaps see me soon, if my wish is granted, so that I can visit you, my pleasure and pride.

Farewell.

To the book.[5]

Go straightway, little book, on my behalf, to wherever you are bidden; [sig. a6r] if you inquire what you should do, listen for a moment to my orders. When you leave the city of Venice you will hasten to Trent; but first you must make for the land on the lake-shore governed by Francesco, glory of the Tron family.

---

[1] Like Maecenas, C. Proculeius was a literary patron and friend of Augustus: see Horace, *Odes* 2. 2. 5, and Juvenal, *Satires* 7. 94.

[2] This time the reference is to M. Porcius Cato 'the Censor' (234–149 BC), so called because of his rigorous insistence on traditional Roman morality when he held the office of censor in 184 BC.

[3] Publius Cornelius Scipio Africanus Major (237–183 BC), so famous for his defeat of Carthage in the Second Punic War (218–201 BC) that the 'Scipionic legend', which arose during his lifetime, in its later form made him the son of Jupiter. The Venetian clan (or 'house') of the Corner claimed descent from the *gens Cornelii*.

[4] The town in Numidia where Scipio defeated Hannibal in 202 BC.

[5] The classical precedent for this address 'to the book' (envoi) is Ovid's *Tristia* 1. 1, comprising 128 lines and, like the present poem, written in elegiac couplets; a shorter example is *Tristia* 3. 7, and there are more than a dozen in Martial's *Epigrams* (e. g., 1. 3 and 1. 70), though not all are in elegiacs.

Hunc salvere iube; sit procul inde pudor!
Protinus agnoscet[1] prudens, tibique oscula laetus
    Calphurni[i] lecto nomine multa dabit.
Te leget, hincque viae comitem praestabit amandum,
    quo duce Pontificis regia tecta petes.   10
Non gravitas moveat vultus spectata verendi,
    dum genibus flexis hunc veneraris humi:
mitior hoc nemo est, nec qui mage[2] pectore toto
    et Phoebi et vatum carmina docta colat.
Qui dum te excipiet, nomen si forte rogabit   15
    auctoris, titulo dic legat ille, tui.
Me com[m]endatum facias, et protinus illi
    carmine si non es, mente disertus eris.
I, liber! Ecce, vocat qui te vult ferre viator;
    responsum, saltem perbreve, redde mihi!   20
    Finis.

Divo Simoni martiri Tridentino innocentissimo Raphael Romeus Hister, poeta laureatus, dedicavit.

Dic age, sancte puer, Christi morientis[3] imago,
    Iud[a]eis medio quid tibi cordis erat?
Quippe loqui obductum collo diadema vetabat,
    et praeter mama dicere quid poteras?
Quid poteras, miserande puer, dic, cuius in ore[4]   5
    tunc et materni guttula[5] lactis erat?
Carnifices verpos orabas lumine tantum,
    lumine quo tigris mota vel orba foret.
Ast illi contra laniabant[6] forcipe corpus,
    multaque trans corpus, trans cerebrum ibat[7] acus.   10
Infermentatis[8] miscet qui vina placentis [sig. a6v]
    iam tuus imbuerat plurima vasa cruor:

---

[1] *correxi*: agnoscaet *L*
[2] *correxi*: magne *L*
[3] morientis *O* inocentis *L*
[4] [cuius] in ore *O* more *L*
[5] [et] materni guttula *O* mrm gutulla *L*
[6] laniabant *O* Lamabant *L*
[7] [multaque] transcorpus transcerebrum ibat *O* trans cerebrum trans corpus ibrie *L*
[8] In fermentatis *O* Infermentatis *L*

Pay him your respects; put aside any shyness! Prudent as he is, he will recognize you at once and, glad to read Calfurnio's name, will shower kisses on you. He will read you, and then give you a lovable companion for your journey, with whose guidance you will make for the pope's princely dwelling. Do not let the seriousness you see in his respected countenance distress you as, kneeling on the ground, you pay him homage: no one is kinder than he, nor anyone a more whole-hearted cherisher of the learned lays of Apollo and the poets. If, as he greets you, he should ask your author's name, tell him to read it in the title. Recommend me to him, and at once you will speak eloquently to him, by your purport if not by your poetry. Go, book! Behold, the traveler who wants to take you is calling; bring me back an answer, a short one at least!

The End.

To godly Simon, wholly innocent martyr of Trent, Raffaele Romeo of Istria, poet laureate, has dedicated this.[1]

Come now, holy boy, image of the dying Christ, tell me, what were your feelings amid the Jews? To be sure, the band fastened round your neck stopped you from speaking, and what could you have said except 'Mama'? What could you have said, pitiful boy, tell me, you whose mouth even had a drop of mother's milk in it then? You pleaded with your circumcised murderers only with your gaze, a gaze which would have moved even a bereaved tigress.[2] They, however, were mutilating your body with pincers, and many a needle was going through your body and skull. Your gore, mingling its 'wine' in unleavened cakes, [sig. a6v] had already stained a great many vessels: you raised your eyes more earnestly to the citadels above,

---

[1] For the present edition *O*'s version of this poem has been collated with *L*'s.

[2] Cf. Ovid, *Metamorphoses* 13. 547–549, where the Trojan queen Hecuba, enraged by the murder of her son Polydorus, is likened to a lioness robbed of her nursing cub: "utque furit catulo lactente orbata leaena, / . . . / sic Hecube . . ."

coniicis[1] ad superas oculos[2] ardentius arces,
    quo fugit angelicis umbra beata choris.[3]
Unde precor[4] te, sancte Simon, nova gloria nostrae   15
    et robur fidei, solque Tridentigenis,[5]
hic tibi sit curae meus Hinderbac[c]hius heros,
    qui nuper tuam vindicat iniuriam
in perfidos[6] hostes fidei trucesque Iudaeos,
    qui innocuae necis causa fuere tuae.   20
Et si fas miseris est te praebere patronum
    vatibus, excipias, quaeso, Iovenzonium.

Eiusdem.

Obductis tenebris oculos,[7] iam morte propinqua,
    Bartholomaea, tuus flebat uterque parens:
iam locus optatus tumulo, iam carmen habebas,
    parva licet, cordis maxima cura mei!
Concepto—mirum!—nobis es reddita voto;   5
    quod tibi nunc solvi, sancte patrone Simon.
Crudeles postquam sensisti, infantule, cultros,
    inque tuo lota est sanguine verpa manus,
arsit amans animus venerandum visere corpus
    hancque tuis lacrimam fundere vulneribus.   10
At veni tandem voto supplexque sepulchrum,
    membraque cum flavis cerno iacere comis.
Quae fera tam duris laniavit morsibus artus,
    lactantes artus? Quae fera, quae feritas?
Victima sancta Dei manibus mandata prophanis,   15
    accipe cum lacrymis oscula nostra, Simon!
    Finis.
    G[iovanni] L[eonardo Longo]

---

[1] coniicis *O* conmicis *L*
[2] oculos *O* occulos *L*
[3] choris *O* coris *L*
[4] precor *O* praecor *L*
[5] tridentigenis *O* trigentigenis *L*
[6] In perfidos *O* Imperfidos *L*
[7] *correxi*: occulos *L*

to which with choirs of angels your blessed shade flew. Therefore I beg you, holy Simon, new glory and bulwark of our faith, and sun of those who are Trent-born, take care of my hero Hinderbach here, who has lately taken vengeance on those faithless and pitiless foes, the Jews, for the harm they did you when they caused your innocent death. And if it is right for you to patronize poets, take Zovenzoni under your wing, I implore you.

By the same author. [1]

With darkness clouding your eyes, with your death already close, both your parents, Bartolomea, were weeping: already a place had been chosen for your grave, already you had an epitaph, mighty darling of my heart, small though you are! When we made a vow—marvelous!—you were given back to us; I have now discharged this vow to you, holy patron Simon. After you felt the cruel knives, tiny infant, and the hands of the circumcised were bathed in your blood, my loving mind burned to see your venerable corpse and shed these tears on your wounds. But at last I have come to your tomb with a vow and a supplication, and I see your body lying there with your golden hair. What wild beast mutilated your limbs with such harsh bites, the limbs of a nursing child? What wild beast, what bestiality? God's holy victim consigned to sacrilegious hands, receive our tearful kisses, Simon!

The End.

Giovanni Leonardo Longo

---

[1] This poem is an 'ex voto' , that is, an offering made in fulfillment of a vow.

Section III

SECTION III

[sig. 1r] Ubertini Pusculi Brixiensis duo libri *Symonidos*.

De Iudaeorum perfidia. Quo modo Ihesum Christum crucifixerunt, divos Ricardum Parisiensem, Symonem Tridentinum afflixere martyrio sup[p]liciaque dedere.

Ut serpens inimica homini mordere parata
        in letum semper fervida colla tumet;
sic gens Iudaeum nobis nostraeque saluti
        insidians odium non satiata gerit.

[sig. 1v] **Othmari Prognei Trebotis endecasyllabon ad lectorem. Libellus loquitur.**

Qui sacro sitiunt cruore buccas
implere, et lacerant, premunt, prophanant
nomen Christicolum, impios, furentes
Iudaeos meritas dedisse poenas
describo, puero necem Tridenti   5
dum pergunt struere optimo Simoni.
Me quondam ediderat probe disertus
Ubertinus; adire docta saepta
fecit Curtius, eximens tenebris.

Section III

[sig. ir] The two books of the *Simonis* of Ubertino Pusculo of Brescia.

About the faithlessness of the Jews. How they crucified Jesus Christ, subjected godly Richard of Paris and Simon of Trent to martyrdom, and suffered punishments.[1]

As a serpent, hostile to humankind and ready to bite, always puffs up its hot neck for the kill, so the Jewish race, lying in wait for us and our salvation, bears insatiable hatred towards us.

[sig. iv] **A hendecasyllabic poem of Othmar Progneus [Nachtigall] Trebos[2] addressed to the reader. The little book speaks.**[3]

Those who thirst to fill their mouths with sacred gore, and who torture, harass, and profane the name of Christ-worshipers: those impious, fury-filled Jews do I describe—how they suffered condign punishment when they pursued their plan to murder the noble boy Simon of Trent. Earlier, the truly eloquent Ubertino had given me birth; Kurtz,[4] bringing me out of the darkness, gave me entry to

---

[1] The texts included in this section are all in *O*, whose signature numbers are therefore inserted throughout.

[2] Othmar Nachtigall (1478/80–1537) was a jurist, humanist, theologian, and musician who spent some time in Augsburg in 1510–1511. 'Trebos' (of which 'Trebotis' is here taken as the genitive, agreeing with the two preceding ones) seems to be some sort of nickname, but there was also a German humanist/philologist called Torquatius Februarius Trebotis (1485–1512), so we may perhaps have three surnames here: that of the printer Othmar, that of Progneus (Latin for Nachtigall), and that of Trebotis. On the printer Johann Othmar, active in Augsburg during 1502–1514, and his involvement in the production of religious literature see Hans-Jörg Künast, *'Getruckt zu Augspurg': Buchdruck und Buchhandel in Augsburg zwischen 1468 und 1555* (Tübingen: Max Niemeyer Verlag, 1997), 74. See also Appendix 2.

The meter of this poem (the hendecasyllable, i.e., a line of eleven syllables) is a favourite of Catullus, who uses it in no fewer than forty of his poems.

[3] As with Calfurnio's envoi addressed 'to the book' (cf. 103 n. 5), the precedents for this short poem and the next, spoken 'by the book', are found, first, in Ovid (*Tristia* 3. 1 and 5. 4) and, second, in Martial (*Epigrams* 10. 1).

[4] Johannes Kurtz von Eberspach, whose address to the reader follows on sig. iiiir. On him see Appendix 2. The literal meaning of *docta saepta* is "learned closets", which we

Me pulvis cariesque—blatta nostra[1]—   10
extinguat celeri furore iamiam:
me iam, lector, eme et, scio, probabis.

Ioannis Piniciani. Ad lectorem libellus.

Si quaeris, lector, qui sim, quae munera portem,
    hoc lege; non magno carmine certus eris.
Qui me scribebat primusque Symonida dixit
    a sancto nomen rite Symone dedit.
Arma fero quibus infantis turba improba quondam
    Iudaeum morti membra tenella dabat.
Crimina praeterea recutitae plurima gentis
    excutiam, mores, et sine fine dolos.
Me finxit docte sic Ubertinus; in umbra
    delitui, paucis cognitus ante viris.

[sig. iir] **Divo Ioanni, quarto pontifici et domino Tridentino, Caesari suo, Ioannes Mathias Thyberinus, e[ques] R[omanus], D[ei] s[acerdos] et filius, inter curarum fluctus raptissime confecit in arce silvarum sexto nonas Iuli[as] MCCCCLXXV.**

De sancto Simone Tridentino.

[Sum puer ille Simon, quem nuper in urbe Tridenti . . .
. . . qui mandunt tepida [et] membra cruenta virum.]

[sig. iiir] **Divo Simoni martyri Tridentino, infanti innocentissimo, Raphael Romeus Hyster, Poeta Laureatus, dedicavit.**

Aliud carmen de Symone puero Tridentino.

[Dic age, sancte puer, Christi morientis ymago. . .
. . . excipias, quaeso, Iovenzonium.]

---

[1] *correxi*: nostram *O*

the closets of the learned. Dust and decay—the worms that eat us up—may in their furious haste destroy me very soon: so buy me now, reader, and I know you will approve of me.

A poem of Johann Pinicianus.[1] The little book addresses the reader.

If, reader, you ask who I am, what gifts I bear, read this; a short poem will tell you. He who wrote me and first called me *Simonis* duly took that title from holy Simon. I carry the weapons[2] with which a wicked Jewish mob once put to death an infant's tender body. I shall, besides, examine the circumcised race's many, many crimes, its customs, and its endless wiles. Thus did Ubertino skillfully compose me; I have lain hidden in the shade, known to few men till now.

[sig. iir] For godly Johannes, fourth bishop and lord of Trent—his own prince—Giovanni Mattia Tiberino, Roman knight, God's priest and son, amidst floods of responsibilities hurriedly completed this poem at the castle of the woods on July 2nd 1475.

About holy Simon of Trent.

[For this poem, which occupies sig. iir–v and part of sig. iiir, see above, 64–69]

[sig. iiir] To the godly martyr Simon of Trent, wholly innocent infant, Raffaele Romeo of Istria,[3] poet laureate, has dedicated this.

Another poem about the boy Simon of Trent.

[For this poem, which occupies the rest of sig. iiir and the top half of sig. iiiv—the bottom half is blank—see above, 104–7]

---

take as referring to Eberspach's scholarly acquaintances in their 'dens'.

[1] A humanist known only in connection with the Othmar press: Künast, *'Getruckt zu Augspurg'*, 240. See also Appendix 2.

[2] The pincers, needles, and noose associated with Simon's martyrdom are shown in the illustration on *O*'s title-page (sig. ir). See also above, 12, fig. 2. The words *Arma fero* recall the opening of Vergil's *Aeneid*: "Arma virumque cano . . ."

[3] Raffaele Zovenzoni of Trieste. See Appendix 2.

[sig. iiiir] Ioannes Curtius Eberspachius lectori salutem.

Quoniam, lector candidissime, recentia vetustis auditu iucundiora sunt, quod quae audimus nostra tempestate facta, quaeque explorare possumus, ita se habere minime dubitamus, quodque animus humanus natura quasi novorum avidior sit—hac ductus ratione eloquentissimi viri Ubertini Pusculi duos Symonidis libros impressum iri curavi, hunc librum ratus non modice tibi voluptati iucunditatique fore; quippe qui non illecebrosa carmina—insani amorum illicia—non vanas fabulas contineat,[1] sed sancti martyris Simonis Tridentini dira tormenta a perfidis Iudaeis in Christi ipsiusque dedecus illata, imprecationem eorum in Christianam fidem, miracula quibus sanctum suum martyrem Christus ornare voluit, poenas Iudaeis pro tanto crimine illatas.

Quae cuncta mire, non minus oratorie quam poetice, Ubertinus ille prosecutus est. Quare age, candide lector: cum iste liber antea plurimis latuerit annis, viris quorum opera in lucem prodiit magnas agere gratias debebis. Venit nempe de manibus facundissimi viri Christiani[2] Umhauser, Doctoris et Laureati Poetae, ad inclitum Christophorum Romer, qui prope Bulsonum, vulgo dictum Botzen, in castro Maresco residet; unde in manus devenit meas, de qua quidem re plurimum exhilarabar.[3] Quia placuit, cogitavi ac exactissimam dedi operam ut in lucem prodiret, non diffidens quod[4] et tu, lector, probabis. Vale. Datum in Augusta Vindelicorum, anno MDXI tertio ydus Aprilis.

[sig. iiiiv] Ad lectorem. Hexastichon Ioannis Vögelin Haylbrunnen.

Aeneam celebrat Maro, Achillem doctus Homerus;
     sic Ubertinus ille Symona suum.
Illic ficta simul veris confusa videntur;
     hic rem sinceram, candide lector, habes.
Quo veris ficta et sinceris oblita fuco
     cedunt,[5] hoc liber hic sit tibi corde magis!

---

[1]   *supplevi*: contineat
[2]   *correxi*: Christanni *O*
[3]   *correxi*: exhylerabar *O*
[4]   *correxi*: quin *O*
[5]   *correxi*: caedunt *O*

[sig. iiiir] Johannes Kurtz von Eberspach sends greetings to the reader.

It is true, most sincere reader, that recent news is pleasanter to hear than old news, because we have no doubts at all that events of our own time which we hear of, and can look into, really are as described, and because the human mind would naturally be thirstier for what is fairly new. Prompted by this thought, I have arranged for the printing of the two books of that most eloquent man Ubertino Pusculo's *Simonis*, considering that this volume will give you no small amount of pleasure and enjoyment. For it contains, *not* alluring verses — the allurements of a madman's loves[1] — *not* empty tales,[2] but the dreadful torments inflicted on the holy martyr Simon of Trent by the faithless Jews in order to dishonor Christ and Simon himself; their imprecations against the Christian faith; the miracles by which Christ wished to honor his holy martyr; and the punishments inflicted on the Jews for such a serious offense.

All these themes Ubertino has wonderfully followed through, no less rhetorically than poetically.[3] So come now, sincere reader: since this book has for many, many years lain hidden, you will owe a big debt of thanks to the men by whose efforts it has emerged into the light. It came, that is to say, from the hands of a most articulate man, Christian Umhauser, Doctor and Poet Laureate, to the renowned Christopher Romer, who resides near Bolzano (commonly called Bozen) in the town of Maresco. From there it passed into my hands, and I was indeed overjoyed at this turn of events. Because I liked it, I have planned and painstakingly striven to ensure its emergence into the light, confident that you too, reader, will approve of it. Farewell. Issued at Augsburg, April 11th, 1511.

[sig. iiiiv] To the reader: a hexastich of Johannes Vögelin Heilbrunnen.[4]

Vergil celebrates Aeneas; learned Homer celebrates Achilles. Thus does famed Ubertino celebrate his hero, Simon. In the former works fiction appears mixed up with truth; here, sincere reader, you have genuine fact. In so far as fiction and pretentious artifice yield to genuine truth, may this book appeal to you all the more!

---

[1] Perhaps a dig at the Ovid of the *Amores*, the *Ars Amatoria*, and the *Remedia Amoris*.

[2] An allusion to Ovid's *Metamorphoses*, perhaps.

[3] For the *studia humanitatis*, see above, 99 n. 2.

[4] On him see Appendix 2.

Ad Reverendissimum Dominum, Dominum Ioannem Hinderbach, episcopum Tridentinum,[1] Ubertini Pusculi Brixiensis[2] oratio.

[sig. vr] Cum antea, reverendissime praesul princepsque clementissime, rerum tu-
arum fama, quae clarissime per terras perferuntur, me ut Dominationi Tuae no-
tum me redderem invitasset, cumque id animo frequenter voluissem meo, timidi-
tas quaedam—haud sane illiberalis, neque inconsiderata—me ab hoc animi mei
proposito quippe deterruit, nec iniuria profecto. Cogitabam enim id quod quisque,
qui aliquid sapiat, cogitaret: principibus magnis ac dominis viros magnos, singu-
larique aliqua virtute praestantes scientiave claros praecipua, gratos acceptosque
esse solere, eosque demum dignos esse, qui gratiae principum complexu teneren-
tur, qui de se aliquid edere valerent, quo eorum gloria vel augeri vel immortalitati
mandari posset. Hoc mihi cogitanti tenuitatis meae in mentem[3] veniebat. Anim-
advertebam namque in me non eas esse animi virtutes, non eam ingenii prae-
stantiam, non eam denique litterarum scientiam, ut me dignum existimarem, qui
a te—tanto principe—inter familiares ac notos susciperer tuos, cui et animarum
cura, tanquam pastori optimo, et regendorum populorum potestas, tanquam sapi-
entissimo ac iustissimo viro, recto Dei ac principum iudicio delata est.

   Quid igitur agerem? Pauperne ac nudus ad Reverendissimam Dominatio-
nem Tuam accederem? At prohibebat pudor. Incognitusne atque obscurus ei, sic
praeterirem? At ambitiosa mea ut ei notus fierem cupiditas me stimulabat. Evenit
divina, ut arbitror, ordinatione—nec aliter[4] profecto credendum est—ut, cum
Dominus Deus nova Passionis suae figura fidelium suorum animos erigere, ip-
sosque ardentiores ad fidem quae frigescit suscitare [sig. vv] vellet, tui simul in
se pietatem, divini cultus Christianaeque religionis ardorem illustraret. Qui hac
tempestate suae Passionis memoriam caede novi agni renovari permisit, quo et
immanitas Iudaeorum obstinataque perfidia denuo innotesceret—qui, cum in

---

   [1] Tridentinum *V* Tridentiuum *O*
   [2] Brixiuensis *O om. V*
   [3] in mentem *V* in in mentem *O*
   [4] aliter *V* alter *O*

To the Most Reverend Lord, Lord Johannes Hinderbach, bishop of Trent: the address of Ubertino Pusculo of Brescia.[1]

[sig. vr] Although earlier, most reverend bishop and most merciful prince, the fame of your achievements — which are very clearly reported throughout the world — had urged me to make myself known to Your Lordship, and although I had frequently had the intention of doing so, a certain timidity (surely not ignoble or ill-advised) did in fact — and surely not unjustifiably — deter me from this idea. For I thought, as any sensible person would think, that to great princes and lords it is great men, preeminent for some remarkable virtue or famous for exceptional knowledge, who are normally pleasing and acceptable, and that those men especially deserve to be held in the gracious embrace of princes who of themselves could produce something by which those princes' glory could be either increased or committed to posterity. Whenever I thought of this, I was reminded of my own insignificance. For I observed that I did not have such mental virtues, or such intellectual preeminence, or, in a word, such literary knowledge, as would lead me to think I deserved adoption by you — so great a prince — as one of your friends and acquaintances. For you, by the right judgment of God and princes, have been entrusted both with the care of souls — as you are an excellent shepherd — and with the power of governing peoples — as you are a supremely wise and just man.

What, then, was I to do? Poor and naked,[2] was I to approach Your Most Reverend Lordship? But shyness prevented it. Unknown and obscure, was I to pass him by, just like that? But my ambitious desire to become known to him spurred me on. It happened, as I think, by divine ordaining — nor, surely, should one believe otherwise — that when the Lord God wished to encourage the minds of his faithful people by a new symbol of his passion, and to rouse them to greater enthusiasm for their faith, which is growing cold, [sig. vv] he also illuminated your own devotion to him, your own enthusiasm for divine worship and the Christian religion. At this time he allowed the memory of his own passion to be renewed by the murder of a new lamb, so that the monstrous obstinacy and faithlessness of the Jews might become known afresh — those who, since they cannot

---

[1] For the present edition, *V*'s version of this letter has been collated with *O*'s.

[2] This phrase has scriptural overtones (see Job 1: 21) of nakedness as the badge of the human condition which the incarnation espoused. It also adumbrates the presentation of Simon as the imitation of Christ in his naked and tortured body in the text and in accompanying woodcuts (above, 12, fig. 2). The bleeding genitalia recall Christ's own circumcision when his redeeming blood first flowed. Franciscans stressed Christ's human nature and imitation of Christ through a vow of poverty and the slogan "naked to follow the naked Christ" taken from Jerome (*PL* 22. 1085). See Leo Steinberg, *The Sexuality of Christ in Renaissance Art and in Modern Oblivion* (London: Faber and Faber, 1983).

Christum ipsum adhuc saevire[1] non possint,[2] in innocentes Christi agnos infantes clam (si palam non licet) crudelissime saeviunt. Idque in civitate tua Simonis, innocentissimi martyris, ab ipsis Iudaeis sanguine exhausti ac dilaniati caede fieri voluit, ut, si (quod factum est)[3] tam dirum atque horrendum facinus palam fieret, tu esses unus qui latrones Iudaeos sanguinem Christianum sitientes—Christi Dei infensissimos hostes, divinaeque gloriae inimicissimos obtrectatores—in tam crudeli atque impio scelere deprehensos pie, iuste constanterque puniri curares: qui te invictum pecunia principem invenirent!

Qua quantum ipsi perfidi valeant Iudaei, tu sane testis locupletissimus ac certissimus es. Nam dum iusticiae[4] cultor severus esse vis, tantum tibi eorum pecunia—qua sola freti scelera aggrediuntur maxima—suscitavit bellum, ut non solum contra ipsos immanissimos Iudaeos, sed etiam contra multos Christianum nomen falso gerentes, opibus potentes, pecunia hostium captos, pugnare tibi fuerit necesse. Et nisi divino fultus fuisses auxilio, fideique lorica armatus fortis proeliator extitisses, profecto iusticia ipsa, pro qua pugnabas, victa pecuniae cessisset inanis. Sed desuper spectans Deus nec iusticiam suam deficere, nec te, suum gloriaeque suae propugnatorem acerrimum, destitui voluit. Qui clarissimis pueri martyris sui miraculis ardorem principibus fidelibus multis—in pri- [sig. vir] misque invicto Christianissimoque Austriae duci Sigismundo—ut nominis sui gloriam veritatemque tutarentur immisit. Ita demum divina ope effectum est ut iusticia suum obtineret locum, scelera Iudaeorum immania punita forent, honor Deo ac martyri suo remaneret illaesus. Vobis vero, qui persecutionem propter iusticiam sustinuistis, cum apud homines laudes erunt, tum vero apud Deum corona iusticiae vos manet.

Quae res cum omnium videretur memoranda praeconiis, mihi quoque illam memoriae mandare atque—si tantum ingenium posset meum—immortalitati dicare visum est, quo et Christianis qui Iudaeorum consuetudines[5] amant, seque ab ipsis amari putant, error maximus denudetur, qui si non Christi Dei amore

---

[1] *correxi*: scaeuire *O* sceuire *V*

[2] possint *V* possit *O*

[3] est *V om. O*

[4] iusticiae *O* iustitiae *V* (*ut passim*)

[5] consuetudines *V* consuetunes *O*

still vent their rage[1] on Christ himself, most cruelly vent it (in secret, if they cannot openly do so) on Christ's innocent infant lambs. And he wished that to happen in your city through the murder of Simon, wholly innocent martyr, drained of blood and torn apart by those same Jews. God's object was that, if (as happened) such a dreadful and horrible outrage came to light, *you* alone might see to the pious, just, and resolute punishment of the Jewish felons who in their thirst for Christian blood—being the fiercest foes of Christ our God, and the most hostile detractors of divine glory—had been caught red-handed in so cruel and impious a crime: so that they might find in you a prince unconquered by money!

As to how much power money gives the faithless Jews themselves, you are surely the most trustworthy and reliable witness. For while *your* wish is to be a strict observer of justice, so great a war has *their* money—their sole standby when they embark on their huge crimes   stirred up against you, that you have had to fight not only against the utterly brutal Jews themselves but also against many who falsely bear the name 'Christian', people strong in resources but slaves to the enemy's money. And had you not had God's powerful support, and not stood out as a brave warrior armed with the breastplate of faith,[2] then certainly that very justice which you were defending would have yielded—worsted and wasted—to money. But God, looking down from above, wanted neither his justice to fail, nor you, the keenest champion of him and his glory, to be deserted. By means of his boy-martyr's bright-shining miracles he inspired many faithful princes—and especially [sig. vir] the invincible and most Christian archduke of Austria, Sigismund—with enthusiasm to protect the glory and truth of his name. So at last divine aid ensured that justice was upheld, the brutal crimes of the Jews were punished, and the honor paid to God and his martyr remained undiminished. But as for people like you who have endured persecution for justice's sake,[3] not only will humankind give you praise, but also God has a crown of justice in store for you.[4]

Since this affair seemed worthy of public record, I too decided to record it and—if I had sufficient talent—to dedicate it to immortality. My purpose was, first, to bring home to those Christians who love fraternizing with Jews, and think themselves loved by them, their own gross error, so that, if they are not deterred from befriending them by love of Christ our God (from whom we take our name, whom those seven men[5] have crucified, and whom they pursue

---

[1] Throughout Section III both sources of the text (*V* and *O*) consistently misspell *saevus* and its derivatives as *scaevus*, etc. This feature's first occurrence is noted in the text here; later ones are not.

[2] Cf. 1 Thess. 5: 8: "induti loricam fidei et charitatis."

[3] Cf. Matt. 5: 10: "beati qui persecutionem patiuntur propter iustitiam."

[4] Cf. 2 Tim. 4: 8: "reposita est mihi corona iustitiae."

[5] Presumably the seven men who are supposed to have tortured and killed Simon as Christ's surrogate, i.e., Engel, Israel, Mayer, Moses, Samuel, Tobias, and Vital.

(a quo nomen ducimus, quem illi septem crucifixerunt et blasphemiis continuis insectantur) ab eorum familiaritatibus non deterrentur, saltem—cum ipsorum in Christianum nomen odium ardentissimum viderint, ut et nostrum bibere sanguinem sitiant—eorum fraudes, dolos ac simulationes devitent non minus quam serpentes; et ut Christo Deo honor redderetur suus, qui nostra aetate gloriam suam novi martyris sui miraculis manifestare voluit, utque pietatis tuae in Deum ac fidei constantissimae monumentum servaretur, eorumque omnium qui una[1] tecum eodem certamine laborarunt.

Hanc rem ordine totam carmine scriptam libellis duobus comprehendi, quos non prius ego edere constitui, quam eos Reverendissima Dominatio Tua dignos qui edantur esse censuerit. Hos igitur tibi iudicio tuo pensandos offero, Hinderbach, praesul ac princeps clementissime: quos si a te probatos benignoque a te acceptos animo intellexero, et studiorum meorum labo- [sig. viv] res mitigaveris, et mihi gaudium perpetuum adiunxeris, ut in dies magis magisque opusculum hoc confecisse gaudeam.

De beato Simone, martyre.[2]

Versus:
Ora pro nobis, beate Simon, martyr Christi, ut digni efficiamur promissione Christi.
Oratio:
Deus, qui beatum Simonem martyrem tuum ineffabilibus miraculis in puerili infantia, ut Iudaeorum detestanda feritas pateret, inenarrabiliter ostendisti, fac nos, quaesumus, ipsius meritis et passione veritatem agnoscere, et caelestia semper amare. Per Dominum nostrum Iesum Christum.

Ubertini Pusculi Brixiensis *Simonidos* liber primus incipit.
[sig. ar]

Qui quondam duro cecini sub Marte cadentem
Constantini urbem magnam Graiumque ruinam
imperii, secum populos in fata trahentem,
nunc immane mihi facinus—fatuque tremendum

---

[1] *correxi*: unam *VO*
[2] *correxi*: martyris *O*

with continued blasphemies), they may at least—when they see their blazing hatred for the name 'Christian', which even makes them thirst to drink our blood—steer clear of their deceptions, wiles, and pretenses no less than they would steer clear of serpents. Secondly, my purpose was to ensure that Christ our Lord, who wished to reveal his glory in our own age by the miracles of his new martyr, be paid the honor due to him, and that a record be preserved of your own devotion to God and most resolute faith, and of the same virtues shown by all those who labored together with you in the same struggle.

I have described this whole affair, in order, in a poem, and have enclosed it in two books, which I have decided not to publish until Your Most Reverend Lordship deems them worthy of publication. These, therefore, I offer to you for your discerning scrutiny, Hinderbach, most merciful bishop and prince: if I learn that you have approved them and received them kindly, you will have succeeded not only in lightening [sig. viv] my scholarly labors, but also in bringing me lasting happiness, so that each day I am increasingly happy to have completed this little work.

On blessed Simon, martyr. [1]

Verse:
Pray for us, blessed Simon, Christ's martyr, that we may be made worthy of Christ's promise.
Prayer:
God, who beyond all telling declared blessed Simon your martyr by ineffable miracles in his boyish infancy, so that the detestable savagery of the Jews might be revealed, enable us, we ask, through his merits and suffering to acknowledge the truth, and always to love heavenly things. Through our Lord Jesus Christ.

Here begins the first book of the *Simonis* of Ubertino Pusculo of Brescia. [2] [sig. ar]

To me, who once sang of Constantine's great city falling prey to harsh warfare, and of the Greek Empire's collapse that dragged peoples to their doom with it,[3] now comes the duty to sing in sorrowful tones of the Jewish race's brutal

---

[1] This prayer appears only in *O*.

[2] As with Pusculo's address to Hinderbach (see above), the whole text of the *Simonis* occurs in *V* as well as in *O*, so the two versions have been collated for this edition.

[3] Pusculo was in Constantinople studying Greek when it was captured by the Ottoman Turks in 1453. After being jailed by the Turks, ransomed by a Florentine merchant, and captured by pirates who took him to Rhodes, he escaped via Crete to Rome, where (*c.* 1455–1457) he wrote *Constantinopolis*, a four-book poem in Latin hexameters describing the fall of the city: Donald M. Nicol, *The Immortal Emperor* (Cambridge: Cambridge

admissumque nefas nullo memorabile in aevo—   5
gentis Iudaeae maesto venit ore canendum;
infantisque dolo capti—qui tractus ad aram,
victima stans toto perfossus corpore vivus,
spectavit vitam fugientem sanguine venis
manante in longam poenam—fera dicere fata   10
cogor, et infandum scelus hoc differre per orbem.
Non mihi nunc vatum Musa est de more vocanda,
pectora quae magno ducat detenta furore
in carmenque iuvet. Sed tu, qui maximus orbis
conditor es, cuiusque aeterna lege tenentur   15
omnia (namque tibi tanta haec iniuria facta est),
te precor ad veros cantus (non ficta canuntur)
ingenium tu tolle meum; similique favore,
virgo Dei, mater C[h]risti intemerata Maria,
da mihi, da plenas ducenda in carmina vires.   20
Vera mihi Musa es: veros mihi suggere cantus.
Tuque puer, parvo qui corpore tanta tulisti
tormenta et duris cruciatibus alta petisti [sig. av]
sidera, quique potes magnum iam flectere numen,
desuper et votis potes exaudire vocantes,   25
adsis, meque tuum praeconem versibus orna.
        Est urbs extremis in finibus alta Tridentum
Italiae, arctoas contingens moenibus Alpes
commiscensque Italis Germanos gentibus. Illas
dux pius alta potens tenet Austria fortis in armis.   30
Hinderbach divus princeps praesulque Ioannes
sceptra habet; hic sanctum praetorem elegerat urbi,
quem gens Sala virum clarum virtute Ioannem
Brixia magna tulit, legum iurisque magistrum
Caesarei iuris doctum canonumque sacrorum.   35
        Hebdomada in Magna—nostrum praecedere Pascha
quae solet et Christi mortis monumenta referre—
tempus erat quo sacra sui sollennia Paschae
Iudaei de more solent celebrare quot annis.
Quem servant ex lege, sibi quam tradidit olim   40
Moyses Aegypti monumentum, ut serva tyranni
pressa iugo gens tota fuit Iudaea per altum
Rubrum ducta Fretum: virga percussa potenti
aequora cesserunt populo (res mira!); per ipsa
ima patens Pelagi patuit via sicca Rubentis.   45
Parietibus similes dextra laevaque fuerunt

crime—a memorable offense, terrible to tell and without precedent in any previous age; and I am forced to describe the cruel fate of a cunningly captured infant—who, dragged to the altar as a victim, and still alive after his whole body had been pierced, saw his life speeding away as the blood dripped from his veins, causing prolonged pain—and to spread news of this unspeakable outrage throughout the world. I do not now have to follow custom by calling on the poetic Muse to direct a heart already gripped by great fervor and help it make verse. But You, the world's mighty creator, by whose eternal law all things are bound (for this grievous injury has been done to you), raise up, I pray you, my understanding to make true songs (their subject is no fiction); and with similar favor you, God's virgin and Christ's spotless mother Mary, grant me, pray grant me full strength to shape my verses. You are my true Muse: suggest true songs to me. And you, boy who in your small body have endured such great torments and through harsh sufferings have flown up [sig. av] to the stars on high, and who can now sway the Almighty and listen from above to those who invoke you in prayer, may you assist me and furnish me, your herald, with poetry.

There is at the edge of Italy's territories a lofty city,[1] Trent, touching with its walls the Alps to the north and mingling Germans with Italians. The pious archduke, strong in arms, who holds power in lofty Austria governs those races. Godly Prince-Bishop Johannes Hinderbach holds sway [in Trent]; he had chosen as the city's holy *podestà* Giovanni, a famously virtuous man born of the de Salis family and of great Brescia, a master of statutes and law, learned in Roman law and in the sacred canons.

It was the time in Holy Week—our accustomed prelude to Easter and reminder of Christ's death—when the Jews traditionally celebrate each year the solemn rites of their Passover. They observe that tradition according to the law which Moses delivered to them long ago to remind them of Egypt, when the whole Jewish race, enslaved under a tyrant's yoke, was led through the deep Red Sea: the waters, struck by a rod, made way for the empowered people (marvelous event!); a clear dry path opened up through the very depths of the Red Sea. The waves on either side became motionless like walls, and stood still like beaches,

---

University Press, 1992), 82; *Ubertini Pusculi Brixiensis Constantinopoleos Libri IV*, ed. V. Ellissen, in *Analekten der mittel- und neugriechischen Literatur*, III (Leipzig: Wigand, 1857). A new edition is reportedly being prepared by M. J. McGann and Estelle Haan of the Queen's University, Belfast. See above, 28 n. 113.

[1] Cf. Vergil, *Aeneid* 1. 12.

immoti fluctus, steteruntque ut littora,[1] donec
integer evasit totus, contraria et undis
vidit mersa suum repetentibus agmina motum
cum duce, dum tentant fugientem per maris alti   50
sicca sequi, medioque illum deprendere cursu [sig. aiir].
Transitus hic Phase[2] Solymorum voce vocatus
Pasc[h]a facit, quod sic peragunt de more vetusto.
Primo mense domus capit agnum quaeque novellum
atque marem, macula mundum; non hunc coquit unda,   55
sed torrere igni divina lege iubentur
cum capite et pedibus totum, nec frangitur illi
quicquam. Sic coctus celeri consumitur esu
stantibus in baculum; lactucae sunt quoque agrestes.
Quod totum in Christi voluit Deus ire figuram.   60
       Ante haec sacra gregem cuncti coguntur in unum
Iudaei, qui tunc altum coluere Tridentum,
dum comedunt azimos, venit et dum Pascha propinquum;
consultantque simul facienda piacula vivi
Christicolae pueri (scelus ingens!). Sanguinis haustum   65
dira sitis rabiesque furens odiumque malignum
flagitat humani, sacro baptismate loti
innocui infantis, fidei in ludibria nostrae
contemptumque Dei Christi, quem vera per orbem
relligio observat. Colitur Deus atque Redemptor   70
humani generis, qui fecit quique redemit.
       Hos inter princeps duri horrendique sedebat
concilii barbam fusus per pectora Mo[y]ses,
Saxoniae ad sacrum solitum sibi missus ab oris
illuc, ut strueret tantum scelus urbe Tridenti.   75
Hunc sibi pro summo gentis suffragia saevae
pontifice extulerant, dederantque hoc nomen inane.
Nam postquam invidia Christum ausi morte, Mesias
qui sonat, in ligno damnarunt, versa fuerunt [sig. aiiv]
iura sui cum gente loci. Rerumque potestas   80
et status amissus: verus nec mansit in illis
pontificatus, habent stabiles nec ponere sedes,
gentibus invisi cunctis, dictante propheta:
"Venerit ut sanctus sanctorum, tum unctio vestra
cessabit." Quid enim vobis[3] sperare relictum est?   85

---

[1] littora *V* lictora *O*
[2] phase *O* pasce *V*
[3] uobis *V* nobis *O*

until the whole [people] escaped unharmed and saw—as the waters resumed their motion—the enemy columns, together with their leader, drowned as they tried to pursue the fleeing host through the deep sea's dry bed and overtake it in mid-course. [sig. aiir]

This crossing, called 'Phase' in the Hebrew language, produces the word 'Passover',[1] which they reenact in accordance with ancient tradition, as follows. In the first month [of the year] each household takes a newborn, unblemished male lamb; they do not boil it in water, but are bidden by divine law to roast it whole—including head and feet—over a fire, nor is any bit of it broken. Thus cooked, it is eaten quickly as they stand leaning on their staffs; wild herbs are added. God meant the whole ceremony to become a representation of Christ.[2]

Before these rites, all the Jews who then dwelt in lofty Trent gathered in a single group as they ate the unleavened cakes, and as the Passover drew near; and at the same time they discussed making an expiatory offering of a live Christ-worshiping boy (enormous crime!). A dreadful thirst, a raging madness, and a malign hatred demanded the drinking of human blood, that of an innocent infant washed in holy baptism, in mockery of our faith and contempt of Christ our God, whom true religion throughout the world respects. He is worshiped as humankind's God and Redeemer, who made it and redeemed it.

Amongst these Jews sat Moses, leader of their harsh and horrible council, his beard flowing over his breast, sent to them there from the lands of Saxony for the accustomed ritual, so that he might plan such a serious crime in the city of Trent. By their votes he had been promoted to be high priest of their savage race, and had been given this empty title.[3] For after the Jews spitefully and presumptuously condemned Christ, which means 'the Anointed One', to death on a tree,[4] their rights [sig. aiiv] were exchanged with the people of their country.[5] Their material power and status were lost: neither did the true priesthood remain among them, nor could they establish stable abodes, being detested by all peoples, in the words of the prophet: "When the holy of holies comes, then will your anointing cease."[6] What, indeed, could you still hope for?

---

[1] In fact, the word probably derives from the Hebrew verb *pasach*, used in Exodus 12: 11–13 in reference to God's 'passing over' the Hebrews' houses while striking down the first-born in every Egyptian house. This has nothing to do with the crossing of the Red Sea. However, the two are conflated in the night liturgy of Easter even with its baptismal component.

[2] Exodus 12 details the institution of the Jewish Passover festival; 1 Corinthians 5: 7–8 describes its reinterpretation as a foreshadowing of Christ's supreme sacrifice.

[3] On Moses, who lived in the house of Samuel, see Appendix 2.

[4] Cf. Acts 5: 30, where Peter and the apostles address the Sanhedrin: "Deus patrum nostrorum suscitavit Iesum, quem vos interemistis, suspendentes in ligno."

[5] That is, with the non-Jewish inhabitants of Palestine.

[6] A misquotation of Daniel 9: 24 which seems to derive from Pseudo-Augustine, *Sermo contra iudaeos, paganos et arianos*, 12 (*PL* 42. 1124): "cum venerit Sanctus

Aegyptus, Babylon, tenuit vos Syria captos;
inde tamen iuga dura Deus miseratus ab alto
depulit. In patriam reduces vos fecit, opesque
immensas late, in populos gentesque subactas
iura dedit. Reges armis opibusque potentes   90
gens Iudaea habuit, claros qui saepe triumphos
hostibus ex victis duxerunt. Oppida multa
capta manu, multique duces regesque perempti.
    Sola Deum noras vivum per quem omnia vivunt,
electique Dei populi tu nomen habebas.   95
Lex tibi dicta fuit divina mente profecta,
per servum delata pium de vertice Moysen,[1]
de C[h]ristoque Deo sacro cecinere prophetae
ore tui. Qui cum natus de virgine sancta,
praedictum ut fuerat, Iesse de stirpe fuisset,   100
Filius aeternus supremi Patris, et ipse
factus homo Deus in mundum[2] venisset, ut hostis
tolleret antiqui insidias, et morsibus atri
sanaret laesos serpentis, morte redemptos
duceret in vitam, mirandaque facta probarent   105
lepros mundari, surdos audire, loquique
mutos, et caecos pulsis spectare tenebris, [sig. aiiir]
funebrique thoro elati clausique sepulchris
surgunt ad iussum devicta morte vocantis.
    Atque haec in populo fieri miracula cernis,   110
ast ingrata Deo meritorumque immemor in te
caeca ruis, rapta invidia, vesana furore,
gens Iudaea! Tuum regem suspendis amaro
ligno, qui dulcis vitae donaverat usum.
Tu mixtis potas sitientem felle et aceto,   115
qui te de saxo dulci potaverat unda.
Spinea tu capiti perfigis serta decoro,
qui dum serva fores fecit te insignia ferre
regia, te gemmis pulchras gestare coronas.
Morte tuum damnas Christum sanctumque Mesiam,   120
qui te serpentum pereuntem morsibus atris

---

[1] moysen *V* syna *O*
[2] mundum *O* mondum *V*

Egypt, Babylon, and Assyria held you captive; but then God showed pity from on high and cast off your harsh yokes. He brought you back to your native land, and gave you immense resources far and wide, rights over conquered peoples and races. The Jewish race had kings strong in arms and resources who often led splendid triumphal processions of conquered foes. Many towns were captured at its hands, and many leaders and kings killed.

You alone knew the living God, through whom all things live, and you were called God's chosen people. To you was the divinely-inspired law declared, sent down from the mountain through God's pious servant Moses, and yours were the prophets who from their sacred lips sang of Christ our God. When, as had been foretold, the eternal Son of the supreme Father had been born of a holy virgin from the stem of Jesse, and God himself, made man, had come into the world, so that he might destroy the snares of the ancient enemy and heal those hurt by the deadly serpent's bites, and lead to life those redeemed by his death, and so that marvelous deeds might prove that lepers were made clean, the deaf could hear, the dumb could speak, and the blind could see, their darkness dispelled [sig. aiiir]—*then* both those lifted up on the funeral bier and those enclosed in graves rose up at the command of him who, having vanquished death, was calling them.[1]

And you saw these miracles occurring among your people, yet, ungrateful to God and unmindful of his favors towards you, you rushed blindly on, seized by spite and crazed by fury, Jewish race! You hanged your king on a bitter tree, him who had granted you the enjoyment of sweet life. When he thirsted, you gave him a mixture of gall and vinegar to drink, him who had given you sweet water from the rock to drink.[2] You pierced his beauteous head with a garland of thorns, the head of him who while you were still slaves enabled you to carry kingly emblems and wear crowns resplendent with jewels. You condemned to death your Christ and holy Messiah, him who healed you when you were dying from the

---

sanctorum, cessabit unctio [vestra]." The text is actually by Quodvultdeus: *Clavis Patristica Pseudepigraphorum Medii Aevi* 1A, ed. J. Machielsen (Turnhout: Brepols, 1990), 264–65 (no. 1205). The meaning given to this statement there is that Christ will silence his enemies who failed to recognize him on earth, such as the Pharisees in John 8: 13, which is quoted.

[1] The idea seems to be that Christ's 'lesser' miracles are proved by the 'greater' ones (involving dead people being restored to life, such as the widow of Nain and Lazarus of Bethany). Cf. the dialogue about the veracity of the apostles' eyewitness reports of Christ's miracles by Pusculo's friend and Brescian contemporary Elia Capriolo, *De confirmatione Christianae fidei* (Brescia: Bernardino Misinta, 31 May 1497).

[2] Cf. Matthew 27: 34: "et dederunt ei vinum bibere cum felle mixtum." In Exodus 17: 6 Moses is commanded by God to strike the rock at Horeb, from which water then flows. This section recalls the *Improperia* or 'Reproaches' of the Good Friday Liturgy.

sanavit deserta loca atque inculta tenentum.
Ante etenim servos, crudelis et impia, missos
cum perimas, Iudaea, Deo sanctosque prophetas,
nempe graves poenas captivaque dira luisti   125
supplicia; in terras hostiles rapta coacta es
servire a dulci longe patriaque domoque.
Haec mala sed finem tandem invenere: misertus
estque tui Deus, atque habuit fortuna regressum
ad meliora; prior rediit status; acta dolore   130
delicti veniam meruisti. Crimine sed nunc
maiestate Dei laesa graviore teneris.
    Non tantum mandata eius legemque refringens
es deprensa — satis non est violasse ministros —
sed Dominum, sub forma hominis qui venerat ad te, [sig. aiiiv] 135
insectata neci dirae turpique dedisti
horrendae crucis in ligno, mediumque duorum
latronum regem posuisti, cuius in ore
non dolus inventus: non peccatum fuit illi.
Nec contenta manes scelus admisisse, dolesve[1]   140
his ausis, non corda subit quantum scelus hoc sit,
nec peccasse semel satis[2] est, sed et acrius instas,
admissumque foves, crimen defendis; et ardes
ira, odiumque atrox dictis factisque fateris
in Christum Christique fidem, substantia Patris   145
una eadem cum sit summi: Genitus Deus ipsi
aequalis Patri regnat cum Pneumate Sancto.
Hae tres personae Deus est idem: omnipotensque
est Pater, est Genitus, Sanctus quoque Spiritus unus.
Hic Iesus Christus Deus, a te qui est cruce fixus,   150
mortuus in ligno, voluit tormenta subire
mortis, ut ad vitam surgens de morte vocaret
mundum,[3] quem primi captum delicta parentis
subdiderant culpae, stabatque obnoxius illi
omnis homo. "Nostros gessit vere ipse dolores   155
languoresque tulit," cecinit sacro ore propheta.
    Hac rabie cum tu perstes saevissima, nullus
peccati dolor immensi tua viscera tangat,
non sperare tibi fas ad meliora regressum,
sed sparsa in terras omnis cum faenore vivas   160

---

[1] dolesue *V* dolosue *O*
[2] semel satis *O* satis semel *V*
[3] mundum *O* mondum *V*

deadly bites of the serpents that dwell in wild and deserted places.[1] For indeed, because earlier, cruel and impious Judea, you killed the servants and holy prophets sent by God, it is true that you suffered severe penalties and dreadful punishments in captivity; carried off to enemy lands, you were forced to be slaves far from your native land and home. But these evils did at last come to an end: God took pity on you, and your fortune reverted to a better state; your former status was restored; sorrow-driven, you earned forgiveness of your misdeed. But now you were held on a graver charge, having offended God's majesty.

Not only were you caught infringing his commands and his law—it was not enough to have dishonored his ministers—but you pursued the Lord who had come to you in human form [sig. aiiiv] and put him to a dreadful and ignoble death on the tree of a horrible cross, and placed your king between two felons, him in whose mouth no guile was found: he was without sin.[2] You were not sat isfied with perpetrating a crime, nor did you regret these outrages—it did not enter your minds how serious a crime this was—nor was it enough to sin once, but you pressed on even more keenly, cherished the offense and defended the wrongdoing; and you blazed with anger, and by your words and deeds confessed your fierce hatred of Christ and the Christian faith, although the supreme Father's substance is one and the same [as Christ's]: God the Son, together with the Holy Spirit,[3] reigns equally with the Father himself. These three persons are the same God, and the almighty Father, the Son, and the Holy Spirit are one. This Jesus Christ our God, who was crucified by you and died on a tree, was willing to undergo the torments of death, in order that, rising to life, he might summon from death the world which the misdeeds of our first parent[4] had enslaved and subjected to blame, and every human being remained liable to that blame. "Truly he himself carried our sorrows and bore our weaknesses," the prophet sang from sacred lips.[5]

Since you most savagely persisted in this madness, and felt no sorrow for your boundless sin, it was right, not that you should hope for a return to a better state, but that, dispersed into all lands, you should live on the proceeds of usury, with princes as your servants. They do not protect you for love, detested as you

---

[1] In Numbers 21: 6–9 God punishes the Israelites' complaints by inflicting fiery serpents on them, but after Moses has made a bronze serpent and raised it as a standard, those who look at it survive their snake-bites.

[2] 1 Peter 2: 22: "qui peccatum non fecit, nec inventus est dolus in ore eius."

[3] *Pneuma*, the normal New Testament Greek word for '[Holy] Spirit' but rare in its Latinised form, is used here partly for reasons of scansion, since *Pneumate* (unlike *Spiritu*) suits the hexameter's dactylic rhythm.

[4] That is, Adam.

[5] Isaiah 53: 4: "vere languores nostros ipse tulit, et dolores nostros ipse portavit."

principibus servis; qui te haud tutantur amore
invisam populis, laceras quos faenore. Num[m]i
te servant soli, pereas quod non male, pendis [sig. aiiiir]
quos dominis partos de faenore. Pro,[1] sitis auri
quantum dira valet! Pedibus supponit honestum,   165
ut vero infandum statuit de caede futura
concilium. Si quis facinus tantum audeat ultro
perquirunt, tentantque animos impellere: centum
promittunt auri num[m]os dare, quisquis ad ipsos
infantem sacro lotum baptismate ducat.   170
       At quanquam est animus cunctis auroque trahuntur[2]
in facinus, se quisque tamen formidine pressus
continet, ac tanto nulli se offerre periclo
fert animus: facti ante oculos stat cognita[3] poena.
Pectora pulsantur mortis discrimine, apertum   175
si facinus fiat. Tobiam munere tandem
sollicitant magno, sedes nam longa Tridenti
huic fuerat, notusque urbi fuit arte medendi,
et poterat tunc solus eo securus obire
scrutarique vias et quaerere furta sine ulla   180
suspicione: alii clausos cum tempore tali
contineant sese domibus, nec in urbe vagari
ausint Iudaei. Cui cum promissa darentur—
magna quidem, non certa tamen—sic rettulit ille:
"Quod petitis magnum est: maius discrimen in ipso   185
impendet capitique meo capitique meorum.
Aggrediar tamen hoc, vobis nec deerit et artis
quicquid opisque mihi est, nostro feliciter hoc si
cesserit[4] ex animo, puerumque impune repertum
quem cupimus fortuna dabit, res dextera vobis   190
manserit in longum. Sin nostrum adversa reflectet [sig. aiiiiv]
conatum sors saeva, manet nos exitus idem
infelix. Nam morte luam conamen inane,
vel fuga me tollet. Pauper sum; munere vivo
artis, alitque domum merces quaesita medendo.   195
Haec me destituat, mecum est peritura meorum
tota domus confecta fame. Vos dicere nolim,

---

[1] pro *V* proch *O*
[2] *correxi*: trahantur *VO*
[3] *correxi*: conscia *VO*
[4] cesserit *V* caessit *O*

are by their peoples, whom you torture with usury. Only the money—drawn from usury—that you pay to your masters saves you from an evil doom. [sig. aiiiir] Ah, what power the dreadful thirst for gold wields![1] It tramples virtue underfoot, as indeed happened when the abominable council planned the forthcoming murder. They inquired whether anyone would volunteer for so daring a crime, and tried to give an incentive: they promised to give a hundred gold coins to whoever brought them an infant washed in holy baptism.

But although all were keen, and were attracted to the crime by gold, yet each one, gripped by fear, held back, and no one had the courage to expose himself to so great a danger: before his eyes loomed the known punishment of the deed. Their hearts were pounding at the danger of death if the crime were uncovered. At last, they tried to tempt Tobias with a large reward, for he had long resided at Trent, was well known to the city for his skill in medicine, and so could safely go about alone then,[2] and could search the streets and prospect for kidnappings without any suspicion: since the others kept themselves shut away in their homes at such a time, nor did Jews dare to wander about in the city. When these promises—large ones indeed, but vague—were given him, he replied: "You are asking a big thing: bigger still is the danger it would involve, threatening my family's lives as well as my own. I *will* undertake it, though, nor will whatever skill and ability I possess let you down, so long as this job has the happy outcome we desire, and fortune gives us the boy we want—one acquired with impunity—and the situation long continues in your favor. But if adversity savagely thwarts our [sig. aiiiiv] enterprise, the same unhappy fate awaits us [all]. For I shall pay with my death for a wasted effort, or else make a quick getaway. I am poor; I live on my professional earnings, and my household depends on the income from my medical practice. Should I lose that income, my whole family household will die of hunger with me. When I demand payment of the reward I was promised for such a mighty deed, I would *not* want you to say:

---

[1] A rephrasing of Vergil, *Aeneid* 3. 56–57: see below, 195 n. 2.

[2] During the Christian Holy Week, when Jews would have felt especially marginalized and vulnerable to the hostility of Christian neighbors.

cum poscam promissa dari mihi praemia tanto[1]
pro facto: 'Ius est: reddemus debita verbis.'
Sic solvar vanis." Uno tunc ore futurum   200
confirmant cuncti: tantum mercedis habendum
vectigalque sibi, quantum sua vita domusque
exigat ipsius, nec rerum copia desit.
    His verbis animum sumit: spe suscitat hac se,
egressusque domo Samuelis corde volutat   205
quo pergat, qua seque ferat regione viarum.
Diversisque locis agitur. Modo fertur ad illam,
nunc hanc ire viam, petit et fora; deinde revertens
vestigansque oculis, ad raptum com[m]oda quaerit
tempora, si puerum videat quem forte relictum   210
solum. Nam clausis regionum ad sacra tabernis
contulerant de more gradum matresque virique:
magna dies Iovis illa fuit. Tandem, ecce, petitum
conspicit infantem, longo qui forte sedebat
codice, stratus humi ante viam qui pondus inane   215
stabat. Eo fessum solus se adduxerat infans,
hicque diem laetus puerili more terebat.
Menses ter denos nondum compleverat; illi
nomen erat Simon, plebeio[2] utroque parente [sig. avr]
ingenua sed stirpe satus. Carissima proles   220
unicaque ambobus; se hoc oblectabat uterque
filiolo pater et mater, pariterque ferebant
pauperiem laeti. Manuum mercede suarum
vivebant, natumque pio dulcique labore
nutribant, pariter clari pietate fideque   225
Garbarius pater Andreas materque Maria.
    Continuo petit hunc Tobias; lustrat et ante[3]
circum, huc atque illuc convolvens lumina. Abunde
ut vidit loca sola suo conducere furto,
blanditias puero tendit, mulcetque capillos   230
atque genas manibus, formosum appellat. Et inde
porrexit digitum, quo sese apprendere dextra
infantem invitat, splendentem monstrat et assem
argenti. Captus nummo comitatur euntem
Iudaeum Simon, quem laetus et accipit ultro;   235
longius accepto procedere velle recusat

---

[1] tanto *V* tantn *O*
[2] plebeio *V* phebeio *O*
[3] ante *O* an *V*

'The right thing is this: we shall repay our debt in words.' That way, I would be paid with mere nothings." Then with one voice they all confirmed what would happen: he was to have as much regular income as he and his household needed for their subsistence, nor was he to go short of material means.

From these words he took courage: with this hope he roused himself and, leaving Samuel's house, turned over in his mind where to proceed and which quarter of the streets to visit. He walked in various places. Now he headed towards one street, now he went along another, and made for the public square; then, turning back and looking carefully around, he sought opportunities for an abduction, in case he happened to see a boy left on his own. For, with the shops of the urban districts closed, mothers and their husbands had as usual gone off to religious services: that day was Maundy Thursday. At last, behold, he saw the infant he wanted sitting, as it happened, on a long tree-trunk which, laid on the ground facing the street, remained there, a useless heavy log. To it the tired, lonely infant had taken himself, and here he was happily whiling away the day as children do. He was not yet thirty months old; he was called Simon, the son of a lower-class couple [sig. avr] but free-born. For both of them he was their darling only child; each of them, father and mother, delighted in this little son, and both equally bore their poverty happily. They lived on the income from their manual work and nurtured their son by dint of pious, sweet toil, Andreas Garbarius,[1] the boy's father, and Mary, his mother, being equally noted for their piety and faith.

Tobias went straight after him; and first he looked all round, glancing this way and that. When he saw that the deserted place gave ample scope for a kidnapping, he tried to cajole the boy, stroked his hair and cheeks, and called him beautiful. And then he held out a finger, inviting the infant to grasp him with his right hand, and showed him a shining silver penny. Captivated by the coin, which he happily and spontaneously accepted, Simon accompanied the Jew on his way; once he had taken it, the boy was reluctant to go any further, struggled to extricate himself from his enemy's hands, and refused to walk.

---

[1] The surname appears as Unferdorben (literally 'uncorrupted') in other contemporary records of the case.

asse puer, manibusque hostis subducere sese
contendit, gressumque negat. Sed percitus atro
daemone Tobias blanditur, et altera dona
promittit, statimque alium sibi porrigit assem.   240
    Hisque dolis ducit puerum. Iam venerat usque
Tobias, ubi saeva cohors habitabat,[1] et ipsis
iam manibus praedam optatam se ferre putabat,
fundere cum lacrymas coepit, matremque vocare
absentem Simon, mamam et clamore ciere.   245
Tum trepidus celerat Iudaeus. Cyclade longa
Simona contexit parvum, blanditus[2] et una [sig. avv]
fert modo, nuncque trahit puerum; et, ne clamor ad auras
sublatus furtum prodat, celer in Samuelis
(eius namque domo tollendi capta fuere   250
consilia infantis, fundendi et sanguinis agni)
tendit iter tectum. Sub cuius limina postquam
pervenit, genibus nolentem intrare coegit
Simona; quem, clausis foribus Samuele vocato,
tradit ei actutum, gaudens quod vota secunda   255
ex animo sibi cesserunt, prout facta maligna.
Laetantur scelere[3] hoc; cuius quae poena secuta
si tunc nota foret, nollent tetigisse, nec unquam
Simona novisse, ac magno non verba fuisse
optarent pretio faciendae caedis in illum.   260
    Interea, dum nox veniat tenebrosa, puellum
blanditi servant, dant et munuscula, dulci et
melle fovent, blandoque sinu amplexuque morantur.
Mittuntur taciti puero praedaque potiri
qui referant sociis, moneantque ad limina duri   265
actutum veniant Samuelis. Moyses illic
primus adest: puerum videt observatque, retractans
totum animo scelerisque modum caedisque futurae;
ac residens parvum foeda[4] inter brac[c]hia blandis,
conveniat dum tota cohors scelerata, moratur   270
vocibus. Interea acciti Samuelis ad aedes
accurrunt laeti: Vitalis cum Solomone,
Angelus atque Mohar, Ioph, Isaac Israelque,
Tobias raptorque, nepos tuus, Angele, Lazar,

---

[1] habitabat *V* habitahat *O*
[2] blanditus *V* bladitus *O*
[3] scelere *V* scaelere *O*
[4] *correxi*: genua *VO*

But Tobias, driven by a deadly demon, cajoled him and promised a second gift, and immediately offered him another penny.

With these tricks he led the boy on. Tobias had now come right up to where the savage gang dwelt, and thought that in his very hands he was already carrying the longed-for prey, when Simon began to shed tears, and to call for his absent mother and loudly summon his "Mama". At this, the Jew anxiously hurried on. He covered little Simon with a long cloak, and, while cajoling him, now carried, [sig. avv] now dragged him along; and, fearing that his cries, rising aloft, might betray the kidnapping, he hurried to Samuel's house (for his was the home where the plan to steal an infant and shed 'a lamb's blood' was conceived). When he reached its threshold, he forced the unwilling Simon to enter on his knees; closing the door and summoning Samuel, he handed the boy to him at once, glad that their prayers, like their evil deeds, had turned out favorably for them as they desired. They rejoiced at this crime; if they had known then their subsequent punishment for it, they would have preferred not to have touched Simon or ever known him, and would have chosen to pay a large sum not to have discussed committing murder against him.[1]

Meanwhile, until dark night came, they soothed and watched the little boy, gave him little presents, refreshed him with sweet honey, and diverted him with soothing hugs and embraces. Tight-lipped messengers were sent to tell their comrades that they had boy and prey in their grasp, and to warn them to come at once to harsh Samuel's home. Moses was there first: he saw the boy and looked him over, rehearsing in his mind the whole procedure of the forthcoming murderous crime; and, as he sat there, he diverted with smooth words the child he held in his filthy[2] arms, until the whole criminal gang assembled. They, meanwhile, when summoned, ran joyfully to Samuel's house: Vital with Solomon, Engel and Mayer, Jo[se]ph, Isaac, Israel, the abductor Tobias, Lazarus—your nephew, Engel—and the two Seligmans: the one Mayer's son, [sig. avir]

---

[1] In other words, they would have tried to undo the past.

[2] Both *V* and *O* have the unscannable and unintelligible word *genua* in this line. The word that replaces it here, *foeda* ('filthy'), has been chosen because of its similar usage by Calfurnio. See above, 94, l. 177.

et Bonaventurae gemini: Moharis satus[1] alter [sig. avir]   275
stirpe, alter cocus est Samuelis. Cuius et uxor
audet se Brunetta viris adiungier una,
atque aliae plures aderant; scelerique favebant
multi praeterea, quorum non nomina novi.
    Hi postquam celeres[2] avidique haurire cruorem   280
Christicolae infantis venerunt in Samuelis
tecta domus, cuncti actutum clauduntur in uno
secretoque loco; pueri procul esse iubentur,
atque omnes illi quis non secreta teneri
acta timent. Nox iam terras obscura tenebris   285
sparserat, et nullus strepitus per strata viarum
audiri, clausaeque domus compage silebant.
Ecce, parant mensam ad caedem sacrumque nefandum,
et scyphum argenti, pueri quo rite cruorem
suscipiant, sed nec cultrum de more sacrorum,   290
quo iugulum aperiant, gladium quo pectus adacto
transfodiant tenerum — sed acus ad vulnera longas
his adhibent sacris et aduncae forcipis usum.
His structis,[3] infans Simon ductatur ut agnus
innocuus, rerum ignarus: non noverat ille   295
quid fera turba velit saeptum contracta sub unum
eius in exitium dirum — quae sanguinis haustu
stabat hians pueri, non secius aspera quam si
turba lupum stimulata fame, quae nocte sub atra
expectans ovium foetus tenerosve iuvencos   300
a stabulis ductos dubiae sub tempora lucis
dentibus infrendens rabiem confoverat ira.
Si videt aut agnum longe[4] mollemve iuvencum, [sig. aviv]
cui tutela canum non adsit, morsibus ora
saeva movet, resonant dentes, vix continet ac se   305
insidiis, donec veniat sua praeda sub ora.
Insolitum ut vidit coetum, stetit inscius infans
territus, et matrem puerili nomine mamam
clamavit, lacrymasque genis effudit inanes,
crebra vocans mamam. Ruit impia turba feroxque   310
plorantemque rapit; ne clamor proderet ipsos,
infantis tenero circumdant lintea collo,

---

[1] *correxi*: datus *VO*
[2] celeres *V* sceleres *O*
[3] structis *V* fructis *O*
[4] *correxi*: longae *VO*

the other Samuel's cook. Samuel's wife Brünnlein also presumed to join the men, and several other women were there; and many people besides, whose names I do not know, approved of the crime.[1]

When these people, rushing and gasping to quaff an infant Christ-worshiper's gore, had entered Samuel's house, all were immediately locked in one secret place; children, and all those whose ability to keep a secret they doubted, were told to stay far away. Gloomy night had already scattered darkness over the earth, no noise was heard along the paved streets, and the terraced houses were silent. Behold, the Jews were preparing a table for the heinous ritual murder, and a silver cup in which to ceremonially take up the boy's gore, but no knife with which to slit his throat in proper ritual fashion, no sword to plunge into his tender breast and run him through — rather, for this ritual they brought long needles for wounding, and employed hooked pincers.

These preparations made, infant Simon was led in like an innocent lamb,[2] unaware of the situation: he did not know what the wild mob, bunched into one confined space, intended for his dreadful demise — the mob that stood agog at the draining of a boy's blood, just like a fierce pack of hunger-driven wolves which, waiting under cover of dark night for new-born lambs, or for tender bullocks led from their stalls, and gnashing their teeth[3] as the time of dawn's faint gleam draws near, have fueled their ferocity with rage. If they see in the distance a lamb or a soft bullock [sig. aviv] unguarded by the dogs, they snap their savage jaws, grind their teeth, and can hardly contain themselves as they lie in wait for their prey to come right up to their mouths.[4] When the puzzled infant saw the strange assembly he stood terror-struck, cried out for his mother with the childish word "Mama", and shed futile tears down his cheeks, repeatedly calling "Mama". The impious, savage mob rushed and seized the sobbing infant; lest his cries betray them, they tied a linen cloth round his tender neck, and tightened it enough to stop his cries reaching up above without blocking the airways of his gentle breath.

---

[1] On each of these individuals see Appendix 2.

[2] Cf. Isaiah 53: 7: "He was oppressed, and he was afflicted, yet he opened not his mouth; he is brought as a lamb to the slaughter, and as a sheep before her shearers is dumb, so he openeth not his mouth"; Acts 8: 32: "He was led as sheep to the slaughter; and like a lamb dumb before his shearer, so opened he not his mouth."

[3] Cf. Vergil, *Aeneid* 3. 664, describing the blinded giant Polyphemus.

[4] Cf. Vergil, *Aeneid* 9. 63–64, where Turnus is compared to a prowling wolf; and Ovid, *Metamorphoses* 11. 369–72, where a wolf attacks a whole herd of oxen. For the Vergil reference, see also above, 49 n. 1.

ac tantum astringunt quantum non tendat in auras
clamor nec claudant animae spiramina mollis.
    Tum[1] nudant tracto ad medium velamine corpus   315
infantem, terraque levant, statuuntque levatum
mensae, quam pro ara facienda ad sacra locarant.
Ne iaceat, plantisque pedum contingere solis
cogunt, ac rectum consistere corpore toto;
inque crucis formam dextra laevaque trahuntur   320
brac[c]hia. Sic positum quatere haud sua membra sinebant
Iudaei immanes, voci et via clausa manebat.
Tum, spirans rabiem in C[h]ristum parvumque fidelis
Christicolae natum, voces has ore prophano
Moyses effudit scelerataque vota sacerdos: 325
"Ut manibus quondam nostrorum C[h]ristus in orbe
maiorum interiit cruce fixus—qui mala nostro
multa tulit populo, per quem dispersa per orbem
gens fertur Iudaea opibus depulsa suisque
sedibus e patriis, nunc toto creditur esse   330
in mundo Deus, aequalis tibi filius idem, [sig. aviir]
summe Pater, colitur, falso hunc inimica Mesiam
Christicolum gens tota putat dixisse prophetas—
sic nunc, sancte, tibi, Deus orbis conditor, hunc de
Christicolis natum puerum in ludibria Christi   335
offerimus gens grata tibi Iudaea. Precamur
oblatum accipias sacrum, parvique cruorem
corporis effusum. Sicut haec tibi victima nostris
iam cadet hic dextris, Christi sic nomen inane
dispereat, sic tota simul gens pessima Christum   340
quae colit intereat, stirpis monumenta nec ulla
Christicolae maneant terris inimica; et in omnes
sit, precor, haec nobis talis permissa potestas,
quae data in infantem invisa de stirpe creatum.
Exilium tandem effugiat, patriaque recepta   345
gaudeat electus populus Iudaeus, et acre
hostibus exitium cernat stragemque supremam!"
    Has ubi crudelis voces dedit, inforat atrox
actutum stanti misero praeputia cultro
infanti, primusque cruor de hoc vulnere manat.   350
Continuoque genae partem aufert forcipe adunca
et cruris dextri suram. Haec tria vulnera prima

---

[1] tum *V* tnm *O*

Then, pulling the infant's clothing down to his waist,[1] they stripped him, lifted him off the ground, and stood him on a table which they had placed there as an altar for performing the ritual. To stop him lying down, they forced him to touch it with just the soles of his feet and to stand with his whole body erect; and his right and left arms were pulled out to form a cross [see above, 12, fig. 2]. Thus placed, the brutal Jews did not let him move his limbs, and his voice was denied an outlet. Then the priest Moses, breathing out ferocious hatred[2] of Christ and a faithful Christ-worshiper's little child, poured forth from his profane mouth these pernicious words of prayer: "Just as, long ago, Christ perished in the world at our ancestors' hands, nailed to a cross—the man who brought many evils upon our people, through whom the scattered Jewish race wanders all over the world, thrown out of its property and ancestral homes, *he* is now throughout the world believed to be God, *he* is worshiped as a son equal to you, [sig. aviir] supreme Father, *he* is wrongly thought by the whole hostile Christ-worshiping race to be the one the prophets called 'Messiah'!—so now, holy God, creator of the world, we, the Jewish race you love, offer you this boy, the child of Christ-worshipers, in mockery of Christ. We pray you to accept the sacrifice we offer, and the poured-out gore of his small body. Just as here, at our hands, this victim will now be slain for you, so may the empty name 'Christ' be destroyed, so may the whole utterly evil race that worships Christ perish together, and may no hostile reminders of the Christ-worshiping breed remain on earth; and may such power be allowed us over all people, I pray, as has been given us over an infant born of that detested breed. May the chosen Jewish people at last escape from exile and rejoice in the recovery of their homeland, and may they see bitter doom and total slaughter visited on their foes!"

As soon as he had uttered these cruel words, the brute pierced the poor infant's foreskin with a knife as he stood there, and the first gore trickled from this wound. Straightway he removed part of a cheek and the calf of the right leg with hooked pincers. Simon felt the pain of these first three wounds and their laceration of his body. Samuel repeated the two wounds to the leg and face with

---

[1] Compare the details given at this point by Calfurnio and Tiberino. Here it is Simon's clothing that is pulled down, whereas in Calfurnio's account a similar description is applied to the Jews—and in Tiberino's account either interpretation is possible, depending on which version of the text is followed. See above, 49–51 n. 5, and 95 n. 3.

[2] An allusion to Acts 9: 1: "And Saul yet breathing out threatenings and slaughter against the disciples of the Lord, went unto the high priest."

sensit et his primis laniari corpore Simon.
Haec Samuel iterat duo vulnera cruris et oris
forcipe, et exprimitur sanguis de vulnere utroque,   355
ut fluat in cyathum. Circumstant—pessima turba!—
Iudaei; puero insultant; gaudentque dolentem
cernere, quodque dolens non edere signa doloris
clara sui valeat, nec enim sua membra movere [sig. aviiv]
nec clamare potest. Longas Brunetta per omnes   360
dispertitur acus; his sese ad vulnera quisque
crebra parat, puerumque petit, tenerosque per artus[1]
saevit in immensum rabies, et cuspide acuta
perforat infigens venis. Rapit inde cruorem
certatim sibi quisque: movet nec corporis ullum   365
Iudaeum parvi ante oculos mensura nec aetas
innocua infantis. Medio deprensa tumultu
praeda canum veluti, cui iam fuga nulla salutem
nec vires donare valent—vel caprea vel sit
cerva fugax aut dama pavens—immota cruentis   370
morsibus icta manet; foedat laniatibus illam
ira canum; duros certatim in corpore dentes
infigunt, varioque ferunt fera vulnera morsu,
nec prius absistunt saevire, a corpore vita
quam fugiat praedae; lambunt foedata cruore   375
ora canes. Talis parvus deprensus amaro
Simon erat coetu Iudaeum; vulnere crebro
saevit quisque sitim satians. Iam sanguine totus
haustus erat, tenuisque in corpore vita manebat.
Saevit adhuc scelerata manus, nec destitit ante   380
quam scyphum implevit fluido per membra cruore,
spiritus et puerum liquit. Sublatus ad astra,
evolat in caelum nitidus, coetusque beatos
Simon habet; digna fruitur mercede dolorum,
quos tulit in tenero laniatus corpore Christi   385
nominis ob causam; claris miracula rebus
addita Iudaeos poenae ob commissa vocarunt. [sig. aviiir]
        Dic mihi saeva, mihi dic gens saevissima, quis te
haec sacra ferre Deo docuit? Quis legis et huius
auctor, ut humano gauderet sanguine numen?   390
Nempe prior vitae humanae natura magistra
nos homines iubet esse[2] pios iustosque, benignos,

---

[1] *correxi*: arctus *VO*
[2] esse *V* esset *O*

the pincers, and the blood was squeezed from both wounds so that it flowed
into a ladle. The Jews—utterly evil mob!—stood round; they scoffed at the boy;
and they rejoiced at seeing him in pain and at the fact that, though in pain, he
could show no clear signs of his pain, being unable either to move his limbs [sig.
aviiv] or to cry out. Brünnlein gave out long needles to them all; with these each
man readied himself for frequent blows and went for the boy, and their ferocity
rampaged unbounded all over his tender limbs, piercing him with sharp points
driven into his veins. Then each vied with his neighbor to seize gore for himself:
neither the smallness of the body they saw nor the infant's innocent youth moved
anyone. It was like what happens when the prey of dogs,[1] caught in the midst of
the uproar, now quite unable to gain safety by flight or physical strength—a roe
or scurrying hind perhaps, or else a frightened fallow-deer—stays motionless,
struck by gory bites; the angry dogs tear it to shreds; they vie with one another
to fasten their harsh teeth in its body, and rain fierce biting blows all over it, nor
do they cease their savagery until life flees from the body of their prey; the dogs
then lick their gore-smirched lips.[2] Such a prey was little Simon, caught in the
bitter company of the Jews; each of them, slaking his thirst, violently attacked
him with frequent blows. By now Simon was wholly drained of blood, and only a
flicker of life remained in his body. Still the criminal band kept up their violence,
nor did they cease until they had filled a cup with the gore that bathed his limbs,
and the boy had breathed his last. Raised to the stars, Simon winged his shining
way to heaven, and now dwells in the companies of the blessed; he enjoys a reward worthy of the pains he bore, having had his tender body torn apart for the
sake of Christ's name; and miracles, as well as plain facts, have summoned the
Jews to punishment for their offenses. [sig. aviiir]

Tell me, savage race, tell me, utterly savage race, who taught you to offer
God this sacrifice? And who invented this law, that the deity should take pleasure in human blood? Surely nature, who formerly directed human life, tells
us humans to be pious, just, and kind, and to distance ourselves from brute
beasts; and she orders us to remove life's disadvantages by mutually sharing our

---

[1] Cf. Ovid, *Metamorphoses* 11. 27, where Orpheus, under attack from the Maenads,
is compared to a stag cornered by dogs in the arena. The simultaneous biblical allusion—again a type of Christ—is to Psalm 22: 16 (= Vulgate Ps. 21:17), recited in Holy
Week: "For many dogs have surrounded me."

[2] Cf. Ovid, *Metamorphoses* 3. 57, describing a huge serpent licking the wounds of the
Phoenicians it has just killed. The simultaneous biblical allusion is to 1 Kings 21: 19: "In
the place where dogs licked the blood of Naboth shall dogs lick thy blood, even thine."

ac distare feris immanibus; utque vicissim
alternis opibus nobis incommoda vitae
tollamus—damnis alienis corde dolere,[1]   395
laetarique bonis—mandat. Sed proxima Mo[y]ses—
Moyses ille pius, iustus magnusque propheta,
huius dissimilis, pueri qui sanguine laetus
foedavit sese caesi crudeliter—arcae[2]
in tabulis praecepta dedit legesque beatas,   400
quae prohibent a caede manus hominisque cruore.
Melchisedech primus, magnus sanctusque sacerdos,
non haec sacra Deo fieri, non caede litare
humana, insontis pueri non sanguinis haustu,
monstrat; sed vituli[3] hircorum pecudumve piari   405
caede docet culpas Solymorum more vetusto.
Tu puerum insontem, gens crudelissima, mactas,
nec[4] nisi C[h]risticolae pueri tibi victima grata est;
nec mors grata tibi subita est, sed perdere longa
morte placet, vivi calidumque haurire cruorem;   410
quem bibitis vino mixtum, sollennia mensae
cum facitis, libis azimis miscetis et illum.

   Hoc agitis laeti Paschalia sacra, bibentes
vescentesque simul, namque huius sanguinis usus
non novus est ipsis Iudaeis. Saecula iam sunt [sig. aviiiv]   415
acta octo, Carr[h]is cum toto ex orbe frequentes
concilium fecere, piam dum crescere Christi
relligione fidem populis terrisque viderent,
quamvis per multas illam delere tyranni
quaesissent poenas, magnisque inhibere parati   420
tormentis varia saevissent morte per orbem
contra Christicolas. Ubinam cruciamina non sunt
sanctorum gladios ignesque, venena rotasque
passorum, et proprio testantum sanguine veram
esse fidem Christi? Laniari corpora ferreis   425
unguibus, et vivos uri mediosque secari,
offerrique feris pro Christi nomine votum
tunc erat, intexique rotis mortisque per omne
ire genus. Nec tanta viris patientia solis,
haec ut dura pati pro Christi nomine vellent: 430

---

[1] dolere *V* dolore *O*
[2] *correxi*: arae *VO*
[3] *correxi*: uitulum *VO*
[4] *correxi*: naec *VO*

resources—to be saddened by other people's losses and gladdened by their successes. But Moses—that pious, just, and great prophet, unlike *this* Moses, who happily smirched himself with the blood of a cruelly slain boy—gave the next commandments on the tables of the Ark,[1] as well as blessed laws which keep our hands well away from murder and human gore. Melchizedek, a great and holy priest,[2] first showed that *this* sacrifice is not performed for God, that one propitiates him not by slaying a human being, not by draining the blood of an innocent boy; rather, he teaches that according to ancient Jewish tradition wrongdoings are expiated by slaying a kid or a calf. But *you*, most cruel race, slaughter an innocent boy, and the only sacrificial offering pleasing to *you* is that of a Christ-worshiping boy; neither does his instant death please you, but you think fit to destroy him by a drawn-out one, and to drain his warm gore while he lives; you drink it mixed with wine when you carry out the rituals of the [Seder] table, and you mix it in the unleavened cakes.

With this you happily perform the Passover rites, drinking and eating it at the same time, for the use of this blood is not new to the Jews themselves. Eight centuries have already [sig. aviiiv] passed since, flocking from all over the world, they held a council at Carr[h]ae,[3] when they saw in peoples and countries the growth of pious faith brought by Christianity, although by many penalties tyrants had sought to wipe it out and, prepared as they were to repress it by mighty torments, had vented their rage on Christ-worshipers throughout the world by various modes of death. What place anywhere has not seen tortures done to saints who suffered sword and fire, poison and the wheel, and who with their own blood testified that the Christian faith is true? Their prayer then was to have their bodies torn by iron hooks, and to be burnt alive and cleft in twain, and to be offered to wild animals for Christ's sake, and to be strapped on wheels and endure every form of death. Nor was such great fortitude confined to men, inspiring them to suffer these hardships for Christ's sake: virgins, married women, and widows had the will to suffer torments for Christ's sake.

---

[1] A wooden box containing the stone tablets of the Law, the Ark (of the Covenant) was carried by the Israelites as they traveled through the desert as a symbol of God's presence with his people: for its construction and contents see Exodus 25: 10–16.

[2] Genesis 14: 18, but Pusculo uses Melchizedek as an epitome of Jewish priestly lore in general. There is also a parallel to the eucharist, the bloodless sacrifice, since the Old Testament figure Melchizedek offers bread and wine: frequent in typological exegesis.

[3] The Mesopotamian town famous as the site of Rome's defeat by the Parthians (53 B.C), but previously known as Haran, Abraham's home town (Genesis 11: 31). This link with Abraham may be why Pusculo mentions it here. In fact, the council in question is the mythical Council of Jamnia, supposed to have fixed the Old Testament canon and added the 'condemnation of the *minim*,' or apostates. See D. Boyarin, *Border Lines* (Philadelphia: University of Pennsylvania Press, 2004).

virginibus nuptisque inerat mulieribus haec mens
ac viduis, tormenta pati pro nomine Christi.
His crevere malis fidei primordia nostrae:
non opibus, mundi illecebris non dulcibus, huius
orta nec aucta fides Christi, sed dura fuere   435
principia in Christo petra fundata. Nec aucta
deliciis: ferro, vinclis et carcere tetro,
verberibus saevis primi coepere fideles
ire viam, signis miris comitantibus illos!
    Illo concilio, fidei in ludibria nostrae   440
contemptumque Dei Christi, per saecla quot annis[1]
decrevere satum puerum de gente fideli
quaerere Christicola, cui non sit septimus annus [sig. br]
exactus, furtimque novo consumere leto,
qui teneram exhausto vitam cum sanguine linquat.   445
Hoc, Iudaea, tibi placet, hoc, gens perfida, quod non
Busyris faciat, duro qui robore victus
Herculis occubuit, non Taurica saeva Dianae
templa ferant, hominum quamvis manantia caede.
Laetitiaeque diem iobelaeumque[2] vocant hunc   450
quo tetrum hoc facinus peragunt; hoc sanguine contra
fetorem innatum tollendum utuntur Hebraei;
hoc vice paschalis sparguntur sanguinis agni;
hunc—quocunque[3] loco scelus hoc crudele peractum est—
dimittunt varias in terras ac synagogas.   455
Ipsorum nostrum potant comeduntque cruorem
Iudaei, ac nostris insultant urbibus in nos.
    Hocque ferunt populi! Tanta haec iniuria inulta est
Christicolis? Nummi dominantur in[4] omnibus! At nos
cogimur Hebraeis populi servire, domique   460
et patria in nostra infensos tolerare trucesque
hostes, dilacerant crudeli faenore qui nos,
qui nostros rident cultus, qui dogmata nostrae
relligionis habent odio ludoque, Deumque
Christum blasphemant—nostri quis victima nati   465
fiunt, et nostro ludunt qui in sanguine! Christe,
nate Patris summi, mundi[5] Deus atque Redemptor,

---

[1] *correxi*: quot quatuor annis *VO*
[2] iobelaeumque *V* iobelaeamque *O*
[3] quocunque *V* quoque *O*
[4] *supplevi*: in
[5] mundi *O* mondi *V*

By these evils the germs of our faith grew: not from wealth, not from the world's sweet enticements, did the Christian faith arise and increase, but its origins were hard, founded on Christ its rock. Nor did it increase because of its charms: it was with the sword, with jail and vile dungeon, with savage beatings, that the first believers began their journey, attended by wondrous signs!

At that [Jewish] council, in mockery of our faith and contempt of Christ our God, they decided every year in perpetuity[1] to seek a boy from a faithful Christ-worshiping family who was not yet seven years old, [sig. br] and secretly destroy him by a new mode of death, so that he gave up his tender life as well as his drained-out blood. You like this, faithless Jewish race, this [sacrifice] which Busiris,[2] who fell worsted by Hercules' harsh strength, would not perform, which even savage Taurian[3] temples dripping with human gore would not offer to Diana. The Jews call it a day of joy and a jubilee when they carry out this vile deed; this blood is what the Hebrews use to counteract their inborn stench; this blood, instead of a paschal lamb's, is what they are sprinkled with; this blood—wherever this cruel crime has been carried out—is what they send off to various lands and synagogues. The Jews drink and eat our very own gore, and scoff at us in our own cities.

And our peoples endure this! Do Christ-worshipers leave such a great injury unavenged? Money lords it over them all! Yet we peoples are forced to be slaves to the Hebrews, and at home, even in our own native land, to tolerate relentless and pitiless foes who tear us apart with cruel usury, who deride our worship, who hate and ridicule the tenets of our religion and blaspheme against Christ our God—those to whom our sons fall victim, and who ridicule our blood! Christ, son of the supreme Father, God and Redeemer of the world, whom we worship and piously adore at sacred altars, I pray you: just as,

---

[1] Emending the text's impossible *quot quatuor annis* to *per saecla quotannis*. Perhaps the scribe missed out *per saecla* and then tried to fill the gap by inserting *quatuor* in the middle of *quotannis*.

[2] An Egyptian king who sacrificed strangers and was killed by Hercules.

[3] The Taurians were a barbarous people living on the Black Sea coast who sacrificed foreigners to Diana. They and Busiris both appear (together with the Gauls and the Carthaginians) in Cicero, *Republic* 3. 15, as examples of peoples who have practised human sacrifice and thought it pleasing to the gods.

quem colimus sacrasque pie[1] veneramur ad aras,
te precor: ut gentem Iudaeam criminis in te
ob causam mortisque tuae depellere regno,   470
sedibus et pulsam patriis errare per orbem [sig. bv]
exiliumque pati voluisti—sic quoque tollas
hanc pestem diram nostris de finibus, ac nos
vivere securos liceat tutosque per aevum!
Aut sana mentes dominorum, lumine recta   475
ut videant puro, nec ament contraria propter
aurum atque argentum; populisve fidelibus adde—
adde animos populis—communes omnibus hostis
quique suos abigant Hebraeos finibus, acri
seque metu eripiant generandae ad sacra prophana   480
Iudaeum sobolis. Mittantur in ultima mundi,[2]
sive per arctoas glatiali frigore terras,
trans Scyt[h]iam et gelidae Serpentis sidera, sive
solis ubi extremi signorum brac[c]hia Cancri
perpetuis ardent flam[m]is, calidique Draconis   485
nigra venena furunt nimio perfusa calore;
aut ubi claustra decem memorant ut Caspia gentis
conclusere tribus Solymorum! Barbara longe
ac deserta colant loca late, vel iuga collo
dura ferant tristi! Naturae arctentur ut hostes   490

---

[1] pie *O* piae *V*
[2] mundi *O* mondi V

on account of their crime against you, and your death, you wanted to expel the Jewish race from their kingdom, and to make them wander all over the world, driven from their ancestral homes, [sig. bv] and to suffer exile—so too, I pray, may you remove this dreadful plague from our territories, and may we be allowed to live secure and safe for ever! Or else heal the minds of our lords, so that they clearly discern what is right, and do not love its opposite for the sake of gold and silver; or, [I pray you,] give, *do* give, to your faithful peoples the courage to drive the Hebrews, the universal enemy and their own, out of their territories, and thereby dispel their bitter fear of Jewish offspring being procreated to perform such profane rites. Let them be sent to the ends of the earth, whether through ice-cold arctic lands, beyond Scythia and the stars of the chill Serpent,[1] or where the claws of the Crab,[2] outermost of the constellations, blaze with the sun's perpetual flames, and where the fiery Dragon's[3] noisome poisons rage, bathed in unbearable heat; or else where, so they say, the Caspian Gates[4] enclosed ten tribes of the Jewish race![5] May they inhabit rude wildernesses far and wide, or may they carry harsh yokes on their sorrowful necks! May they be confined as enemies

---

[1] Cf. Ovid, *Metamorphoses* 2. 173: "quaeque polo posita est glaciali proxima Serpens."

[2] The fourth sign of the Zodiac, appearing when the sun has reached its highest northern limit. Cf. Ovid, *Metamorphoses* 4. 625, describing Perseus as he brings back the Gorgon's head: "ter gelidas Arctos, ter Cancri bracchia vidit."

[3] The dragon guarding the apples of the Hesperides, whose garden was traditionally located beyond the Atlas mountains at the Ocean's western border. Cf. Vergil, *Aeneid* 4. 484; Propertius, *Elegies* 2. 24B.10.

[4] Probably the set of defiles lying to the south of the Caspian Sea between the ancient kingdoms of Media and Parthia and beginning *c.* 50 miles south-east of Rhagae (now Rey in Iran), though—confusingly—two places in or near the Caucasus (i.e., to the west of the Caspian) were also called by this name in classical times. See Pliny the Elder, *Natural History* 6. 30, 6. 40, and 6. 43–45; A. R. Anderson, "Alexander at the Caspian Gates," *Transactions and Proceedings of the American Philological Association* 59 (1928): 130–63; and R. Stoneman, *Alexander the Great: A Life in Legend* (New Haven: Yale University Press, 2008), 77–78. Pusculo's purpose is clearly to balance 'the furthest possible point west' of the previous reference with 'the furthest possible point east' of this one.

[5] In the medieval 'Alexander Romance' Alexander is supposed to have enclosed the nations of Gog and Magog in the Caspian or Caucasus Mountains: see Stoneman, *Alexander the Great*, 170–85. The medieval French historian Peter Comestor (*c.* 1110–79) seems to have been the first to identify Gog and Magog with the lost ten tribes of Israel, in his *Historia Scholastica*, Liber Esther, chap. 5, 'De reclusione decem tribuum, et morte Alexandri' (*PL* 198. 1498), where the mountains miraculously come together as the result of Alexander's prayers. The lost Hebrew tribes were the ten northern ones called by biblical writers 'Israel' (Asher, Dan, Ephraim, Gad, Issachar, Manasseh, Naphtali, Reuben, Simeon, and Zebulun) which, in contrast to the other two (Judah and Benjamin), attached themselves to Jeroboam I on the death of Solomon (*c.* 930 BC), and were carried away to Assyria two centuries later (*c.* 721 BC).

humanae, qui hominum vescuntur sanguine vivi
educto pueri venis! Hac Gallia causa
clausa manet populo Iudaeo, nam fuit olim
turba nocens omnis Solymorum sparsa feraces
Gallorum in terras, longa quos pace fovebant   495
otia, divitiis plenos opibusque potentes.

    Nec regum deerat favor illis, emerat auro
quos scelerata manus—populos sic, Christe, tuentur,[1] [sig. biir]
sic sua bella gerunt! Indicti[2] saepe[3] fuerunt
Hebdomada in Magna puerum iugulare quot annis   500
Christicolam in cryptis noctu foveisque profundis
deprensi ante dies Paschae; quae sacra vocabant
contemptum in Christi fideique opprobria nostrae.
Saepius et poenas, damnati crimine tanto,
igne graves dederant combusti, nec tamen huius   505
linquebant morem sacri, nec caede vacabant.
Tantum odium rabiesque animos invasit Hebraeos
ut sitiant nostri satiari sanguinis haustu!

    Nunc quoque Parisiis stat sacra corpus in aede
martyris occisi pueri, quem tempore in illo   510
gens Iudaea cruci fixit rabiosa, Ricardi.
Hunc Deus et multis insignem reddere signis
dignatus, sanctumque suum miracula magna
condecorant. Tandem regni successor aviti,
quod veritus vivente patre et quod pectore[4] clausum   515
iamdudum tulerat, factus rex edidit: omnes
iussit septena comprendi luce Philippus
Iudaeos solitis collectos in synagogis,
veste, auro, argento spoliatos cedere lato
e regno; et cunctos exactos finibus egit   520
Gallorum actutum, mundatas et synagogas
Christi templa Dei fecit. Tunc Gallia felix
tali rege fuit, felix et tempore nostro,
quod vivit secura. Timet nec perdere natos
occisos manibus Solymorum in sacra prophana,   525
ut vero in nostramque fidem infantisque cruorem [sig. biiv]

---

[1] *correxi*: victe tentatur *VO*
[2] *correxi*: infandi *VO*
[3] saepe *V* sepae *O*
[4] et quod pectore *V* et quod in pectore *O*

of human nature who devour human blood drawn from a live boy's veins! This is why France stays closed to the Jewish people,[1] for once the noxious Hebrew horde was scattered all over France's fertile lands, pampered by leisure in long-lasting peace, replete with riches and powerful in resources.

Nor did they lack the favor of kings, whom the criminal band had bought with gold—this, Christ, is how kings protect their peoples, [sig. biir] this is how they wage their wars! The Jews were often charged with murdering a Christ-worshiping boy every year during Holy Week, after being caught red-handed at night in crypts and deep pits before the Passover season; in contempt of Christ and reproach of our faith they called such murder a sacrifice. And often, condemned and burnt for so serious a crime, they had paid a heavy penalty, yet they neither abandoned this customary rite nor abstained from murder. Hebrew minds were seized by such a hate-filled, insane craving to slake their thirst by drinking our blood!

Now, too, in a holy church in Paris rests the body of the slain boy-martyr Richard,[2] whom at that [Passover] season the raving Jewish race nailed to a cross. Not only did God by many signs see fit to make him famous, but also mighty miracles glorify his saint. The successor to the ancestral kingdom, Philip,[3] when he became king, at last did what he was afraid to do with his father alive and had long since kept locked in his breast: he ordered that on the seventh morning all the Jews, assembled in their usual synagogues, should be arrested and, stripped of their clothing, gold, and silver, should depart from his wide realm; and at once he forcibly removed them all from French territory, and, cleansing their synagogues, made them churches of Christ our God. With such a king, France was blessed then, and she is blessed today, because she lives secure. Nor is she afraid of losing children slain by Jewish hands for their profane rites, as indeed they ridiculed our faith and an infant's gore [sig. biiv]

---

[1] Referring to the final expulsion of Jews from France in 1394, after earlier expulsions of 1182 and 1306.

[2] Richard of Pontoise, who was supposed to have been murdered by Jews in the later twelfth century.

[3] Philip II Augustus of France (reigned 1180–1223), who at the age of fifteen succeeded his father Louis VII. The Jews in the crown lands who were arrested in 1180 were ransomed for the huge sum of 15,000 marks.

luserunt. Corpusque nihil iam sanguinis edit
exanimum. Rursus maternis vestibus illum
circumdant, discoque locant quo monstra levatum
stare coegerunt vivum, dum sanguis acuta   530
exhauritur acu et laniatur forcipe dura.
     Scrynium erat, quae mensa fuit, crudelis et ara.
Ponitur hic Simon caesus; spectare iacentem
cuique erat intranti puerum, nam lumina claram
praebebant accensa domum, noctemque fugabant.   535
Hic synagoga locus namque est, quem lumine multo
et lychnis adolere solent dum sacra frequentant
Iudaei. Demum collecto sanguine, corpus
tunc Bonaventurae Samuel iubet inde moveri
inque penum primo deferri[1] (namque timebat   540
deprendi puerum ac facinus); mox ipse propinquum
defert in stabulum. Samuel sub cyclade longa
parietis ad partem dextri faenoque sepultum
hic tenet occultumque die; sed nocte relatum
in synagogam iterum servat sol[l]enniter actis   545
quae mos est fieri Paschalibus in synagogis.
     Interea pater Andreas atque anxia mater
amissum quaerunt natum. Discurrit uterque
per varias urbis partes, per strata viarum,
per fora, perque domos. Cogitant si viderit illum   550
quisquam, aut vocem si forte audiverit eius
clamantis: nusquam inveniunt. Iam cesserat atrae
nocti clara dies; miseri rediere parentes
cum lacrimis maestique domum. Qui luce propinqua [sig. biiir]
quaesitum surgunt iterum; per templa feruntur   555
plena hominum (nam sexta dies ea maxima Sacrae
Hebdomadae populum sacrata in templa fidelem
accierat). Clara differtur voce per omnis
conventus—ubicunque[2] aderat celeberrima turba—
Garbarii natum Andreae, cui tertius annus   560
nondum erat, amissum esse. Hoc ipsum per regiones
urbis sublata praeconis voce tubarum
ad sonitum clamatur.[3] Tum si forte fluentem
urbis per medium rapidum sit lapsus in amnem
quaeritur, ac nulla cessatur parte: cloacas   565

---

[1] deferri *V* deferre *O*
[2] ubicunque *V* uerusque *O*
[3] *correxi*: clamantur *VO*

Simon's lifeless body now gave out no blood. They put back on him the clothes his mother gave him, and placed him on the dish[1] where, after lifting him, the monsters had forcibly stood him alive, as his blood was drained out with sharp needles and torn out with harsh pincers.

There was a chest which served as a table and a cruel altar. Here slain Simon was put; everyone who entered could look at the boy as he lay, for the lamps they had lit brightened the house and chased night away. For this place was their synagogue, which the Jews customarily honored with blazing lamp-light when they celebrated their rites. The blood finally gathered, Samuel ordered Seligman to have the corpse removed and taken first to the store-room (for he feared the discovery of the boy and the crime); he soon took it into a nearby shed. When it had been buried and hidden in the hay under a long cloak near part of the right-hand wall, Samuel kept it here during the day; but, bringing it back again into the synagogue at night, he stored it there after the solemn Passover celebrations which traditionally take place in synagogues.

Meanwhile the boy's father Andreas and his anxious mother were searching for their lost son. They both rushed about through various parts of the city, through the paved streets,[2] through the public squares, and through houses. They wondered if anyone had seen him, or else had perhaps heard the sound of his crying: nowhere did they find anyone. Bright day had now yielded to dark night; the parents returned home in tears, wretched and rueful. Next morning [sig. biiir] they roused themselves to search again; they passed through churches full of people (for that most important sixth day of Holy Week [Good Friday] had summoned the faithful populace to hallowed churches). To every congregation—wherever a very large crowd had assembled—it was loudly announced that the son of Andreas Garbarius, not yet three years old, had been lost. This same message was shouted out in every urban district by the town-crier's high-pitched voice to the sound of trumpets. Then people asked whether he might have fallen into the fast-moving river which flowed through the city center, and no area was left out:

---

[1] Perhaps significantly, the same word for 'dish' (*discus*) is used here as the Vulgate uses in the description of John the Baptist's beheading (Matthew 14: 8, 11).

[2] Cf. Juvencus, 289–291: "Illum per vicos urbis perque abdita tecta / Perque iteris stratas per notos perque propinquos / Quaerebat genetrix . . ."

scrutantur, rivos qui deducuntur[1] in aedes,
quos vulgo fossata vocant. Sed dum omnia tentant,
et nusquam infantem inveniunt, tum denique nata
suspitio est animis[2] hominum quod raptus Hebraeis
sit puer infidis, manibus miser occidendus   570
ipsorum ad sacrum, quo vox iam sparsa ferebat
gaudere Hebraeos festis Paschalibus. Ante,
ante est[3] auditum scelus hoc patrasse per urbes
Germanas siquidem multis de partibus orbis
Iudaeos pulsos, poenasque dedisse nefandas   575
crimine pro tali punitos. Gallia testis
hoc pacto Hebraeis crucefixi membra Ricardi
martyris ostentat; divus quae innoxius aede
Parisiis servat praeclara. Hac urbe Tridenti
nondum ter lustrum tempus compleverat, ex quo   580
tentarant facinus tetrum, similemque pararant
Iudaei caedem infantis; quem sedula mater [sig. biiiv]
explorans triduum totum quaesivit, et ipso
invenit stabulo Hebraeum, incolumemque recepit.
Suspicio his causis aucta est magis; itur ad ipsum   585
praesulem, eoque dari petitur[4] qui claustra domosque
Iudaeum exquirant, cogantque[5] aperire recessus
invitos secreta sui. Praetoria turba
est data continuo, rectaque venitur ad aedes —
Garbario comitante simul — Samuelis, habebat   590
qui[6] solus synagogam intus. Nam grandior omni[7]
Iudaeum numero qui tunc coluere Tridentum
ille erat, et dives: capiebat faenora plura.
Praeterea hinc voces auditas fama[8] ferebat
plorantis pueri prima atra noctis in hora.   595
          Quidnam animi credas ipsis mentisque fuisse
Iudaeis,[9] an quod crudelia facta moverent?
Paeniteatque metu sceleris, quod conscia caedis

---

[1] deducuntur *O* diducuntur *V*
[2] animis *V* animus *O*
[3] *correxi*: et *VO*
[4] petitur *V* petit *O*
[5] cogantque *V* cogitantque *O*
[6] qui *V* quis *O*
[7] *correxi*: amnis *VO*
[8] fama *O* phama *V* (*ut passim*)
[9] Iudaeis *V* Iudaei *O*

they examined the sewers, the streams, commonly called "ditches", which go down into the houses. But then, when, despite all their efforts, they did not find the infant anywhere, a suspicion was finally born in people's minds that the boy had been seized by infidel Hebrews, to be miserably murdered by their own hands for a ritual which—so went an already widespread rumor—the Hebrews enjoyed at their Passover festivals. For indeed earlier, earlier still, it had been reported that the Jews, driven from many parts of the world, had perpetrated this crime in cities all over Germany, and had been punished with terrible penalties for such an offense. France, as witness, displays the body of the martyr Richard, whom the Hebrews crucified in this way; the godly innocent preserves it intact in a famous church in Paris. In this city of Trent fifteen years had not yet passed since the Jews had attempted the vile crime, and had similarly planned to murder an infant; his attentive mother [sig. biiiv] painstakingly sought him for three whole days, and then found him in the very same Hebrew shed, and recovered him unharmed.[1] These cases increased suspicion still further; people went to the bishop himself and asked that he provide men to make a thorough search of the Jews' closets and houses, and to force the unwilling ones to open up their secret hideaways. The *podestà*'s troop was immediately provided, and came straightway—with Garbarius also in attendance—to the house of Samuel, who alone had an indoor synagogue. For he was the most distinguished member of the whole Jewish community then resident in Trent, and a wealthy man: he charged a higher rate of interest. Besides, it was rumored that the sounds of a sobbing boy had been heard coming from here in the first dark hour of night.

Tell me, what sort of feelings and thoughts would you believe the Jews themselves had—or which their cruel deeds were prompting in them? And would they repent of their crime through fear, because their hearts—conscious of the dreadful

---

[1] Cf. Luke 2: 46 on the young Christ being found by his parents in the temple at Jerusalem after going missing for three days.

pectora turbentur dirae, cum intrare cohortem[1]
praetoris videant aedes? Audacia vultu   600
sumitur in trepido. Sceleri scelus additur. Audent
ingressos caesum quaesitum Simona saevis,
si prohibere queant quaerendo,[2] incessere dictis.
Ast mandata sui praetoris turba ministra
exequitur, subigitque locos monstrare reclusos,   605
ac synagogam adit. Inquirunt secreta domorum;
nil intentatum linquunt infraque supraque.
Omittunt solo in stabulo conquirere, quo tunc
Simonis in faeno corpus stipulisque latebat
contectum. In mentem talis non venerat ulli [sig. biiiir]   610
suspicio, ut latebras sceleris stabulum esse putaret
Iudaeis. Redeunt retro ipsi: singula quaeque
scrutatos quaesisse putant loca, protinus et se
praetori referunt nil invenisse. Monebat
hunc[3] animus, vates cui certus, non bene cuncta   615
lustravisse[4] viros, nec eis monstrata fuisse
claustra domus secreta dolo. Stat[5] rursus eodem
tendere, cum totaque ipsum explorare cohorte,
ne lateat verum: facinus ne linquat inultum
tam diri exempli, insontes vel solvat Hebraeos   620
hac culpa vana—fuerit si percita[6] fama.
     Talia versanti secum sententia sedit:
nil sibi inexcussum tanto de crimine linqui.
Pergit et ipse domum Samuelis. Venit ut illo,[7]
ingreditur quaeritque locos; scrutatur et instat.   625
Cuncta patere iubet sibi tunc penetralia. Parent
inviti quamquam Iudaei: dicere contra
iussa timent. Explorat, adit, loca singula cernit,
at non quaesitum in stabulo, quo furta latebant!
Sed quia decurrit fossatum per Samuelis   630
vicinasque domos, illius et id[8] regionis
intra tecta fluit ductum torrente—vocatur

---

[1] cohortem *V* corhortem *O*
[2] *correxi*: querant ne *VO*
[3] *correxi*: manebat huic *VO*
[4] lustrauisse *V* lustrasse *O*
[5] stat *V* stas *O*
[6] percita *V* parcita *O*
[7] venit ut illo *O* om. *V*
[8] *correxi*: et *V* stet *O*

murder—were troubled when they saw the *podestà*'s squad enter the house? Boldness masked an anxious countenance. Crime was added to crime. They presumed to assail with savage words the men who had entered to search for slain Simon, in an attempt to prevent them from searching. But the *podestà*'s assisting troop carried out his orders, forced the Jews to unlock and reveal the premises, and approached the synagogue. They investigated the house's secret places; they left nothing untouched either below or above. Only in the shed, where Simon's body then lay completely hidden in the hay and straw, did they fail to make a thorough search. Such a suspicion had not dawned on anyone, [sig. biiiir] that the Jews might be using the shed as a hiding-place for their crime. The *podestà*'s men went back: they thought they had examined and searched each and every place, and immediately reported to him that they had found nothing. *His* mind—for him a sure prophet[1]—warned him that the men had not ransacked the whole house properly, nor had its artfully isolated closets been revealed to them. He was determined to go back there himself and reconnoiter with his whole squad, lest the truth lie hidden: lest he leave unavenged a crime of so dreadful a precedent, or absolve the "innocent" Jews of this "unfounded" blame—[which would be said] if rumor were stirred up.

As he mulled these things over, he made a firm decision: to leave no aspect of so great a crime unscrutinized. And he himself proceeded to Samuel's house. When he came there, he walked in and searched the rooms; he strenuously examined them. He then ordered all the inner rooms to be opened up for him. The Jews obeyed, albeit reluctantly: they were afraid to object to his orders. He reconnoitered, entered, and looked at every room, yet did not search the shed, where the kidnapped boy lay hidden! But because a ditch ran down along Samuel's house and those nearby, and also flowed inside the dwellings of that district, carried down by a torrent—called "Rugia", it was divided into many streams,

---

[1] Cf. Livy 26. 41. 19, where Scipio Africanus, just appointed Rome's general in Spain, addresses his army (210 BC): "animus . . . meus, maximus mihi ad hoc tempus vates, praesagit nostram Hispaniam esse."

Rugia qui in rivos multos diductus, at ille
obsequium largitur aquae, domibusque ministrat—
labitur hic tenuis Samuelis rivus in aedes,   635
praesulis at praetor mentemque animumque secutus
quaerere constituit, si caesus forsitan undis[1]
proiectus iaceat puer usquam fluminis alveo. [sig. biiiiv]
 Continuoque viros iubet huc descendere binos;
qui[2] penetrent longe diversa ex parte fluentum,   640
fornicibus tecti delato lumine cuncta
perlustrent partisque oculi volvantur in omnes.
Adversi pergant, inter se occurrat uterque
imperat, utque domum contendant in Samuelis.
Iussa[3] viri peragunt celeres, infraque supraque   645
descendunt in aquam delata luce fluentem;
cumque his ipse pater pueri descendit in undas.
 Hic sequitur labentem undam, contendit ab ima
alter in adversam, contra et vestigia ponunt.
Vestigant ripas vigili ambo lumine utrasque;   650
nunc medias scrutantur aquas, amboque propinquant
rimantes domibus Samuelis. Venerat illuc
adverso annixus fluctu, sed parte suprema
qui sequebatur aquas passu contendere eodem
haud valuit. Forti invenit retinacula vallo   655
supra aedes falsi Samuelis, et obice tali
non poterat quicquam deferri flumine tectis
ipsius. Alter adit figens per singula visum,
obicibus donec interpellatus acutis
constitit, et socium astantem convenit inertem.   660
 Sic demum egressi rediere[4] ad lumen inanes
et non invento repetit praetoria praetor
Simone, corde agitans versansque in pectore multa:
quid faciat, quave ipse via perquirat. Habendam
rem tantam haud parvi, sed magna exempla daturam   665
cogitat, atque animum curis mordacibus angit. [sig. cr]

---

[1] undis *V* vncis *O*
[2] qui *V* qni *O*
[3] iussa *V* iussi *O*
[4] rediere *V* redire *O*

yet obediently provided generous amounts of water, and supplied them to the houses — because this shallow stream ran into Samuel's house, the bishop's *podestà*, following his thoughts and feelings, nevertheless decided to make a search in case the slain boy, thrown to the waves, lay anywhere on the river-bed. [sig. biiiiv]

Immediately he ordered two men to go down here; they were to make their way into the stream at widely separated points, and, with the aid of a lamp lowered from the arches of the roof, they were to scour everything and look carefully in every direction. He commanded them to proceed in opposite directions, to rendezvous, and to struggle on to Samuel's house. The men speedily carried out his orders, and when a lamp had been lowered they went down, upstream and downstream, into the flowing water; and the boy's father himself went down into the waves with them.

One man followed the downward stream, the other struggled against the current from below, and they walked in opposite directions. Both of them, with the aid of the ever burning lamp, scanned both riverbanks; now they examined the midstream, and both, as they searched, approached Samuel's house. The man who had battled against the current had now arrived there, but the one who had been following the waters downstream was unable to struggle on at the same pace. He came across cables forming a strong barrier above false Samuel's home, and with such an obstacle nothing could float downstream to his house. The other man came up, gazing intently at everything until, obstructed by the sharp obstacles, he halted, and joined his ineffectual comrade standing there.

So, having finally emerged, they returned to the light empty-handed, and the *podestà*, not having found Simon, went back to his *podestà*'s quarters, pondering in his heart and revolving in his mind many things:[1] what he should do, or what method of inquiry he should himself pursue. He reflected that so great a matter should not be regarded as unimportant, but rather as a future source of great precedents, and his mind was beset by gnawing anxieties.[2]

---

[1] Cf. Vergil, *Aeneid* 5. 701–702: "nunc illuc pectore curas / mutabat versans . . ."

[2] Cf. Lucan, *Pharsalia* 2. 681: ". . . curis animum mordacibus angit . . ."

Simonidos liber secundus

Septimus, ecce, dies oritur qui maximus ipsis
Iudaeis colitur: molli quo vescitur agno,
Pascha suum celebrans, Solymorum sparsa[1] per orbem
gens fera, contaminans humano festa cruore.
Angelus et Samuel, Moyses ac caetera turba   5
vespertina parant agno convivia sumpto.
Constituunt mensas lautas; cenacula sternunt.
Ponuntur tria liba infantis mixta cruore;
ponuntur magna perfuso vina phiala
sanguine. Tum, cunctis ad cenam rite vocatis,   10
ipse domus pater haec in Ihesum verba prophana
fundens ore Deum diro sic pectore fatur:
   "Summe Deus, quem nos Iudaei credimus unum
esse Deum—nec te Trinum veneramur, ut illi
qui tecum Christum Sancto cum Pneumate adorant—   15
Christi tolle, precor, nomen, populumque colentem
Christum perde; decemque illis immitte flagella
quae quondam Egypti Pharao rex sensit acerba
in populum dimissa suum! Sit sanguis inundans
fusus Christicolis; sint ranae, lepra famesque;   20
sint pulices, tenebrae, vastantes cuncta locustae! [sig. cv]
Corpora tabescant letali[2] languida morbo,
et muscae infestent[3] homines; animalia leto[4]
strage gravi dentur, vitae iumenta futurae!
Hunc tibi, sancte Pater, puerum mactavimus, et nunc   25
hunc tibi libamus laticem, de corpore fusum
infantis viventis adhuc de nomine Christi.
Da, Genitor, nobis: sacra haec ut saecula multa
viderunt tibi coepta novo de more, per aevum
aeternum fiant fidei in ludibria Christi!"   30
   Talia dicta fremens in Christum, sanguine mixto
mensam irroravit vino, et quae mensa ferebat.[5]
Post hinc astantes vinum divisit in omnis,
libaque gustarunt illo de sanguine, potu
atque cibo; hinc[6] epulis convivia facta paratis.   35

---

[1] sparsa *V* spersa *O*
[2] letali *V* laetali *O*
[3] infestent *V* inuestent *O*
[4] leto *V* laeto *O*
[5] ferebat *V* ferebant *O*
[6] *correxi:* dehinc *VO*

[sig. cr] The second book of the *Simonis*

Behold, the seventh day was dawning, which the Jews themselves cherish as the greatest: the day when the wild Jewish race, scattered across the world, in celebration of its Passover feeds on a tender 'lamb', defiling the festival with human gore. Engel and Samuel, Moses and the rest of the gang, taking the 'lamb', prepared the evening banquet. They set up clean tables; they arranged the dining-room. Three cakes containing the infant's mingled gore were put out; blood-laced wine was also put out in a large flask. Then, when all had been duly called to the meal, the father of the house himself spoke with dreadful passion, pouring forth from his lips these profanities against Jesus our God:

"Supreme God, whom we Jews believe to be one God—nor, unlike those who adore Christ with you and the Holy Spirit, do we venerate you as Triune—do away with the name 'Christ', I beseech you, and destroy the Christ-worshiping people; inflict on them the ten bitter scourges[1] which Pharaoh, king of Egypt, once saw loosed on his own people. May the Christ-worshipers have an overflowing stream of blood; may they have frogs, leprosy, and famine; may they have fleas, darkness, all-destroying locusts! [sig. cv] May their weary bodies be wasted by a deadly disease, and may flies infest their persons; may a severe plague consign their livestock to death, their pack-animals to a future life! Here is the boy we have sacrificed to you, holy Father, and here now is the liquid we pour out for you, shed from the body of a still-living Christian infant. Grant us this, Father: just as this rite, initiated for you, has seen many centuries, so let it be performed everlastingly in mockery of the Christian faith!"

Rasping out such words against Christ, he sprinkled the table, and the things on it, with the blood-laced wine. Afterwards he gave out the wine to all the bystanders, and they partook of cakes containing that blood, their meat and drink; then, when the food was served, the banquet took place.

---

[1] All the ten plagues of Egypt described in Exodus 7–11 are mentioned here except the seventh (hail) and the tenth (death of the first-born). This prayer bears no resemblance to either the Twelfth Benediction or the prayer supposedly uttered by the Jews of Trent given in Tiberino's letter. See above, 57 n. 2.

At postquam illusum triduo iam luce carenti
est puero, nostrae et fidei, Christoque Patrique,[1]
ac celebrata suo Paschalia more fuerunt,
consilium inter se Samuel sociique futurum
quid sit de puero versant: pulsantur amaro   40
corda metu sceleris tanti nam conscia corpus
deprendi atque ipsos suspectos, aedibus ultra
si teneant triduo caesum.[2] Expectare nec audent.
Cuncta timent: merito seque observarier omni
a populo, versosque oculos pro crimine tanto   45
cunctorum credunt quid agant spectare. Quiescit
haud animus, nec mens illis consistit: Erinnys
Tisiphone turbat pavidos accincta flagello.
    Tum demum proprio auxilium tentatur ab auro. [sig. ciir]
Forte vicina fuit habitans loca cognitus ipsis,   50
Angellinus erat cui nomen, pauper, ab ortu
Teutonus. Hunc adeunt secreto, blandaque verba
dant cauti, obsequiumque petunt,[3] mercede parata
ingenti. "Exanimis nostris stat in aedibus infans;
cernat ne quis eum sacco conclusimus. Hunc tu   55
clam si efferre velis, dabimus tibi praemia," dicunt,
"quae poscas. Auri tibi tres vel quinque dabuntur
num[m]i. Sis[4] tacitus modo tu, ne sentiat alter,
tu lucrum a nobis habeas impune petendum
votis." Continuo respondit Teutonus ille: 60
"Forsitan hic puer est, tota qui quaeritur urbe,
aedibus et nostris quaesitus. Si mihi centum
a vobis num[m]i sint aurei—si mihi mille,
si plures etiam[5]—tanto in discrimine nunquam
efferrem infantem. Tali ne involvite culpae   65
insontem pretio! Contemno munera vestra."
    Talibus actutum trepida sunt mente locuti:
"Non puer est quem tu quaesitum dicis, at[6] alter,
de stirpe Hebraeum non circumcisus, acerba
raptus morte iacet; pro qua ratione sepulchro   70
est gentis mandare nefas. Tu tolle, ferasque,

---

[1] *correxi*: parenti et *VO*
[2] caesum *V* caesam *O*
[3] petunt *V* petuut *O*
[4] sis *V* si *O*
[5] etiam *V* essent *O*
[6] at *V* ac *O*

But when they had mocked the boy—now three days dead—and our faith, and Christ and the Father, and when the Passover had been celebrated according to their tradition, Samuel and his comrades discussed what was to happen to the boy: for their hearts, guiltily conscious of so great a crime, were assailed by bitter dread lest the body be discovered and they themselves suspected, if they kept the slain boy more than three days in their house. Nor did they dare look forward. They feared everything: they rightly believed that all the people were watching them, and that because of the seriousness of their offense everyone's eyes were focused on what they did. Their minds were not at peace, nor was their resolve unshaken: the avenging Fury Tisiphone, armed with her scourge, confounded them in their terror.[1]

Then at last they sought help from their own gold. [sig. ciir] Living near them, as it happened, was a poor man they knew called Anzelino, German by birth. They secretly approached him, cautiously flattered him, and, producing a large fee, sought his compliance: "A dead infant lies in our house; we have tied him up in a sack, lest anyone see him. Should you be willing to secretly remove him, we will give you whatever reward you ask for," they said. "You will be given three or five gold coins. So long as you keep quiet, so that no one else notices, *you* could safely make the sort of profit that *we* have to pray for." Straightway the German replied: "Perhaps this is the boy who is being sought all over the city, and has already been sought in our houses. If you gave me a hundred gold coins—if you gave me a thousand, or even more—you would never see me removing the infant at so great a risk. Do not involve an innocent man in such mischief by bribery! I despise your gifts."

Alarmed, they immediately responded: "It is not the boy you say has been sought, but another, an uncircumcised Hebrew child, who lies struck down by a cruel death; that is why it is sacrilege to put him in a gentile grave.[2] *You* remove him,

---

[1] Cf. Vergil, *Aeneid* 6. 570–571: "continuo sontis ultrix accincta flagello / Tisiphone quatit insultans . . . ."

[2] Since ancient times, the proper treatment of the body of an uncircumcised Jewish child has been postmortem circumcision followed by burial in a Jewish cemetery.

in fluvium iacias Athesis, mercesque parata
est tibi. Clam volumus portari, namque timemus
exeat in populum ne res in tempore tali
quod[1] periit puer hic amissus, crescat et inde   75
in nos suspitio[2] maior." Non ille movetur[3]
verbis nec precio; facturum se negat[4] illis [sig. ciiv]
quicquam. Sic illos liquit, secreta precatos
haec fieri saltem, tacitus sitque ipse rogantes.
[Iuratusque fidem dedit haec secreta futura.][5]   80
　　His actis Samuel sceleris se eripere tanti
suspicione volens — nec enim celare,[6] sed a se
ac sociis crimen sperat devolvere posse —
clam Bonaventuram vocat ad se, ac talia mandat:
"Vade age, et e stabulo pueri fer corpus, et undae   85
proiice quae nostras deducta interfluit aedes
(nam cocus es) tum, cum latices haurire recentes
inde petes. Dicas: 'Inventum corpus in amni
quaesiti infantis iamdudum an forte sit illud?'
Exequitur mandata cocus, faenoque sepultum   90
clam stabulo[7] pueri corpus rapit, inque fluentum
proiicit; inde redit tacitus. Subitoque lebete
rapto pergit aquas liquidas haurire; revertens
continuo dicit: "Liquidis albescere in undis
per dubiam lucem visum est mihi corpus, et an sit   95
infantis dubito quaesiti." Censet eundum,
haud mora, quaesitum Samuel, qui iusserat ipsum
nuper aquae mitti; vacuatum sanguine per tot
vulnera conspicitur. Tobias, Angelus una
ac Samuel secum consultant crimen acerbum   100
patratum Hebraeis avertere; conscia caedis
fronte parant tegere ac simulata pectora voce.
　　Postridieque petunt arcem, quo praesulis aures
vocibus obtundant fictis; fidumque ministrum
principis arte petunt, aditum facilemque precantur [sig. ciiir] 105
his usi verbis: "Suspectos novimus hoc nos

---

[1] *correxi*: quo *VO*
[2] suspitio *O* suspicio *V* (*ut passim*)
[3] mouetur *V* mouerur *O*
[4] negat *V* denegat *O*
[5] iuratusque . . . futura *O om. V*
[6] *correxi*: caelare *VO*
[7] faenoque sepultum / clam stabulo *O* clam fronde sepultum / e stabulo *V*

take him away, and throw him into the River Adige, and the fee awaits you. We want him carried away in secret, for we are afraid that news of this lost boy's death may leak out to the people at such a time as this, and that, as a result, even greater suspicion may build up against us." He was not swayed by their words or money; he refused to do anything for them. [sig. ciiv] So he left them, after they had begged him to at least hush up these matters and had asked him to keep quiet about them himself. [And, under oath, he gave his word that they *would* be hushed up.][1]

After this Samuel, wishing to free himself from suspicion of such a serious crime—for indeed he hoped, not to hide the offense, but to distance it from himself and his comrades—secretly summoned Seligman and gave him these orders: "Come now, take the boy's corpse out of the shed, and throw it into the stream that flows down through our house when (in your capacity as cook) you go down to draw fresh water from there. You are to say: 'Could the corpse I've found in the river be that of the long-sought infant?'" The cook carried out these orders, hurriedly took the boy's corpse out of the shed where it had been secretly buried in the hay, and threw it into the stream; then he returned in silence. And suddenly, taking a cauldron, he went off to draw some clear-flowing water; returning, he said at once: "In the faint light I saw a corpse gleaming in the clear-flowing waves, and I think it could be the missing infant's." Samuel, who had just ordered it to be put in the water, thought they should lose no time in going to look for it; and they did see it, drained of blood by so many wounds. Tobias, Engel, and Samuel conspired to steer responsibility for the Hebrews' cruel crime away from them; guiltily conscious of the murder, they prepared to mask their feelings with effrontery and feigned words.

And next day they made for the castle, to deafen the bishop with their lies; they cunningly sought out the prince's trusty lieutenant and begged for easy access [to Hinderbach], [sig. ciiir] saying: "We know that we Jews have been suspected of this crime against the boy: a vain rumor has gone through the city,

---

[1] This line is present in *O* but absent in *V.*

crimine de pueri Iudaeos: vana per urbem
fama fuit, crescitque magis, periisse nefanda
caede dolis captum nostris. Accedimus huc nos
purgatum tanto nos crimine. Vidimus unda   110
submersum infantem; sitne is quaesitus an[1] alter
incerti nescimus adhuc. Extractus ab unda
fossati stat quod[2] nostras perlabitur aedes.
Suspicio in Hebraeos iam cesset falsa: patescit
iam nullum admisisse nefas. Timor omnis abesto   115
innocuis; liceat nos tutos vivere in urbe!"
     Haec[3] conficta rogant deferri ad praesulis aures,
qui iubeat statim tolli condique sepulchro
corpus defuncti pueri, ne fama peremptum
ipsis per populum volitet moveatque tumultum.   120
Promittuntque decem famulo sese dare num[m]os
auri, purpureumque simul thoraca daturos
sericeum, exorent hoc tantum. Praesul ut ista
sunt delata[4] sibi, praetori mittit eosdem,
et nisi visat eum, puerum vetat inde moveri.   125
Praetor ut audivit Iudaeos, quaerere verum
ipse animum firmat; rogat hos in singula quemque
divisos. Audit vario sermone loquentes
haud constare simul; vetat hos abscedere donec
iusserit ipse. Domum Samuelis pergit, et una   130
tota cohors. Pueri iubet illuc ire vocatos
Garbarium patrem Andream matremque Mariam,
ut videant, natus si sit puer ille repertus. [sig. ciiiv]
     Quo postquam est ventum, stabat iam tractus ab undis
ipse puer, toto confossus corpore. At illum   135
ut vidit praetor[5] crudeli morte peremptum —
fascia nam tenerum constrinxerat inclita collum,
ac laniata genae dextrae stat vulnere duro,
et cruris[6] dextri pars rapta est forcipe adunca,
virgulaque in summo penetrata videtur, et omne   140
perfossum crebro, tenui sed vulnere corpus;
huic humeri et coxae demissaque crura latusque,

---

[1] *correxi*: at *VO*
[2] quod *V* qui *O*
[3] haec *V* hae *O*
[4] delata *V* celata *O*
[5] praetor *V* praetos *O*
[6] cruris *V* crucis *O*

and is increasing, that, caught by our wiles, he was heinously murdered. We come here to clear ourselves from so grave a charge. We saw an infant drowned in the waves; we still do not know for certain whether he is the missing one or another. He is still there, pulled from the waves of the ditch that passes through our house. Now let false suspicion of the Hebrews cease: it is clear now that they have done no wrong. Let the innocent be relieved of all fear; let us be allowed to live safely in the city!"

They asked that this fictitious account be reported to the bishop, so that he might order the immediate removal and burial of the dead boy's corpse, lest the rumor that they had dispatched him fly through the populace and cause a riot. Should this plea of theirs only succeed, they promised to give the attendant ten gold coins, and also a purple silken waistcoat. When the bishop had been told this, he sent the Jews to the *podestà*, and forbade the boy to be moved from there unless he saw him. The *podestà*, when he had heard the Jews, steeled his mind to seek out the truth himself; he asked them individually about every single thing. In their various spoken accounts he heard inconsistencies; he forbade them to leave until he himself ordered it. He proceeded to Samuel's house, and so did his whole squad. Summoning the boy's father, Andreas Garbarius, and his mother Maria, he ordered them to go there, to see if the boy who had been found was their son. [sig. ciiiv]

When they arrived, there the boy himself now was, drawn from the waves, stabbed all over his body. But when the *podestà* saw that he had been cruelly murdered—for the famous[1] ribbon had been tied tightly round his tender neck, part of his right cheek had been torn by a harsh blow, part of his right leg had been pulled out with hooked pincers, his penis had seemingly been pierced at its tip, and his whole body had been stabbed with dense but tiny wounds; his shoulders, his hips, his drooping legs, his side, his whole chest, and his pierced arms all showed red bruises amid their pallor, bristling as if struck by the sharp

---

[1] The length of cloth with which Simon was allegedly strangled appears in most contemporary representations of his martyrdom.

et pectus totum confossa et brac[c]hia rubras
cum pallore notas monstrabant, horrida tanquam
sint telis percussa aspri[1] crabronis acutis —   145
hoc facinus dirum versat secum, omnia confert
indicia, auctores quibus arguat. Illita tolli
membra notis densis crudeli caede perempti
imperat, in Petri deferri et protinus aedem,
qua Simon sacro fuerat baptismate lotus.   150
    Postea Pascha Dies nostra est celebrata.[2] Per urbem
fama volat, puerum crudeli morte peremptum,
Garbarii natum, Solymorum sede repertum,
gut[t]ure constricto ac laniato corpore, in undam
proiectum. Accurrunt visum iuvenesque senesque.   155
Nec minus et princeps divus praesulque Ioannes
postea cum magna procerum stipante[3] caterva
atque sacerdotum cinctus sacro ordine venit,
praefecto Iacobo Sporo claroque Ioanne
praetore hunc primis comitantibus. Altera turba   160
subsequitur numerosa virum. Qui venit ut illo, [sig. ciiiir]
infantem et vidit confossum corpore toto,
constrictum et collum nexo velamine, cruris[4]
avulsam[5] dextri partem, dextrae quoque malae
carnem vi raptam, tactus pietate dolorem   165
sensit; et ingemuit, vocesque has edidit ore
cum lacrymis: "Tantas nullo pro crimine poenas
quis voluit te ferre, infans? Quae monstra feraeve
te petiere? Velint[6] infantis sanguine pasci
quae fera? Quive homines? Exhaustum sanguine cerno   170
corpus: an hic regnat Busiris vel Diomedes?
Hi periere quidem poenasque dedere, quod ausi —
ut memorant — satiare deos hic sanguine ad aram
caesorum sitiens hominum, praesepia[7] dura
artubus[8] humanis alter repleta fovere.   175
At quamquam immanes fuerint, immania monstra

---

1   aspri *V* asperi *O*
2   *correxi*: nostrum fuit *VO*
3   stipante *V* stipantte *O*
4   cruris *V* crucis *O*
5   auulsam *V* auulsum *O*
6   velint *V* velit *O*
7   *correxi*: praesepio *VO*
8   *correxi*: arctubus *VO*

stings of a fierce hornet—seeing everything, the *podestà* turned this dreadful crime over in his mind, collating all the clues that might help him to convict its authors. He ordered the cruelly slain infant's badly bruised body to be removed, and taken straightway to St Peter's Church, where Simon had been washed in holy baptism.

Afterwards our Easter Day was celebrated. A rumor flew through the city[1] that a boy, Garbarius's son, cruelly killed, had been found in a Jewish house, strangled and mutilated, thrown in the waves. Young men and old rushed to see him. And, not to be outdone, godly Prince-Bishop Johannes [Hinderbach] came later, surrounded by a great crowd of dignitaries and encircled by a holy train of priests, with Jakob von Sporo the captain and renowned Giovanni [de Salis] the *podestà* as his chief attendants. Another large throng of men followed behind. When he came there [ciiiir] and saw the infant—his whole body stabbed, his neck tied tightly with his cloak, part of his right leg torn off, and the flesh of his right cheek wrenched out—Johannes, moved by piety, was grief-stricken; and he groaned, and said tearfully: "Who wished you, child, to suffer such grievous punishment for no crime at all? What monsters or wild beasts sought you out? What wild creatures would wish to feed on an infant's blood? Or what human beings would? I see your body has been drained of blood: does Busiris[2] or Diomedes[3] reign here? They indeed were punished with death for their presumption, because—so the story goes—the former craved to gratify the gods with blood from men slain at the altar, the other craved to heat his harsh stable by stuffing it with human limbs. But brutal though they were, still those brutal monsters did not seek a tender infant's death.

---

[1] Cf. Vergil, *Aeneid* 8. 554: "Fama volat parvam subito vulgata per urbem . . ."

[2] See above, 145 n. 2.

[3] A king of Thrace who kept a stable of man-eating mares.

non tamen infantis mortem[1] petiere tenelli.
Non fera, parve, tuum confecit vulnere corpus—
heu, doleo!—sed homo vincens feritate leones
et rapidas tigres. Monstra haec nascuntur in oris   180
aut vivunt nostris? Audent hac talia nostra
urbe viri? Haud certe Nilus, non Thracia sunt hic!
Hic certe[2] colitur Christus Deus, et pia Christi
lex bene servatur, populusque fidelis in huius
stat regione poli. Nempe extra foedera legis   185
hostis et est nostrae, quicunque haec—horrida visu,
asperaque affatu, cuiquam haud audita virorum—
admisit. Testor, Iesu pie, te—crucifixum[3]
Iudaeis, clausum devicta morte sepulchro, [sig. ciiiiv]
surrexisse hodie quem ecclesia concinit alma   190
credimus et vere—scelus haud impune laturum
quicunque in parvum infantem saeviverit istum.
Et te, parve puer, testor—cui regia caeli
est data—pro meritis, pro Christi sanguine sacro:
crudelis quicunque tuum violaverit ullo   195
vulnere, vel proprio foedarit sanguine corpus,
factis digna feret pretia, et pro crimine poenas."
    His dictis, mandat praetori imponere curam—
ut facit—ac studium, scelus hoc exquirere quinam
patrarint. Samuel, Tobias, Angelus una   200
ad puerum veniunt[4] praetoris voce vocati.
Hos rogat an[ne] hic sit puer is[5] quem gurgite mersum
inventum dixere sibi; affirmantibus esse,
tum petit unde illi sint vulnera, quidve ligatum
sic fuerit collum. "Quid crebra foramina?" poscit.   205
"Quis virgam summam ferro transfixit acuto?"
Hii gelido tremuere metu; pavor occupat ingens
corda mali tanti sibi conscia; pallor et ora
inficit. Hoc solum respondent, gurgite mersum
invenisse. Negant se caetera scire petita.   210
    Res miranda quidem! Caedis manifestius ipse
edidit inditium sanguis, nam vulnere fusus
exiit, ut primum tetigerunt limina Hebraei,

---

[1] mortem *O* morte *V*
[2] *correxi*: certae *VO*
[3] crucifixum *O* cruce fixum *V*
[4] ueniunt *V* ueuiunt *O*
[5] is *V* his *O*

No wild beast, little one, wounded *your* body—alas, I grieve for you!—but a man far more bestial than lions and fleet-footed tigers. Are these monsters born or living in our country? Do men presume to do such things in this city of ours? Surely this is not the [land of the] Nile, nor is it Thrace! Here, surely, Christ our God is worshiped, and Christ's sacred law is observed well, and on this continent the people remain faithful! Whoever committed these deeds—horrendous to behold, bitter to relate, unheard of by any man—is surely beyond the pale of our law and hostile to it. I call you to witness, holy Jesus—you, crucified by the Jews, shut in the grave when you vanquished death, [sig. ciiiiv] whose resurrection our gracious church hymns today, and we truly believe in it—that whoever vented his rage on this little child will not escape punishment for his crime. You too I call to witness—little boy now dwelling in heaven—by your merits, by Christ's sacred blood: whoever cruelly violated your body with any wound, or smirched it with its own blood, will pay a price worthy of his deeds, and a penalty equal to his offense."

This said, he commanded the *podestà* to apply care and zeal—as he was doing—to the task of finding out who exactly perpetrated this crime. In answer to the *podestà*'s call, Samuel, Tobias, and Engel came in a body to see the boy. He asked them whether this was the boy they said they had found drowned in the stream; when they confirmed that it was, he then wanted to know how he came by his wounds, or why his neck had been bound like this. "Why the dense incisions?" he demanded. "Who pierced the tip of his penis with a sharp knife?" An icy fear made them tremble; a mighty dread seized their hearts, guiltily conscious of so evil a deed; and pallor spread over their faces. Their only answer was this, that they had found the boy drowned in the stream. They denied any knowledge of the other things he wanted to know.

A wondrous thing indeed! The blood itself gave still clearer proof of the murder, for it came pouring out of a wound as soon as the Hebrews reached the threshold[1] and saw, lying inside, the body their own hands had stabbed. Now, three days since he was slain, Simon's body preserved its beauty;

---

[1] It was a common medieval belief that the body of a murdered man or woman would bleed when the murderer was present. Blood might flow from inanimate objects such as church walls and hosts in accusation against the sinful. In the context of Simon's death as *imitatio Christi* it is interesting to note that Christ's wounds were also regarded as a reproach to sinful men and women, and particularly the Jews. See Caroline Walker Bynum, *Wonderful Blood*, 180–85. On blood 'crying to Heaven' see Bettina Bildhauer, *Medieval Blood* (Cardiff: University of Wales Press, 2006), 41–50.

confossum et propriis manibus videre iacentem.
Iam triduo caesi servabant membra decorem;   215
signa quoque[1] infantis formosi clara tenebant
et nuper occisi — visum mirabile cunctis, [sig. cvr]
indiciumque patens, scelus hoc qui admiserit atrox.
Hic aderant urbis primi, praefectus et ipse
cum praetore aderat. Cuncti stupuere fluentem   220
cernentes laticem de vulnere sanguinis atrum
Iudaeum adventu. Portendere adesse homicidas
talia monstra ferunt. Rursus de vulnere caesi
sanguis ad aspectum factoris caedis abundat.
    Talibus indiciis motus non credere inanem   225
suspitionem ortam praetor, durare in Hebraeos,
carceris hos primum tres duci in vincula mandat:
Angelum, et inde simul Tobiam cum Samuele.
At Iacobus Sporus praefectus mandat in arcem
duci, concludique loco pro carcere honesto.   230
Continuo et numerum medicorum colligit omnem,
quos urbs tunc habuit praestantis arte medendi,
consulit atque ipsos iuratos, num puer ille
Simon mersus aquis vitam exhalaverit, aut vi.
Una eademque fuit medicis sententia cunctis   235
enectum ferro puerum, vel gutture presso
emisisse animam: tumidum fore corpus et undae
viscera plena, viam vitae si clauserit unda;
sed neque corpus aqua tumidum, neque viscera turgent.
In promptu ac facili dicunt hoc posse probari,   240
si medium scindant uterum et de ventre retecta
intestina trahant. Scissus puer arte magistra
praetore ac Sporo praefecto astantibus una,
civibus et multis; lympha est inventus inanis.
    Audiit ut mater laniato corpore natum [sig.cvv] 245
Simona Iudaeum manibus colloque repertum
constricto infelix, celeris[2] — sed sera — cucurrit
cum clamore vocans natum ad crudelia tecta.
Sed puer hinc sacram fuerat sublatus in aedem
compositusque toro[3] sacro, stratoque iacebat   250
ante oculos procerum miserantum ac dura precantum
supplicia ausorum tantorum auctoribus. Ingens

---

[1] quoque *V* qnoque *O*
[2] celeris *V* sceleris *O*
[3] *correxi*: thoro *VO*

it also retained clear signs of the infant's good looks and recent murder—a marvelous sight for all, [sig. cvr] and an obvious clue as to who committed this brutal crime. The city's leaders were at the scene, and so was the captain himself, as well as the *podestà*. All were amazed when they saw the dark stream of blood flowing from the wound at the Jews' approach. People say that such portents indicate the presence of homicides. Once again blood gushed out from the slain boy's wound at the sight of his slayer.

Prompted by such clues to believe that the nascent suspicion of the Hebrews was not unfounded, and to treat them sternly, the *podestà* first commanded that these three be taken in chains to jail: [first] Engel, and then Tobias together with Samuel. But Jakob von Sporo the captain commanded that they be taken to the castle and confined in a respectable place as their prison. And at once he gathered the whole complement of doctors the city then possessed, outstanding medical practitioners, and consulted them under oath as to whether drowning or violence had caused the boy Simon's death. All the doctors were of one and the same opinion: that the boy had been stabbed to death or strangled. "If water has blocked the windpipe," they said, "a body will be bloated and the intestines full of water; but neither is this body bloated with water, nor are its intestines distended." And, they said, this could very easily be proved if they cut right into the abdomen and drew the exposed intestines out of the belly. With masterly skill the boy was cut open as the *podestà* and von Sporo the captain both stood by, and many citizens too; he was found empty of water.

When the unhappy mother heard that her son Simon's body had been found mutilated [sig. cvv] and strangled at the Jews' hands, she ran quickly—but too late—to their cruel houses, loudly calling for him. But the boy had been taken hence to a holy church and placed on a holy bier, and lay on a blanket, watched by dignitaries sorrowfully praying for harsh punishment of the authors of such outrages. A huge crowd of onlookers had already flooded in. Behold, here was his mother, tossing her hair, beating her breast, and scoring her cheeks with her nails, weeping and moaning. At the dignitaries'

visentis populi iam turba affluxerat. Ecce,
mater adest, iactansque comas et pectora pulsans,
unguibus atque genas foedans, lacrimansque gemensque.   255
Clamanti procerum iussu cessere, viamque
ad natum miserae matri—pia turba!—dedere.
Quem postquam aspexit lacerum crudeliter ora,
dum stat in amplexu, dum figit et oscula nato,
concidit, et sensus labentia membra reliquit.   260
     Spiritus ut rediit tandem, et vox aegra dolori
est concessa, pio fletu lacrimisque soluta,
has voces miseranda dedit: "Pro!¹ fata sinistra
quae te,² parve puer, quae nos tenuere parentes—
te, quod parvus adhuc infans sic morte perires   265
crudeli; nos, quod raptum fleremus iniqua
incerta sed morte tamen! Te quippe iacentem
conspicimus lacerum, sed non letalia membris
vulnera sunt infixa tuis, quae magna videntur,
haec tria. Sed quantum penetrent quae plurima cerno—   270
parva quidem,³ sed crebra nimis, sed caeca—per omne
corpus, adhuc nescimus. Adhuc quod mortis ademit
te genus incertum est nobis. Saevissima nobis [sig. cvir]
te rapuit, certo scimus, mors saeva. 'Tenellum,
hei mihi, namque meum constrinxit fascia collum!'   275
Hocne modo es forsan privatus, parvule, vita?
Sanguinis exhaustu te mors an⁴ cruda peremit?
Spiritus anne⁵ extinctus aquis tibi gurgite merso?
An triplex genus hoc mortis tibi fata tulere,
ut non morte una, triplici sed morte perires?   280
     "Sed quis tam durus, crudelis, barbarus hostis
in te, nate, suam satiare optaverit iram?
Scilicet infensus nobis, matrique patrique.
Viximus innocui, nullius movimus⁶ iram
infesti, sed amant omnes et amamus eosdem.   285
Innocua est aetas tibi; sane publicus hostis
exegit poenas tales de sanguine parvi
Christicolae nati, rabiemque ostendit in uno,

---

¹ *correxi*: proh *VO*
² te *V* ter *O*
³ quidem *V* quid *O*
⁴ an *V* ante *O*
⁵ *correxi*: an *VO*
⁶ mouimus *V* nouissimus *O*

command the people—pious crowd!—yielded to the poor mother's cries and made way for her to reach her child. After seeing him with his face cruelly torn, as she embraced him and showered kisses on him, she collapsed, and feeling forsook her drooping limbs.[1]

When at last she regained her breath, and her grief was given a feeble voice, the wretched woman, weakened by pious wailing and weeping, spoke thus: "Ah! What an ill fate has laid hold on you, little boy, and on us your parents—on you, to make a mere baby like you suffer such a cruel death; on us, to make us mourn you, snatched from us by an unfair but unclear death! We do indeed see you lying torn, but these three seemingly big wounds implanted in your body are not deadly ones. Yet as to the large number I see all over you—small ones indeed, but very dense, and hidden—we still do not know how deep they go. We are still unsure what kind of death took you away. Utterly savage, we know for certain, [sig. cvir] was the savage death that snatched you from us. 'Ah, poor me! a ribbon has squeezed my tender neck!'[2] Could this have been the way you perished, little one? Or were you crudely bled to death? Or did the swirling waters end your life when you sank beneath them? Or did fate ordain for you a threefold death, so that you might suffer three deaths, not just one?

"But what foe would be so harsh, cruel, and barbaric that he wished to sate his wrath on you, child? No doubt he was hostile to us, your mother and father. We have lived innocently, we have provoked the wrath of no enemy, but all love us and we love them. Yours is the age of innocence; surely a public enemy has punished a small Christ-worshiping child's blood so severely, and shown such ferocity to one person, as a way of venting his rage on all the faithful. Oh grief! What brought these torments on you, a mere boy? Oh, would that I had been put in your place! I, child,

---

[1] Here, and in the speech which follows, there may be an echo of the hymns and dramatizations of the anguished lament of Mary at the death of Jesus which spread through Italy from the twelfth century onward and sometimes became a focus for hostility toward the Jews. See Carol Lansing, *Passion and Order: Restraint of Grief in the Medieval Italian Communes* (Ithaca: Cornell University Press, 2008), 148–52.

[2] Here the boy's mother imagines him speaking as he was being choked.

saevire in cunctos qua vellet posse fideles.
O dolor! Unde tibi puero haec tormenta? Fuissem   290
o utinam pro te posita! Has ego, nate, tulissem
crudeles poenas, et vitam[1] morte dedissem;
aut absumpta forem tecum, carissime nate!

    "Nunc ad te, mecum pariter de corde dolentem
et pariter dantem lacrimas, dulcissime coniunx,   295
vertor. Quid[2] nobis dulcis, quae vita futura est?
Perdidimus natum; lenimen dulce laborum
curarumque fuit; nos hoc solamine laeti
vivebamus. Erat nobis leve pondus acerba
paupertas multis. Iacet en spes unica nostrae   300
stirpis, et incassum nostri periere[3] labores! [sig. civ]
Subductus nostrae est baculus columenque senectae;
sed—spero—dabitis poenas, immania[4] monstra,
si caelo Deus haec oculis Pater aspicit aequis!"

    Vocibus his procerum mentes populique ciebat   305
ad lacrymas: animos nati subiere[5] parentum.
Ausi immane nefas Iudaei crimine falso
adiiciunt culpae insontes; nec sufficit illos
crudeli infantem morti duraeque dedisse,
et pateris avidos libisque hausisse cruorem,   310
sed scelere ingenti scelus ingens vertere ab ipsis
conantur, fraudesque novas contexere contra
Christicolas audent. Insontes perdere possint
quaque via tentant—aliena ut crimina dura
morte luant (nostro exultant sic sanguine fuso!)—   315
peccatumque suum in nostras convertere poenas.

    His vicinus erat, vita famaque probatus,[6]
Svicerus;[7] innocuum culpant, et crimen in illum
convertunt miserum caedis facinusque tremendum.
Confinguntque odium vetus hunc servare in Hebraeos   320
faenoris ob causam, propter quod iurgia dicunt
orta olim secum atque irarum incendia magna
hinc exisse, gravesque minas fecisse frementem.

---

[1] *omisi*: tibi *VO*
[2] quid *V* quae *O*
[3] periere *V* perire *O*
[4] *correxi*: in mania *VO*
[5] subiere *V* subire *O*
[6] vita phamaque probatus *V* pauper at minime diues *O*
[7] *correxi*: ianzarus *VO*

would have borne these cruel pains and given you life by my death; or else I would have met my end with you, dearest child!

"Now, sweetest husband, I turn to you, for your grief is no less heartfelt and your tears no less copious than mine. What sweetness, what life shall we have? We have lost our son; he was the sweet balm of our toils[1] and cares; we lived happily with this solace. Poverty, bitter for many, was a light burden for us. See, our family's sole hope lies dead, and our toils have gone for nothing! [sig. cviv] The prop and pride of our old age[2] has been pulled from under us; but you, brutal monsters, will—I hope—pay the penalty, if with impartial eyes God the Father is looking down from heaven on these events!"

With these words she moved the city's dignitaries and people to tears: parents were reminded of their own children. The Jews, having dared a heinous misdeed, now tried to involve the innocent in their guilt by means of a false charge; nor was it enough that they had sent an infant to a cruel and harsh death, and greedily quaffed his gore from libation-bowls and [Passover] cakes, but they attempted to steer the blame for one huge crime away from themselves by committing another, and dared to embroider fresh falsehoods against Christ-worshipers. In every possible way they tried to destroy the innocent—so that they might expiate their own harsh crimes by other people's deaths (thus do they rejoice in spilling our blood!)—and they tried to turn *their* sin into *our* punishment.

'The Schweizer' was a neighbor of theirs, good-living and well-respected; they blamed the innocent man, and turned against that wretch the dreaded criminal charge of murder.[3] And they pretended that he harbored long-standing hatred against the Hebrews because of interest-payment, because of which, they said, he had once quarreled with them and breathed out great fires of wrath, and in his fury he had made serious threats. They accused him of killing the boy and putting his dead body into the waves that flowed through their house,

---

[1] Cf. Horace, *Odes* 1. 32. 15: "o laborum / dulce lenimen."

[2] In Tobit 10: 4 Anna, mother of Tobias, fears his death and describes him as "baculum senectutis nostrae."

[3] On Johannes 'the Schweizer' see Appendix 2.

Accusant puerum hunc[1] interfecisse, necatum et
immisisse suas aedes quae perfluit undam,   325
ut poenas pro caede darent infantis Hebraei
inventi occisi domibus: sic perderet illos.
      His visum praebere aures absurda locutis;
Svicerus innocua capitur cum coniuge. In arcem [sig. dr]
ducitur, huicque pedes connectunt vincula ferri.   330
Quaeritur et verum pueri de caede: quid ipse
egerit, et si quid sibi conscia noverit uxor.
Sic miseri insontes poenas dant carceris; una
spes Deus est, ac mens nullius conscia culpae.
Quos Deus et salvos fecit, vetuitque perire!   335
Namque ut forte pius princeps praesulque Ioannes
mandasset Christo fieri mysteria sacra,
et Missam de more suo celebrarier arae,
deque loco spectare suo sollennia vinctis
quo clausi stabant (nam Paschae haec sacra) dedisset,   340
[Svicerus[2] haec Christo, dum tollitur hostia, fundit
suspirans lacrimans, facit et pia vota precatus:][3]
"Magne Pater, cui cuncta patent, nec corda latescunt,
nec vis iusticiam violari: crimine falso
carcere contineor cara cum coniuge. Nosti   345
insontes nos esse mali, quo perfida culpat
nos turba Hebraeum, nobis inimica tibique.
Da, precor, auxilium, verum et clarescere praesta
signo aliquo; indignis ac nos his eripe vinclis!"
      Vix haec ediderat: subito — mirabile dictu! —   350
ut glaties resoluta, crepant quae vincula ferri
crura tenent, pedibusque cadunt diffracta levatis.
Continuo, "Ecce, Deus confregit vincula nobis,"
Svicerus exclamat, "meaque est audita precantis
vox pia!" Cuncti aderant; cernunt; mirantur; et ipse   355
praecipue[4] Hinderbach princeps praesulque Ioannes
stat mirans, delapsa videt confractaque vincto [sig. dv]
vincla viro. Monstro hoc motus de carcere laetos
liberat, insontesque domum dimittit utrosque.
      Cogitat et secum Hebraeos struxisse malignos   360
insidias contra insontem, quo crimen acerbum

---

[1] *correxi*: hoc *VO*
[2] *correxi*: Svictus *O*
[3] Svicerus . . . precatus *om. V*
[4] precipue *V* pricipue *O*

so that the Hebrews might pay the penalty for the murder of the infant found slain there: thus might he destroy them.

It seemed best to listen to their ridiculous tale; 'the Schweizer', with his innocent wife, was arrested. [sig. dr] He was taken to the castle, and his feet were clamped together with iron fetters. And he was asked for the truth about the boy's murder: what he himself did, and what knowledge, if any, his wife was privy to. So the wretched innocents bore the penalty of imprisonment; their only hope was God, and a guilt-free conscience. And God did save them, and did forbid their destruction! For since the pious Prince-Bishop Johannes happened to have given orders for the sacrament of the Lord's supper to be offered to Christ, and for the altar to have its usual celebration of Mass, and had allowed the prisoners to look down on the ceremony from their place of confinement (for these were the Easter services), [during the Elevation of the Host 'the Schweizer', sighing and weeping, poured out these words to Christ, and prayerfully made his pious petitions:][1] "Great Father, to whom all things are known, nor are our hearts hidden from you,[2] neither do you want justice to be violated: I, with my dear wife, have been jailed on a false charge. You know that we are innocent of the evil deed for which the faithless Hebrew gang—hostile to us and to you—is blaming us. Give us your help, I pray, and by some sign make the truth shine out; and rescue us from these undeserved chains!"

He had scarcely uttered these words: suddenly—wonderful to relate!—the iron chains holding his legs cracked like melted ice, and fell shattered from his much-relieved feet. Straightway, "Behold!, God has smashed my fetters," exclaimed 'the Schweizer', "and heard the voice of my pious prayer!" All were on the spot; they saw; they were amazed; and, foremost among them, Prince-Bishop Johannes Hinderbach himself stood amazed, and saw that the once-fettered man's fetters [sig. dv] had fallen off smashed. Prompted by this portent, he released the two now joyful innocents from jail and sent them home.

And he pondered the fact that the evil-minded Jews had laid a trap for an innocent man, so as to shift the bitter murder-charge away from themselves. There were further marvels too, and God wanted to show by other signs

---

[1] These two lines are present in *O* but absent in *V*.

[2] Compare the Gregorian Sacramentary: "Deus cui omne cor patet . . . et quem nihil latet" (cf. *PL* 101. 446)

devolvant a se caedis. Sunt altera mira
insuper, atque aliis voluit clarescere signis
infantem Deus hunc fidei sub nomine sanctae
martyrium passum, vitamque hostiliter illi   365
perfidia raptam Hebraeum cruciamine multo.
     Inter quae hoc aliud dicam memorabile toti
conspectum populo: mirum — sed nemo negare
quod valet, obscurum[1] nulli — cui certa Tridenti
urbs testis. Nam dum iacet infans Simon, in aedem   370
delatus divi Petri, dumque undique turba
spectatum accurrit — pueri quam fama ciebat
martyris ob Christi nomen crudeliter ora
et corpus totum laceri, miracula nam iam
fulgebant! — oculis ambobus debilis, acri   375
morbo captus, erat quidam illo tempore, caecus
non penitus: tenebrae volitabant lumina circum,
nec quicquam certo poterat deprendere visu.
Martyris hunc pueri felix devotio cepit:[2]
ducitur huc, iuxtaque illum supraque iacentem   380
ponitur. At frustra declinat lumina; frustra
ante oculos positum queritur[3] non cernere, tangit
quem manibus. Christum tandem sic voce precatur:
"Iesu Christe, mihi videam da martyra parvum
quem signis ornas miris — ut fertur, et aure [sig. diir]   385
accipio — quem turba nocens odioque sitique
sanguinis occidit. Dederis mihi laetus ut illum
cernam, haud visus damno (vel caecus in aevum
vivam!) tristis ero, sed me hinc abiisse fatebor
contentum." Fatus sic tangit corpus, et inde   390
confricat allatis digitis sua lumina. Morbus
tunc abiit[4] tenebrae, rediit lux, vidit et ipsum
martyris infantis corpus. Miratus abacta
nocte oculis, sospesque domum deductus, honorem
clara voce dedit Christo, qui munere parvi   395
martyris optata donavit lumina luce.
Haec tria prima tulit rumor miracula clara
Simonis; hinc multi faciunt iam vota, feruntque
quae poscunt votis, multi sanantur et aegri.

---

[1] obscurum *V* obscrurum *O*

[2] cepit *V* caepit *O*

[3] queritur *V* quaeritur *O*

[4] *correxi*: abit *VO*

that this infant had suffered martyrdom for the sake of the holy faith, and that by grievous torture the faithless Hebrews had viciously destroyed him.

Amongst these signs I shall record this other notable one, seen by the whole populace: a marvel—yet its meaning is undeniable, clear to all—to which the city of Trent bears sure witness. For while the infant Simon, after being taken to St Peter's church, was lying there, and while a crowd was rushing in from all directions to see him—how quickly word was traveling of the boy martyred for Christ's sake, his face and whole body cruelly torn, for already miracles were flashing forth!—a certain man was present, weak-sighted in both eyes, afflicted by a severe disease, not completely blind: darkness floated all round his eyes, nor was his vision clear enough to identify anything. A blessed devotion to the boy martyr seized him: he was brought here, and placed next to and above the boy's body. But in vain did he look downwards; in vain, when the boy was placed in front of him, did he complain that he could not see the person his hands were touching. At last he uttered this prayer to Christ: "Jesus Christ, grant that I may see the little martyr whom—as I am told, and as [sig. diir] I hear—you honor with wondrous signs, whom the noxious gang murdered in their hate and thirst for blood. If you give me the joy of seeing him, I shall not be sad at my loss of sight (or may I live blind for ever!), but will acknowledge that I went from here satisfied." Saying this, he touched the body and then, moving his fingers to his eyes, rubbed them. At that moment the sickly darkness departed, the light returned, and he saw the infant martyr's very body. Amazed at night's enforced departure from his eyes, and taken back home safe and sound, he loudly praised Christ who, thanks to the little martyr, had granted the longed-for light to his eyes. Rumor has reported these as Simon's first three[1] clear miracles; hence many people now offer prayers and say what they request in them, and many sick people are healed.

The weary sun had now removed the horses from his chariot,[2] and dark night had set high heaven alight with flaming stars;[3] and now sleep was soothing

---

[1] The first, presumably, being the spontaneous issue of blood from the corpse as described in lines 211–213. See 168–69, above

[2] The Greek sun-god Helios was regularly portrayed as a charioteer who drives daily from east to west. Cf. Statius, *Thebaid* 2. 45–46.

[3] Cf. Vergil, *Aeneid* 5. 721: "et Nox atra polum bigis subvecta tenebat."

Iam sol fessus equos curru subduxerat, et nox   400
atra polum flammis stellarum incenderat altum;
iamque hominum curas somnus lenibat.[1] Agendum
quidnam esset presul secum versabat, et omnis
in partis animum rapiebat. Aperta videbat
indicia in Solymos patratae caedis, at illis   405
quaerit adhuc maiora, quibus convincat et ipsos
arguat esse necis sontes: si talis Hebraeis
sit mos, ut celebrent Paschalia festa cruore
Christicolae fuso pueri, si tale Tridenti
tentarint olim facinus. Vincentius auctor   410
eximius scribit Solymos a rege Philippo
exactos causa hac, deprensos caede Ricardi
martyris,[2] e terris Gallorum. Venerat aucta [sig. diiv]
sole dies. Mandat praetori haec quaerere signa.
    Audierat quendam Iudaea stirpe creatum   415
ex patre Hebraeo, sacro baptismate lotum,
Christicolam factum, servari in carcere propter
aes alienum. Hunc ad sese de carcere duci
imperat, et multis praesentibus hunc rogat, ante
iuratum, mos an talis servetur Hebraeis,   420
an comedant panes festis Paschalibus, in[3] quis
Christicolae mixtus sit sanguis, vinaque potent
sanguine mixta, necem pueri si audiverit unquam
viderit aut fieri nati de gente fideli.
Ille refert: "Memini viventem lege paterna   425
audivisse patrem narrantem tempore Paschae
ac mihi dicentem, posita dum liba darentur
ad cenam mensa Paschalem, sanguinem in illis
Christicolae pueri mixtum vinoque fuisse.
Et clam dicebat sub eodem tempore Paschae   430
Iudaeis puerum occidi de sanguine cretum
Christicolae; solitum fieri hoc in partibus altis
Germanum." Testis tunc a praetore rogatus
num sibi gustatum fuerit de sanguine, dixit:
"Non quaeri decet hoc a me, nec tale rogari   435
convenit." Hunc puduit, puto, tunc, nec reddidit ullum
responsum. Satis est visum dixisse Ioanni;
carceris ad saeptum testis redit inde vocatus.

---

[1] lenibat *V* leniabat *O*
[2] martyris *V* nartyris *O*
[3] in *V* an *O*

mortals' cares.[1] The bishop was inwardly debating what exactly he should do, and was hurrying his mind in all directions. He saw the obvious clues pointing to the Jews as the murderers, but he sought still greater ones than those, in order to convict them and prove them guilty of homicide: he inquired whether it was the Hebrews' custom to celebrate the Passover feast with a Christ-worshiping boy's poured-out gore, whether they had previously attempted such a crime in Trent. The excellent author Vincent[2] writes that the Jews, caught red-handed in the murder of the martyr Richard, were for this cause driven out of French territory by King Philip. Day had dawned [sig. diiv] with the sun's strengthening light. Hinderbach instructed the *podestà* to search for these signs.

[Giovanni de Salis] had heard that a certain man, of Jewish birth with a Hebrew father, now a Christ-worshiping convert washed in holy baptism, was currently in jail for debt. He commanded that he be brought to him from jail, and before many witnesses asked him, on oath, whether the Hebrews observed such a custom, whether at their Passover feast they ate loaves containing a Christ-worshiper's mingled blood and drank blood-laced wine, whether he had ever heard of or seen the killing of a boy from a faithful [Christian] family. The man replied: "I remember that when I lived under my father's jurisdiction I heard him telling me in detail that in the Passover season, when the cakes were given out after the laying of the table for the Passover meal, they and the wine contained a Christ-worshiping boy's mingled blood. And he used to tell me that at the same Passover season the Jews secretly killed a Christ-worshiper's son; this, he said, happened regularly in Upper Germany." Then, asked by the *podestà* whether he himself had partaken of the blood, the witness said: "It is not right or proper to ask me such a question as this." Shame then filled him, I think, nor did he give any answer. Giovanni thought he had said enough; the witness returned to the prison cell from which he had been summoned.

---

[1] Cf. Vergil, *Aeneid* 9. 225, where, as here, the sleep enjoyed by others is denied to the person or persons involved (in Vergil's case, the Trojan leaders; in Pusculo's case, Hinderbach).

[2] For Vincent of Beauvais' description of King Philip II Augustus of France's action against the Jews, see *Vincentius Bellovacensis Speculum quadruplex: sive Speculum maius: naturale, doctrinale, morale, historiale*, 4 vols. (Douai: B. Beller, 1624), *Historiale*, bk. 29, chap. 25, vol. 4, col. 1194. See above, 149 n. 3.

Non contentus eo est Salus;[1] stat quaerere signum
certius. Audierat quendam[2] tentasse Tridenti   440
alterius pueri furtum caedemque. Sed ante [sig. diiir]
inventus puer ille fuit, nam rumor in urbe
clam rapti Hebraeis illius terruit ipsos:
perdere non ausi, statim abstinuere.[3] Vocari
ipsius infantis matrem iubet; ordine cuncta   445
vera referre sibi iuratam postulat illam,
quae sibi contigerint de[4] nato, de Solymorum
raptu, quoque modo fuerit puer ipse repertus.
        Haec responsa dedit prudens matrona rogatis:
"Ter quinus, praetor, iam lapsus transiit annus,   450
Hebdomada in Magna natum quem mater habebam
amisi infantem carum mihi. Sedula totum
hunc ego quaesivi triduum, scrutata per urbem,
anxia quod raptus Iudaeis filius esset.
Mens maeret[5] vatesque animus; quod tale timerem,   455
tempora Iudaeis Paschalia dicta monebant,[6]
in quibus, ut fama est, furto iugulare quot annis
gens Iudaea solet puerum baptismate lotum,
contemptum in Christi, fidei in ludibria nostrae.
Hac ratione adii praetorem temporis eius,   460
et petii armatam Iudaeum[7] in tecta cohortem
quaesitum mitti, si (quod praesaga videbat
mens mea) conclusum forte intra tecta tenerent.
Quaesitus puer est at non inventus Hebraeis
aedibus. Inde abii magno perculsa dolore;   465
suspicio nec abit tamen, hic quod filius esset,
saepius et vicum Iudaeum tristis obibam.
Dicebam (et memini) clamitans: 'Ubi, nate, moraris?
Quo te, nate, loco quaeram?' Semel, ecce, querenti[8] [sig. diiiv]
talia respondit natus quaesitus, et inquit: 470
'Mama, adsum! Accede—adsum, carissima mama!'
Accessi, vocem infantis sum laeta secuta;

---

[1] Salus *V* salius *O*
[2] *correxi*: quondam *VO*
[3] *correxi*: tenuere *VO*
[4] de *V* dae *O*
[5] *correxi*: merat *VO*
[6] monebant *V* mouebant *O*
[7] Iudeum *V* iudaeam *O*
[8] querenti *V* quaerenti *O*

De Salis was not satisfied with that; he was determined to seek a surer sign. He had heard that someone had attempted to kidnap and murder another boy in Trent. But [sig. diiir] *that* boy was found in time, for the rumor of his secret abduction by Hebrews in the city frightened them: not daring to destroy him, they immediately desisted. De Salis ordered this infant's mother to be summoned; he demanded from her under oath a consecutive account of everything that truly happened to her concerning her son, his abduction by the Jews, and the way the boy himself was found.

This is how the prudent matron answered his questions: "Fifteen years have now passed, *podestà*, since, in Holy Week, I lost the beloved infant boy whose mother I was. I looked for him diligently for a whole three days, searching all over the city,[1] worried that my son had been abducted by the Jews. My mind and spirit were sad with foreboding; I was warned to fear something of the sort by the season the Jews call 'Passover', when, so rumor says, each year the Jewish race has a practice of stealthily slaughtering a baptized [Christian] boy, in contempt of Christ, in mockery of our faith. So I went to the then *podestà* and asked him to send an armed squad to search inside the Jews' houses, in case (as my foreboding mind saw) they were keeping him captive there. The squad did look for the boy in the Hebrew homes but did not find him. Then, utterly sorrow-stricken, I went away; and yet the suspicion did not go away that this was where my son was, and often I would wander sadly through the Jewish quarter. I kept crying out (and I remember this): 'Where are you, child? Where, child, am I to look for you?' Behold, on one occasion [sig. diiiv] the child I sought answered my plaintive cries, and said: 'Mama, here I am! Come to me—here I am, dearest mama!' I went to him, joyfully following his childish voice;

---

[1] Cf. Luke 2: 45–46 on the young Christ being found by his parents in the temple at Jerusalem after going missing for three days.

accitosque viros ducens mecum, in Samuelis
inveni stabulo tenebroso ligna sedentem
atque[1] inter paleas natum; quem laeta recepi. 475
Haec sunt vera, licet quae te novisse relata,
et quorum fama est." Audit ut talia praetor,
est firmata sibi sententia, de Solymorum
quaerere caede ullum non ultra ducere tempus.

Moysen actutum, Isaac imperat, Israelem 480
et Bonaventuras geminos, Moharem et Samuelis
Brunettam uxorem, Vitalem cum Solomone,
Ioph Lazarumque una[2] captos ad carceris atri
duci saepta.[3] Cohors paret praetoria iussis;
carceris hos ducunt in vincula. Non tamen uno 485
coniunctos posuere loco — sic iusserat ipse
praetor — seiunctos[4] omnes statuere locatos.

Inditia haec animo subeunt praetoris aperta:
confossum Hebraeis infantem Simona dextris;
tempus; fama odiumque vetus; mos actaque retro 490
facta; locus. Fortique movent retinacula vallo
fossatum supra Iudaeum; vulnera crebra;
quod virga infantis transfixa; vincula collo;
non ante inventum quaesitum corpus ibidem,
deferri quo non potuit, nunc esse repertum 495
aedibus Hebraeis. Praetor secum omnia confert;
praesulem adit; pueri caedis clarissima monstrat [sig. diiiir]
indicia in Solymos. Cogi cruciatibus ipsos
esse reos dicit iustum[5] commissa fateri;
praefectumque dari socium sibi postulat urbis 500
Sporum, dum quaerit, sontes dum fune rigentes[6]
cogit, qui secum videat, dicta audiatque.

Haec ait. Antistes responsum reddidit heros:
"Brixigena interpres legum, clarissime Sale,
consilio elegi te certo, ut[7] praetor in ista[8] 505
urbe fores nostra, nec me mea cura fefellit.

---

[1] *correxi*: ac *VO*

[2] *correxi*: unam *VO*

[3] *correxi*: scepta *VO*

[4] seiunctos *V* se uinctos *O*

[5] iustum *V* ustum *O*

[6] *correxi*: tegentes *VO*

[7] *supplevi*: ut

[8] *correxi*: ista *V* istam *O*

and, taking with me some men I had called, I found my son sitting among logs and straw in Samuel's dark shed; joyfully I took him back. These are the true facts, though you know them as stories and subjects of rumor." When the *podestà* heard this account, his opinion, that he should make no further delay in investigating the Jewish murder, was strengthened.

He at once commanded that Moses, Isaac, Israel and the two Seligmans, Mayer and Samuel's wife Brünnlein, Vital with Solomon, Jo[se]ph and Lazarus, after being arrested in a body, be taken to dark prison-cells. The *podestà*'s squad obeyed his orders; they took them in chains to jail. They did not, however, put them together in one place—the *podestà* himself had so ordered—but set all the prisoners in separate places.

These obvious clues occurred to the *podestà*: the fact that the infant Simon had been stabbed by Hebrew hands; the season; rumor and long-standing hatred; tradition and retrospective actions; and the location. Influencing his thoughts, too, were the cables forming a strong barrier upstream from the Jewish ditch; the dense wounds; the fact that the infant's penis had been pierced; the ligature round his neck; the fact that the missing corpse, not having been found earlier in the same place, had now been discovered in a Hebrew house to which it could not have floated down. The *podestà* mentally collated all these facts; he went to the bishop; he showed him the very clear clues of child-murder [sig. diiiir] pointing to the Jews. He said it was just that these culprits be forced by torture to confess their crimes; and he demanded that he be given von Sporo, the city's captain, as his colleague, so that when he himself questioned the culprits, when he used the numbing force of the rope on them, von Sporo might join him in observing them and hearing what they said.

These were his words. The heroic bishop replied: "Brescia-born interpreter of laws, illustrious de Salis, my judgment was sure when I chose you to be *podestà*

Nam quem fama probat, rebus spectavimus ipsis
egregium, et cui sancta manent pia iura fidesque.
Iusticiam nuper tibi delegavimus; idem
servandam tibi nunc etiam permittimus. Hoc nos   510
optamus, meritis reddantur ut omnibus aequa
praemia; nec sceleri[1] patimur regionibus ullum
esse locum, nostro quaecunque audire videmur[2]
imperio. Inquiras verum; subigasque fateri
sontes ac iustas dent poenas: haec mea mens est.   515
Sumendi socium Sporum tibi, Sale, relinquo
hanc curam; facias tu fidens quod tibi spectat
officium mando." Tali sermone Ioannes
principis Hinderbach firmatus praetor, ab ore
ipsorum proprio Solymorum excudere verum   520
constituit, clausi qui servabantur. Ab artis[3]
vinclis educi iubet[4] ad loca, mos ubi sontes
compelli malefacta diu contecta sub auras
prodere et arcano sensu depromere clausa.

    Quemque loco educunt secretum e carceris unum, [diiiiv] 525
non visum sociis. Rogitatur[5] singulus[6] huius
de caede infantis: quisnam patraverit, et quo
tempore, quoque modo. Quisquam haud impune fateri
sustinuit facinus; torti sed fune, dolore
victi omnes caedis manifestant crimina, et atrox   530
quisque suum scelus expromit,[7] simul et sociorum,
post aliquot sotios confessos gesta. Rogatus
haec Samuel primo praestanti corde negavit;
omnia narravit praetori fune solutus
ordine, praefecto astanti cum testibus. Inde   535
amota turba (hoc petiit) perductus in artum[8]
secretumque locum, infantem rapuisse fatetur
Simona Tobiam, seque admisisse domique
hunc habuisse, dato faciendae ex ordine caedis
consilio et structo super hoc prius. Inde, vocatis   540

---

  [1] sceleri *V* celeri *O*
  [2] *correxi:* fatentur *VO*
  [3] *correxi:* arctis *VO*
  [4] iubet *V* iubct *O*
  [5] *omisi:* et *VO*
  [6] singulus *V* singulis *O*
  [7] expromit *V* exprimit *O*
  [8] *correxi:* arctum *VO*

of our city here, nor has my careful choice misled me.[1] For I have looked on you, with your high repute, as a man of proven excellence, and as one for whom holy laws and faith are sacrosanct. I recently delegated justice to you; now I entrust you with its maintenance too. This is my wish, that fair recompense be given for all deserts; nor do I allow crime any place in my territories, whatever I seem to hear of in my domain. Seek out the truth; compel the culprits to confess and pay the just penalties: this is my will. I give you this commission, de Salis, to take von Sporo as your colleague; I order you to boldly do what your duty demands." Strengthened by these words of Prince Hinderbach, Giovanni the *podestà* decided to hammer the truth out of the very mouths of the Jews who were being held in jail. He ordered them to be brought out of close confinement to the usual place where criminals are compelled to make open confession of their long-hidden crimes[2] and declare their closely-guarded thoughts.[3]

Each man was brought separately from his prison-cell, [sig. diiiiv] unseen by his comrades. Each one was interrogated about this infant's murder: who exactly perpetrated it, and when, and how. Unpunished, not one had the courage to confess his crime; but tortured by the rope, all, overcome by pain, clearly revealed their murderous offenses, and each disclosed his own brutal crime and, at the same time, those of his comrades, after some of them had confessed their deeds. Asked about these things, Samuel at first stoutly denied them; broken by the rope, he told the whole story, in order, to the *podestà*, and to the captain who stood by with witnesses. Then, when, with the crowd removed (at his request), he had been taken to a confined and secret place, he confessed that Tobias had abducted the infant Simon, and that he himself had taken him in and held him at his home, as a step-by-step murder plan had

---

[1] Cf. Vergil, *Aeneid* 6. 691: ". . . nec me mea cura fefellit."

[2] Cf. Vergil, *Aeneid* 2. 158: "fas odisse viros atque omnia ferre sub auras."

[3] Cf. Vergil, *Aeneid* 4. 421–422: "solam nam perfidus ille / te colere, arcanos etiam tibi credere sensus."

ad synagogam aliis Iudaeis, Simona ductum
Moysique esse datum, et cunctis spectantibus illum
nudatum, ad medium tracto velamine. Moyses
ut virgam pueri cultro transfixit acuto,
abripuitque genae dextrae cum forcipe adunca,[1]   545
et cruris[2] dextri carnem abscidit, "Atque ego," dixit,
"haec iterans eadem duo vulnera forcipe feci,
et dum clamaret strinxi velamine collum.
Erectus disco a nobis est stare coactus,
in formamque crucis distendere brac[c]hia dextram   550
ac laevam in partem, pedibus tangentibus imis
discum, vi tractis Moharis, qui apprenderat illos.
Interea longis acubus pertunditur omni [sig. dvr]
a turba infixis penitus." Fixisse fatetur
Moysen atque ipsum tenera intra viscera parvi.   555
      "Non tamen interea in Christum blasphemia cessat
ulla," inquit. "'Iesum veluti cruce fiximus, hunc sic
Christicolam[3] puerum mactemus!' Talia quisque
atque his aequa suo pro voto verba locutus
crebra ferit, ridensque[4] fidem simul inspuit ipsi.   560
Collectus cyat[h]o sanguis fuit," inquit, "ab omni
vulnere qui potuit, tribus est sed maxime ab illis
forcipis et cultri de virga, crure genaque.
Angelus hic mecum inter nos divisimus haustum
totum, partiti pariter. Nam sanguine mixto   565
vescimur hoc libis Paschalibus; hoc quoque cenae
mensam irroramus Paschalis; nosque cruore
hoc vice paschalis mactati aspergimur agni.
Hunc et libantes vino imprecamur in omnes
Christicolas quondam Pharao quae sensit acerba   570
in populum dimissa suum trepidata flagella.
Hic," inquit, "mos est multis servatus ab annis.
Pulveris in morem contritum saepe cruorem
auro emi allatum, longe lateque petitum,
et panem in socios divisi hoc sanguine mixtum."   575
Simona sed postquam defecit vita, locasse
infantem exanimum in disco ac tenuisse fatetur
dum consueta sibi peragunt sollennia noctu,

---

[1] adunca *V* aduncam *O*

[2] cruris *V* crucis *O*

[3] Christicolam *V* Cyristicolam *O*

[4] ridensque *V* vidensque *O*

previously been made and built up on this basis. Then, when the other Jews had been summoned to the synagogue, Simon had been taken there and given to Moses, and, after his clothes had been pulled down to his waist, he had been stripped in full view of everyone. After Moses had pierced the boy's penis with a sharp knife, removed part of his right cheek with hooked pincers, and cut out flesh from his right leg, "I too," Samuel said, "repeating these actions, inflicted the same two wounds with the pincers; and when he cried out I tied his cloak tightly round his neck. Placing him upright on a dish, we forced him to stand up and stretch his arms outwards to right and left to form a cross, with the soles of his feet touching the dish, pulled down by Mayer, who had seized them. Meanwhile the whole crowd was piercing him with long needles [sig. dvr] stuck right into him." He confessed that Moses and himself had stuck them into the infant's tender intestines.

"Yet meanwhile," he said, "blasphemy against Christ by no means ceased. 'Just as we crucified Jesus, so let us sacrifice this Christ-worshiping boy!' Each man, speaking these or equivalent words as his own vow, struck frequent blows, and at the same time, ridiculing the boy's faith, spat on him. The blood," he said, "was collected in a ladle from every possible wound, but mainly from those three wounds inflicted by the pincers and knife on his penis, leg, and cheek. Engel here and myself gave out all the drained blood to us, distributing it equally. For we feed on this blood mingled in the Passover cakes; with this, too, we sprinkle the table used for the Passover meal; and with this gore, instead of a slaughtered paschal lamb's, we ourselves are sprinkled. And as we ritually pour it in the wine, we call down upon all Christ-worshipers the bitter, much-dreaded scourges that Pharaoh once saw loosed on his own people. This custom," he said, "has been observed for many years past. I have often paid gold for dust-like powdered gore, imported here and sought far and wide, and I have given out to my comrades bread containing this mingled blood." But he confessed that after Simon's death they had placed the lifeless infant on the dish and kept him there

inque die primum penore[1] occultasse Lyaei.
    "Faeno deinde fuit stabuli culmoque sepultus,   580
atque ibi contectus fuerat dum quaereret illum [sig. dvv]
miles," ait. "Paschae postquam sollennia finem
nacta fuere suum—cocus est mihi sedulus—" inquit,
"tunc Bonaventurae mando dimittere in undam
quae nostras medias aedes perlabitur, utque   585
hunc dicat sese mersum invenisse petentem
de fluvio lymphas. Fingentes flumine mersum
crimina detulimus stulti, ac patefecimus ipsi
quae fuerant occulta tibi nos,[2] Angelus atque
Tobias mecum." Samuel haec vera fatendo   590
confessis stetit his constans; iterumque rogatus,
haec iterum dixit, confirmans vera relata.
    Moyses haec eadem confessus facta probavit
singula, et[3] ignarus Samuel quid dixerit. Addit
hoc etiam,[4] morem hunc Carr[h]is per saecula ductum   595
acta octo, coetu facto de partibus orbis
Iudaeum, hoc ritu celebrent ut Pascha quot annis,
sanguine mactati pueri, cui septimus annus
nondum[5] adsit, pereat vivi qui sanguinis haustu;
quo spargant mensam Paschalem, libaque mixto   600
degustent, latices Bac[c]hi cum sanguine potent,
contemptum in Christi, fidei ac ludibria nostrae.
    Tobias rapuisse ait ac Samuelis ad aedes
blanditiis ductum et nummo; quod forcipe Moyses
abripuit cruris[6] partem, quod forcipe eadem   605
de dextraque gena carnem abstulit, et quod acuto
transfixit virgam cultro; quod forcipe rapta
haec iterans eadem Samuel duo vulnera fecit,
quae Moyses primo crudelis crure genaque [sig. dvir]
fecerat. Astrinxit durus quod vincula collo   610
infantis dicit, turba confossus ab omni
quod fuerit longis acubus. Cocus ipse fatetur
quod puerum iussu Samuelis iecit in undam,[7]

---

    [1] *correxi*: penu *VO*
    [2] quae fuerant occulta tibi nos *V* quae vobis fuerant oculta haec *O*
    [3] singula et *V* singulaque *O*
    [4] etiam *V* esset *O*
    [5] nondum *V* mundum *O*
    [6] cruris *V* crucis *O*
    [7] undam *V* undas *O*

while they performed their customary night-time rituals, and that in the daytime they had at first hidden him in their wine-store.

"Then," said Samuel, "we buried him in hay and straw in the shed, and that was where he was lying hidden when the soldiers were searching for him. [sig. dvv] After the Passover ceremonies had finished, I ordered Seligman my hard-working cook," he said, "to drop him into the waves that flow right through my house, and to say that he had found him drowned when he went to get water from the stream. Pretending that he had been drowned in the river, we foolishly reported the crime, and we ourselves — Engel, Tobias, and myself — disclosed to you what we had previously kept secret." Samuel stood firmly by this confession, declaring that these things were true; and when questioned again, he repeated them, confirming that he had told the truth.

Moses, when he confessed, vouched for each of these same facts, even though he was unaware of what Samuel said. He also added that, following an international Jewish council held at Carr[h]ae,[1] for the past eight hundred years they had continued this custom, whereby they celebrate the Passover each year with this ritual, using the blood of a slaughtered boy less than seven years old, who dies from the draining of his living blood; they sprinkle the Passover table with this, and eat and drink cakes and wine laced with it, in contempt of Christ and mockery of our faith.[2]

Tobias said that he had abducted the boy and, with the aid of cajolery and a silver coin, had taken him to Samuel's home; that Moses had torn off part of his leg with pincers, had also removed flesh from his right cheek with them, and had pierced the boy's penis with a sharp knife; that Samuel, seizing the pincers, had repeated these actions, inflicting the same two wounds which cruel Moses had first inflicted on his leg and cheek. [sig. dvir] He said that Samuel had roughly tied a tight bandage round the infant's neck, and the whole crowd had stabbed the boy with long needles. Seligman the cook himself

---

[1] Cf. above, 143 n. 3.

[2] Line 602 repeats line 459 (except *in* / *ac* in second phrase).

confictumque dolum, mersum simulasse repertum.
Lazarus haec eadem, Solomon, Mohar, Angelus et Ioph   615
ac Bonaventura, est Moharis qui[1] sanguine cretus,
Israel et Isaac, Vitalis, fune coacti,
confirmant[2] dictis omnes, eademque fatentur
ad caedem pueri factam spectantia: sanguis
quod cyatho fuerit collectus corpore fusus,   620
libaque gustarint omnes, laticemque Lyaeum
sanguine commixtum, facta ut convivia cena
Paschali celebrata Dei in ludibria Christi.
　　Ut vero manifesta manent patrata, nec ulla
suspitio ambigua est, confessi crimina clauso   625
carcere servantur sontes gravibusque catenis.
Famaque per populos facinus diffuderat atrox
Iudaeumque patens odium; scelerataque turba
tam diro deprensa malo trepidatque pavetque
Italiae dispersa locis. Mollire potentes   630
muneribus tentant dominos, precibusque fatigant
nunc hos, nunc illos; proprias vertuntur ad artes
antiquosque dolos. Auro corrumpere multo
aggressi petiere ducem, quo magna potensque
laeta, Sigismundum, divino principe gaudet   635
Austria; promittunt sibi nummum milia multa
auri, si solvat sontes e carcere vinctos [dviv]
Iudaeos, ac plura, velit si munera plura.
Praesulis atque animum tentant qui[3] sceptra Tridenti
urbis habet. Spondentur opes ac pondera multa   640
auri atque argenti. Est medius qui nuntius ultro
offerat ingentes thesauros, quis struat arcem
excelsam atque aurichalco ornet, si placet illam
non plumbo velare, velit dimittere tantum
Iudaeos, ultra sontes nec quaerere contra.   645
　　Conantur quoque praetorem corrumpere magnis
muneribus frustra. Donatus dives habebat
Soncinum Iudaeus opum ditissimus illo
tempore. Tum patriae Salus[4] se contulit urbi,
viseret aut illam, rerum aut poscente suarum   650
fortuna. Donatus adest, sibi maxima dona

---

[1] est moharis qui *V* qui moharis est *O*
[2] *correxi*: conueniunt *VO*
[3] qui *V* quae *O*
[4] Salus *V* salius *O*

confessed that on Samuel's orders he had thrown the boy into the waves, and had dishonestly pretended he had found him drowned. Lazarus, Solomon, Mayer, Engel, Jo[se]ph, the Seligman who was Mayer's son, Israel, Isaac, and Vital, forced by the rope, all explicitly confirmed these statements, and made the same confessions regarding the boy's murder: that the blood shed from his body had been gathered in a ladle, and that all had tasted the cakes and the blood-laced wine, when, on the occasion of the Passover meal, a celebratory banquet was held in mockery of Christ our God.

Now that their deeds were truly revealed, neither was there any shadow of doubt, after confessing their crimes the culprits were kept in close confinement, heavily chained. News of the brutal crime, and open hatred of the Jews, had been spread abroad by word of mouth; the criminal crowd, scattered all over Italy, suffered paroxysms of fear after being caught red-handed in such dreadful evildoing. They tried to soften powerful lords with gifts, and plagued them, one by one, with petitions; they turned to their special skills and ancient wiles. In a bid to bribe him with gold galore, they sought out Archduke Sigismund, whom great and powerful Austria is blissfully happy to have as its godly prince; they promised him many thousands of gold coins if he would release the guilty Jewish prisoners from jail, [sig. dviv] and more gifts still, if he so wished. And they tempted the bishop who governs the city of Trent. They promised him property, and many pounds of gold and silver. There was a go-between who, in addition, offered him huge piles of money wherewith to build a lofty castle and give it a splendid brass roof, if a leaden one did not suit him, so long as he was willing to let the Jews go, and to forgo further proceedings against the culprits.

They also tried to give the *podestà* large bribes, but in vain. A wealthy Jew called Donato, an immensely rich property-owner, was at that time living at Soncino. Just then de Salis went to his native town, either just to visit it or because personal

offert, expandatque sinum[1] iubet accipiatque
quantumvis gremio lato numerumque modumque
nummorum iuvet ut praetor, laxetque nocentes
crimine tantum orat—iuri legumque rigori   655
avertat mentem, sententia mitis ab ore
exeat, ac demum foveatque tegatque merentes
supplicium, nec morte velit damnare latronum!
Non desunt qui se medios in munere tali
Iudaeis ponant, adeantque, precentur et omnes.   660
Nunc ducis invicti pulsant, nunc praesulis aures
occlusas sceleri, nunc et praetoris. Et acrem
Spori animum tentant praefecti: magna[2] daturi
thesauros spondent magnos. Via sola ferebat
haec spem Iudaeis: auro superare potenti [sig.er]   665
iusticiam, et sanctas leges pessumdare nummis!
        Ast ubi nulla datur vitiandi iura facultas,
duxque illos praesulque pius praetorque severus
constantique animo Sporus praefectus ut hostes
rep[p]ulit, invenere viam qua tempora causae   670
longa habeant, si qua interea fortuna salutem
afferat inclusis latronibus. O mala gentis
pectora Iudaeae scelerosae! Facta tueri
impia conductis legum doctoribus audent:
aurum animos tantos dabat illis! Ad quid enim non   675
auri sacra fames mortalia pectora cogit?
Ecce, viros adeunt Patavina ex urbe, magistros
iuris qui, magna vi capti pondere et auri,
adsint Iudaeis; nec opem nec iura negavit
antistes (divus princeps!), sed commoda late   680
defendi dedit; atque in lucem cuncta venire
crimina permisit, verumque inquirier ac ius.
Hi postquam contra ius sanctum fasque verendum
non valuere suo auxilio defendere sontes,
iura suo mansere loco inviolata fidesque.   685
Sic fuit Hebraeis auri spes improba vana!
        Transierantque dies multi, fixumque manebat
consilium magnoque duci divoque Ioanni,
praetori simul et Ioanni: carcere clausos
Iudaeos merita pro crimine tollere poena.   690
Diverso educi de carcere tempore praetor

---

[1] *correxi*: siuum *V* suum *O*
[2] magna *V* magua *O*

circumstances demanded his presence. Donato appeared, offered the *podestà* lavish gifts, told him to open up his pocket and receive in his broad lap whatever number and quantity of coins he liked, and begged him merely to release the miscreants from the charge — let him turn his mind away from justice and rigorous laws,[1] let a mild verdict issue from his lips, and let him at long last support and shelter those who deserved punishment, and not wish to condemn them to the death of felons! Plenty of people offered their services to the Jews as go-betweens for this purpose, and approached and pleaded with everybody. Now they battered the ears of the invincible archduke, now the crime-resistant ears of the bishop, and now the *podestà*'s. And they tempted the astute captain von Sporo: to guarantee their huge promises they pledged huge piles of money. The only hopeful course open to the Jews was this: using the power of gold to defeat justice, [sig. e1] and using coins to destroy holy laws!

But when no chance of perverting the course of justice presented itself, and when the archduke, the pious bishop, the stern *podestà*, and the resolute captain von Sporo repulsed them as enemies, they found a way of dragging out the trial, hoping that in the meantime fortune might bring salvation to the jailed felons. Oh, the evil hearts of the criminal Jewish race! They dared to defend their impious deeds by hiring doctors of law: gold was giving them so much courage! For "what lengths are the hearts of men not driven to by the accursed greed for gold?"[2] Behold, they approached men of the city of Padua, masters of law, to induce them, by a large and heavy quantity of gold, to assist the Jews; nor did the bishop (godly prince!) deny them help or legal rights, but gave them full protection of their privileges; he also granted them an airing of all the charges, and an inquiry into the truth and justness of them. When these people's intervention had failed to protect the criminals against holy law and moral sanction, the laws and the faith remained in place, inviolate. Thus did the Hebrews' wicked gold-driven hope prove vain!

Many days had now passed, and the resolve shared by the great archduke and godly Johannes, and by Giovanni the *podestà* as well, remained irrevocable: to get rid of the imprisoned Jews by imposing the penalty they deserved for their crime.

---

[1] For a similar use of the verb *avertere* in reference to the mind, cf. Statius, *Thebaid* 8. 211: "fracta dehinc cunctis aversaque pectora bello."

[2] Cf. Vergil, *Aeneid* 3. 56–57, where (as in this case) gold-lust is linked with murder (the Thracian king's murder of Polydorus): "quid non mortalia pectora cogis, / auri sacra fames!" See also above, 131 n. 1.

seiunctos, sistique[1] suum iubet ante tribunal;
hosque[2] rogat num vera sibi narrata fuere [sig. ev]
de puero. Magna populi cingente corona
confirmant omnes vera et manifesta fuisse 695
confessos. Caedisque modum causamque soluti
enarrant iterum, et constant[3] sermone; fatentur
haud secus ac pridem praetori[4] dicta fuerunt.
⠀⠀⠀Haec ubi sunt audita, diem quo crimina digna
afficiat poena—dignam si crimina tanta 700
inveniant poenam!—statuit fixitque Ioannes
praetor, et ad populum saevos proferre latrones
incipiat, damnetque reos sententia morte.[5]
Ut venit promissa dies, de more paratis
ad poenam sceleris[6] rebus, ducuntur in alta 705
atria praetoris manibus post terga revinctis
latrones (solio lectis crudelibus actis
ad populum). Quos iusta reos sententia damnat
igne perire rotae coniunctos.[7] At Samuelem
nudatum curru deferri ac forcipe crebra 710
candenti sua membra rapi prius; inde, ligatum
intextumque rotae, subiectis ignibus uri;
Angelus huic sotius poena damnatur eadem.
Sic fera monstra suis pro gestis fata tulere!
⠀⠀⠀Moyses effugit meritam pro crimine poenam; 715
[ac Thobias is[8] raptor, puerique Symonis;][9]
conscius immanis sceleris tactusque furore
daemonis, ante diem letum sibi vindice dextra
conscivit, raptusque sub impia Tartara foedum
horrendum et visu, tetro nec odore[10] ferendum, 720
raptandum liquit pedibus cum fune cadaver, [sig.eiir]
urendumque loco turpi quo morte perire
debuerat vivus, sceleratam et reddere vitam

---

1. sistique *V* sitique *O*
2. hosque *V* nosque *O*
3. constant *V* constanter *O*
4. *correxi*: quaestura *VO*
5. morte *V* mortis *O*
6. *correxi*: sceleri *VO*
7. coniunctos *V* connectos *O*
8. *correxi*: ille *O*
9. ac thobias . . . Symonis *O om. V*
10. *correxi*: horrore *VO*

The *podestà* ordered them to be brought out of jail separately, at different times, and to be placed before his judgment-seat; and he asked them [sig. ev] whether the story they had told him about the boy was true. Surrounded by a large gathering of the people, they all confirmed that they had confessed the plain truth. Released, they again described the means and cause of the murder, and stood by their account; they made the same confessions as they had previously made to the *podestà*.

Having heard these statements, Giovanni the *podestà* fixed a firm date when he might punish the crimes with a fitting penalty—if a fitting penalty could be found for crimes so great!—and might start bringing the savage felons before the people, and when the guilty might by due sentence be condemned to death. On the promised day, after the usual preparations for the punishment of crime, the felons, their hands tied behind their backs, were brought into the *podestà*'s lofty hall (after their cruel acts had been read out to the people from the judge's throne). Found guilty, by just sentence they were condemned to be burnt, fastened to the wheel. But Samuel was first to be carried along naked in a cart, and have his body clawed repeatedly with red-hot pincers; then, tightly bound to the wheel, he was to be burnt at the stake; his comrade Engel was condemned to the same punishment. Thus did the savage monsters suffer the fate that matched their deeds!

Moses escaped the punishment he deserved for his crime; [and so did the boy Simon's abductor Tobias;][1] guiltily conscious of his brutal crime and touched by demonic madness, he took vengeance on himself by committing suicide before execution day, and, hurried down to godless hell,[2] left his foul, repulsive, and unbearably vile-smelling corpse to be seized by the feet with a rope, [sig. eiir] and to be burnt

---

[1] This line is present in *O* but absent in *V*, where it is suggested that Moses was the only suicide.

[2] Cf. Vergil, *Aeneid* 6. 543–43: "at laeva (*sc.* via) malorum / exercet poenas et ad impia Tartara mittit."

criminibus. Tali damnati morte dederunt
supplicia, infernosque lacus Phleget[h]ontis et undas   725
ardentis petiere, alii maiora daturi.
     Sed Bonaventurae soli (cocus hic Samuelis,
hic Moharis natus), tacti gravitate peractae
caedis in[1] infantem, trepidique horrore Gehennae
Tartareae — quod tanta ausi crudelia, quae non   730
permittit lex ulla Dei, non sustinet usquam
barbara gens hominum, non fert natura ferarum —
oravere dari sibi sacrum numen aquarum
purgamen, Christique Dei sibi nomina poni,
sedibus ut saltem fruerentur morte quietis   735
lectorum, et veniam baptismi munere sacri,
sanguinis et Christi mererentur. Speque fideque,
admissi immanis merita se morte perire
confessi, accipiunt baptismum; Sporus et illos,
ignibus atque rota damnatos, colla feriri   740
imperat; ac subitam truncato[2] corpore mortem
senserunt gladii. Hancque in poenam sanguine fuso
spirarunt animas lustratas labe nefandi
peccati. Tumulum praesul decreverat illis,
officioque pio ac celebri sua corpora terrae   745
Christicolum commissa dari, sacroque reponi.
Sed capitis rerum vindex improvida turba
festinans flammis caesos ignique dederunt.
     His deprensa malis, Solymorum sparsa[3] per omnem [sig. eiiv]
Italiam gens prava, timens scelerum dare poenas,   750
atque pavens odium populorum, cogit in unum
concilium non mota locis secreta, fidemque
quisque suam implorat. Magnum conferre tributum
omnibus est animus, decretaque scripta feruntur
per terras, ubicunque forent qui faenore nummos   755
conflarent: taxata darent pro viribus aera
in commune. Parant omnes excire tumultum
atque ingens bellum obstinataque proelia contra

---

[1] in *V om. O*
[2] truncato *V* trunco *O*
[3] sparsa *V* spersa *O*

in the loathsome place where he ought to have gone to his death alive, and to have paid for his crimes with his villainous life. Such were the deaths by which the condemned Jews were punished,[1] and they went down to the infernal lakes and the waves of blazing Phlegethon,[2] to be punished more severely by Another.

But the Seligmans alone (the one Samuel's cook, the other Mayer's son), haunted by the heinousness of the child-murder they had done, and in mortal dread of hellish Gehenna[3]—for they had dared misdeeds more cruel than any law of God permits, than any barbarous human tribe anywhere allows, than any wild beast can abide—begged to be given the sacrament of baptismal water, and to be granted names evoking Christ our God, so that they might at least enjoy a death that gave them rest in the abodes of the elect, and might earn forgiveness through holy baptism and Christ's blood. Having confessed that they were dying the death their brutal offense deserved, in hope and faith they received baptism; and von Sporo commanded that, though condemned to burning and the wheel, they be beheaded; then, their bodies decapitated, they died instantly by the sword. And when their blood was thus shed they breathed out souls cleansed from the taint of their abominable sin. The bishop decreed that they were to have a grave, and that their bodies were to be interred in the Christ-worshipers' burial-ground at a holy and stately funeral-service, and laid to rest in a shrine. But the reckless rabble, taking vengeance on the ringleaders, hastily consigned the corpses to a blazing bonfire.

Caught red-handed in these evil deeds, the depraved Jewish race, scattered all over [sig. eiiv] Italy, fearing punishment of its crimes and dreading popular hatred, pooled its separate, locally held, funds into a single consortium, and each person asked for his own guarantee. All were keen to collect a large levy, and written decrees were carried to all countries, wherever there might be money-lenders at interest: they were to pay means-related contributions into a common fund. All of them prepared to incite a riot, a large-scale war, and long-lasting battles against the

---

[1] We take this statement as summarizing all the Jewish deaths so far mentioned, but since the words *tali morte* are singular, the clause could (grammatically at least) refer specifically to suicide if, but only if, the plural subject and verb were justified by at least two suicides. This may account for the insertion of line 716 in O: perhaps its editor misunderstood the present clause as referring to suicide, and then put in an extra line earlier, so as to make two suicides instead of one—even though this was not the way Tobias died.

[2] One of the rivers of the Underworld. The name itself means 'Blazing'; see Vergil, *Aeneid* 6. 550–551: "quae (*sc.* moenia) rapidus flammis ambit torrentibus amnis, / Tartareus Phlegethon."

[3] Literally (in Hebrew), 'the Valley of Hinnom', where sacrifices to Baal and Moloch were offered (e.g., Jeremiah 19: 6), but in later Jewish thought a divinely appointed place of punishment for apostates and other great sinners (e.g., 2 Esdras 7: 36–38), and in the New Testament the final place of torment for the wicked after the last judgment (e.g., Matthew 5: 29).

pastorem, sotii merita quo principe Hebraei
affecti poena pro factis digna tulere.   760
    Muneribus primo divisa pecunia reges
strangulat et dominos, quibus est devotio nulla
frigida vel fidei, quibus et nil carius auro.
Suscipiunt causam Hebreaeum: tutantur et illos
Simonaque oppugnant. Fiunt edicta per urbes   765
quae prohibent puero divi ut reddantur honores
martyris, et pingi Hebraeum crudelia facta,
praeconesque Dei populis aperire (quid aurum
pollet!)[1] Praeterea hoc fretis Romana petuntur
iudicia Hebraeis, summique vocatur ad altam   770
pontificis sedem causa haec. Tibi, maxime, porro,
Sixte pater, placet ire tuum, Romane, Tridentum
legatum, Hebraeis sumptus facientibus omnes
conductum pretio; fuerat qui frater honesti
ordinis in claustris, divus quem Domnicus olim   775
constituit, fidei robur ingens. Claustra sed ipse
pauperis atque humilis fugiens, exivit, opesque [eiiir]
sectatus tumidas, laxis vivebat habenis.
    Hic venit Hebraeum circumdatus agmine magno
Rofredum, magnis opibus comitantibus illos;   780
atque his interea dimissis ipse Tridentum
pergit, et impugnat pueri miracula parvi,
quae videt ipse oculis auditque, fatentibus aegris
sanatos sese meritis infantis, ad illum
votis ac precibus missis. Non impius illa   785
accipit, irridetque super: patronus Hebraeum
nomine legati manifestus! Strinxerat aurum
illi oculos, atque illud idem sibi clauserat aures:
cor duratum[2] auro fuerat. Satis ast ubi lusit,
Iudaeum et partes fovit, clam sustulit hinc se   790
Rofredumque[3] abiit, quem gaudens excipit hostis
impia turba. Virum ducebat more triumphi
vinctum, qui fuerat quondam invitatus ab ipsis
Iudaeis puerum occisum exportare latenter.
Ille idem, ut fama est, promissis victus et auro,   795
tradiderat se sponte, reum caedis velut, urbem
ducendum Romam, seque accusaret ad ipsum

---

[1] pollet *V* polletur *O*
[2] duratum *V* induratum *O*
[3] Rofredumque *V* Rofredum *O*

shepherd [of souls] in whose principality their Hebrew comrades, having suffered condign punishment, had paid the price their deeds deserved.

At first the money handed out in gifts exerted a stranglehold on kings and lords whose devotion to the faith was non-existent or uninspired, and to whom nothing was dearer than gold. They took up the Hebrews' cause: not only did they protect them, but they also attacked Simon. Edicts were issued in every city prohibiting the conferment of a godly martyr's honors on the boy, the depiction of the Hebrews' cruel deeds, and their disclosure to the people by God's preachers (what power gold wields!). Furthermore, the Hebrews, thus emboldened, sought justice at Rome, and this case was summoned to the supreme pontiff's lofty capital. And then you, mighty Sixtus[1] our Roman father, decided that your envoy[2] should go to Trent as a paid employee, completely at the Hebrews' expense; he had been a friar of the honorable cloistered order founded long ago by godly Dominic, mighty bulwark of the faith. But he himself, fleeing the cloisters of the poor and humble, came out and now, [sig. eiiir] in pursuit of boosted wealth, lived a life free from restraint.

This man, surrounded by a large, greatly augmented, troop of Hebrews, came to Rovereto; then, dismissing them, he meanwhile proceeded to Trent, and challenged the little boy's miracles, which he clearly saw and heard about, for sick people declared that, after making vows and prayers to the infant, they had been healed by his merits. The impious man did not accept those miracles, and laughed at them as well: obviously a Hebrew defender posing as an envoy! Gold had blinkered him, and had also made him deaf: his heart had been hardened by gold. But when he had tired of joking and taking the Jews' side, he secretly left Trent and went off to Rovereto, where the impious enemy mob joyfully greeted him. They were leading along in chains, as though in a [Roman] triumph, a man[3] who had once been invited by the Jews themselves to take the slain boy away secretly. That same man, so the story goes, won over by their promises of gold, had given himself up, supposedly guilty of murder, to be taken to the city of Rome, and, before the supreme pontiff himself, to be his

---

[1] Francesco della Rovere (1414–1484), a Franciscan who became Pope Sixtus IV in 1471 and is noted for his nepotism, his political intrigues, and also for his patronage of the arts.

[2] Giovanni Battista dei Giudici wrote in defence of his conduct in the case of the Jews of Trent. See Appendix 2.

[3] Anzelino Austoch: see above, 160–63, and Appendix 2.

pontificem summum, quod c[a]edis conscius esset
Simonis adiutorque simul, quodque occidisset
Svicerus is, cui vincla pedum cecidere soluta.   800
　　　Nec[1] mortis poena terretur, namque dabatur
spes sibi non poenas Romae pro caede daturum
Simonis, ac nullum puniri sanguine summo
iudice pontifice, et veniam si criminis huius
dicat paenituisse habiturum. Captus et hac spe, [sig. eiiiv]   805
sponte sequebatur, simulans ad moenia Romae
invitum vinctumque trahi; tactus tamen ibat
iusticiae ac veri violati verbere mentem,
paenitet et tandem coepti. Si occasio detur,
mente fugam meditatur. Iter legatus habebat   810
Veronam; quo cum venit, devertit,[2] et unam
noctem egit, tumidus praedam quod victor haberet.
　　　Angellinus ea meditatam, occasio quando
est data, nocte fugam peragit, quo nescius aut qua
se ferret; trepidusque domum quam vidit apertam   815
ingreditur primam latitans, si forsitan ipso
neglecto hinc[3] abeat legatus. Cognita mane
sed fuga legato; famuli celerare iubentur,
eque domo exire, inventumque reducere vinctum.
Ille quidem inventus, Veneti sed fraude retecta,   820
qua vinctus Romam traheretur, multa querentem
reiciunt fratrem rectores ac flagitantem,
liber et ad patrias sedes redit Angellinus
incolumis. Sed vix abiit legatus ab urbe
Veronae, de qua immeritum sperarat honorem   825
(innocuae aetatis velut hostis), sensit ab omni
parte urbis magnum puerorum instare tumultum,
quodque magis mirum est, nullo instigante frementum!
　　　Impubes pueri coeunt, et Simonis ardent
ulcisci letum[4] unanimes, poenasque reposcunt;   830
et moniti tanquam discessus tempus et horam,
occurrunt facienti abitum portaeque propinquo.
Quem stipant medium Iudaei. Protinus, ecce, [sig. eiiiir]
irati incurrunt magno clamore ruuntque;
Iudaeos comites simul execrantur et ipsum,   835

---

[1] nec *V* haec *O*
[2] *correxi*: divertit *VO*
[3] hinc *V* hic *O*
[4] letum *V* laetum *O*

own accuser, alleging that he had been privy to Simon's murder and an accomplice as well, and that 'the Schweizer', the man whose fetters fell off broken, had done the actual killing.

Nor was he frightened by a possible death penalty, for he cherished the hope that he would not be punished at Rome for Simon's murder, that no one suffered capital punishment when the supreme pontiff was the judge, and that he would be pardoned if he said he regretted this crime. And, misled by this hope, [sig. eiiiv] he voluntarily accompanied the Jews, pretending to be dragged to the walls of Rome against his will and in chains; as he went, however, his conscience was pricked by the thought that he had violated justice and truth, and in the end he regretted the enterprise. If he had the chance, he planned to escape. The envoy was on his way to Verona; when he arrived, he found lodgings, and spent one night there, proud that he had succeeded in catching his prey.

Anzelino, since he now had the chance, carried out his planned escape that night, not knowing where or which way to go; keeping out of sight, he anxiously entered the first house he saw open, in the hope that the envoy, not bothering about him, would go away. But in the morning the envoy learned of his escape; he ordered his servants to make haste, get out of the house, and bring the prisoner back when they found him. He was indeed found, but the Venetian rulers, discovering that he had been tricked into being dragged to Rome in chains, rebuffed the querulous and clamorous friar, and Anzelino, free at last, returned to his native abode unscathed. But scarcely had the envoy left the city of Verona, where he had hoped to receive honor he did not deserve (as being hostile to innocent youth), when he noticed a large, seething mob of angry boys advancing on him from every part of the city and, more wonderful still, with no one goading them on!

The young boys crowded round him, unanimous in their zeal to avenge Simon's death, and in their demand for retribution; and, as though apprised of the exact time of the envoy's departure, they confronted him as he took his leave and neared the city gate. The Jews surrounded him. Behold, straightway [sig. eiiiir] the enraged boys, shouting loudly, rushed menacingly towards them; as they did so, they cursed his Jewish companions and him, their supporter,

qui favet his, c[a]esumque obiectant Simona parvum,
hosque petunt crebris nullo discrimine saxis.
Diffugiunt dispersi omnes, cursuque salutem
quaerunt quadrupedum, stimulis fodientibus armos.
At pueri pedites quanquam insectantur, et usque   840
saxa volant,[1] donec certamen[2] territa fugit
fratris turba nocens, mortemque evasit equorum
auxilio, tandem Romanas tendit ad arces!
     Lis nova tunc oritur, longumque pecunia bellum
suscitat hostilis cruciatum Simona[3] contra.   845
Instant Iudaei, qui tutabantur et illos,
ullis non ipsum clarescere martyra[4] signis,
Iudaeumque negant manibus periisse nefandis.
Stat contra Hinderbach[5] praesul; defendit honorem
iusticiae atque suum, scelerum fortissimus ultor,   850
mittit et ipse viros Romam, qui pondera causae
sustineant, fidos: iusto periisse latrones
supplicio ostendant, pueri et miracula caesi.
Hic duo sub magno certant contraria nisu:
iusticia atque aurum, inter se adversantia semper.   855
Confligunt partes ambae, sed dispare causa.
Iudaei certant auro, certatur et auro
contra iusticiam, contra fas, iura fidemque
pro scelere atque dolo caedis, pro perfidiaque.
Ast pro iusticia, pro vero, pro quoque recto   860
altera stat pia pars, caedem insectata dolumque, [sig. eiiiiv]
perfidiam immanem et scelus omnibus acre primendum.
     Sed tandem exacta causa graviterque voluta,
Sixte pater, tibi, sancte, tuo sanctoque senatu—
munera non auri quem nulla pecunia flectit   865
a recto, qui iura Dei inviolata tuetur—
exactos post tris annos sententia fertur
iusta, gravis, pia, cunctorum exoptandaque votis.
Laudatur iuste Hinderbach fecisse latrones
afficiens poena, parvum qui Symona diris   870
contemptum in Christi cruciatibus occiderunt,

---

[1] uolant *V* uolent *O*
[2] *correxi*: aspectum *VO*
[3] simona *V* simonam *O*
[4] martyra *V* martyram *O*
[5] Hinderbach *V* inuictus *O*

upbraided them with little Simon's murder, and pelted them repeatedly and indiscriminately with stones. The envoy's retinue all fled, scattering in all directions, and sought safety in their fleet-footed horses, digging their spurs into their flanks. But although the boyish infantry pursued them, and the rocks still flew at them—until the friar's noxious band fled in terror from the battle, and escaped death by the aid of their horses—they did at last make their way to the Roman citadel!

A fresh dispute then arose, and enemy money stirred up a long war against tortured Simon. The Jews, and their protectors, insisted that there were no signs to prove him a martyr, and they denied that he had died at the Jews' abominable hands. Against them stood bishop Hinderbach; valiant avenger of the crimes, he defended justice's honor and his own, and himself sent trusty men to Rome to shoulder the weight of the case: they were to demonstrate the justice of the felons' death-penalty, and the slain boy's miracles. Here two contrary forces were fighting with great vigor: justice and gold, always at odds with each other. The two sides clashed, but on unequal terms.[1] The weapon the Jews fought with was gold, and that gold fought against justice, against the right, the laws, and the faith, in defense of crime, murderous deceit, and faithlessness. But the other, pious side defended justice, truth, and rectitude, hotly pursuing murder and deceit, [sig. eiiiiv] monstrous faithlessness, and a cruel crime which everyone must stamp out.

But at last, when the case had been examined and weightily pondered by you, holy father Sixtus, and in your holy Curia—which no gifts of gold, no money can twist from rectitude, and which keeps God's laws inviolate—three years later the just, weighty, and pious verdict was pronounced which everyone ought to have fervently prayed for. It praised Hinderbach for having acted justly in punishing the felons, who, in contempt of Christ, had with dreadful tortures

---

[1] For the rare ablative singular *dispare*, cf. Statius, *Thebaid* 4. 214–216: "Taenariis hic celsus equis, quam dispare coetu / Cyllarus ignaro generarat Castore prolem, / quassat humum."

inque alios quiri[1] sotios permittitur[2] omnis
Iudaeos, qui se maculari sanguine parvi
favere assensu, fuerit vel femina vel vir.
    Non ego te indictum transibo carmine, nec fas,   875
qui—virtute tua delectus, praesule[3] divo
Hinderbach contra Iudaeos missus ad urbem
Romanam[4]—duros perfers, Aprovine, labores,
et redis[5] in patriam victor strato hoste, reportans
perpetuam laudem, tanto qui es principe dignus!   880
    Bassano actutum sontes inquirere[6] praesul
mandat Alexandro, Salo successerat is nam
integer et magna praestans virtute, Tridentum
accitus praetor, iuris legumque magister.[7]
[Heus, magna[8] urbs Patavi tanto laetatur alumno!][9]   885
Quo nato de te gaudes, Vincentia, cive.
Hic sancta gravitate reos inquirit Hebraeos,
carcere qui[10] steterant clausi[11] iam tempore ab illo,
quo[12] Romae causa haec agitari coepit ad altam [sig. evr]
pontificis sedem et stetit intermissa Tridenti.   890
Convictos[13] damnat sontes fassosque latronum
morte pari. Meritas poenas sic impia turba
invenit, tandem cessitque pecunia vero!
    Tu tamen in primis celebranda es carmine nostro
ac, fortis Brunetta, tui[14] Patientia victrix: 895
quae trepidata viris vincis tormenta, nec ignis
subiectus pedibus, non funis, non genus omne
tormenti subigit mentis secreta fateri;

---

   [1] *correxi*: inquiri *VO*

   [2] permittitur *V* permittitnr *O*

   [3] praesule *V* a praesule *O*

   [4] Romanam *V* Romam *O*

   [5] redis *V* reddis *O*

   [6] inquirere *V* Inquirere *O*

   [7] integer et magna prestans virtute tridentum / accitus praetor iuris legumque magister *V* accitus praetor iuris legumque magister / integer et magna prestans virtute tridentum *O*

   [8] *correxi*: magia *O*

   [9] Heus . . . alumno *O om. V*

   [10] qui *V* quae *O*

   [11] clausi *V* clause *O*

   [12] quo *V* que *O*

   [13] conuictos *V* conuinctos *O*

   [14] tui *V* tua *O*

killed little Simon, and gave permission for the interrogation of all the other Jews—their comrades, whether male or female—who by their approval of the crime had elected to be stained with an infant's blood.

I shall not omit to mention you, Approvinus,[1] in my poem, nor would that be right, for you—chosen for your virtue, sent to the city of Rome to oppose the Jews when godly Hinderbach was bishop—labored long and hard, and then, vanquishing the foe, you returned victorious to your native city, having won perpetual praise; you are worthy of so great a prince!

Forthwith the bishop commanded Alessandro Bassano to interrogate the criminals, for he, being an upright and outstandingly virtuous master of canon and civil law, had been called to Trent to take de Salis's place as *podestà*. [Ah, the great city of Padua is proud of so great a pupil!][2] He gives you joy, Vicenza, as your own citizen-son. With holy gravity he interrogated the guilty Hebrews who had been kept in jail ever since legal proceedings in this case started in the pope's [sig. evr] lofty capital and were discontinued at Trent. He condemned the convicted criminals, and those who had confessed, to similar felons' deaths. Thus the impious gang got the punishment they deserved, and at long last money yielded to truth!

But you, brave Brünnlein, deserve special praise in my poem, and so does your conqueror, Fortitude:[3] you conquered the tortures men are afraid of, nor did the scorching of your feet, or the rope, or any other kind of torture compel you to

---

[1] The jurist Approvinus de Approvinis, whose letters to Hinderbach (sent from Rome between 24 March 1477 and 1 July 1478) are listed in Paul Oskar Kristeller, "The Alleged Ritual Murder of Simon of Trent (1475) and its Literary Repercussions: A Bibliographical Study," *Proceedings of the American Academy for Jewish Research* 59 (1993): 111–12.

[2] This line is present in *O* but absent in *V*.

[3] Cf. Juvenal, *Satires* 13. 19–20: "magna quidem . . . / victrix fortunae sapientia." Brünnlein, the wife of Samuel, has just been described as 'brave' (*fortis*), but the virtue of fortitude (one of the four cardinal virtues), which Pusculo here personifies as her 'conqueror', cannot be called *fortitudo* because of its non-dactylic rhythm, so Pusculo calls it *patientia* instead.

et, nudata viris detectaque, crimina sola
non prodis, constans animo. Iam coxerat ardens   900
pruna pedes, et odos teter nidorque fugarat
praetorem atque alios, tu prunas subiicientem
accensas[1] pedibus torvo cum lumine spectans
carnificem appellas! Iam spes cruciamine vinci
nulla erat, aut quicquam veri extorquerier ore;   905
clausa tenebatur iam non quaesita, nec illi
poena ferebatur, quae poenas vicerat omnis.
  Tacta Deo, mentem mutat, scelerisque peracti
paenitet, atque animae iam consulit atque saluti;
iam credit Christum esse Deum Dominumque salutis;   910
destinat a Christo nomen baptismate lota
sumere. Clavigeri Petri qui praesidet aedi
ipsa sacerdotem ad sese accersier orat.
Ad quem, dum venit, contrita mente locuta est:
"O (mihi iam pater es) Christi venerande sacerdos,   915
stirpe orta Hebraea vixi sub lege parentum
hactenus, atque mori nostra sub lege stetit mens. [sig. evv]
Sed, video, Deus hac non vult me excedere vita
Hebraeam, nec posse, puto, cruciamina tanta
quae vici — ac tenebras, pedorem et carceris atri.   920
Nempe boni feci quicquam, quo gratia talis
nunc mihi donatur — moriar ne morte perenni![2]
  "Confiteor. Dum me malus error, dum Solymorum
antiquata diu lex coniugis atque parentum
possedit, semper sum inopum miserata labores   925
Christicolum, et placuit semper succurrere egenis.
Saepius et, memini, contendi cum Samuele
coniuge, dum nimios petiisset faenoris usus;
dumque ego torquebar diro quaesita dolore,
auxilium implorans divinum audire videbar   930
vocem corde mihi dicentem: 'Munere matris
(est pia), mente Dei salvabere, voce preceris
certa Dei matrem sanctam intactamque Mariam.'
Nunc damno peiora, sequor meliora; fidelis
Christi serva peto baptismum. Nomine cuius   935
admissi veniam merear Christique cruoris!
Simona confiteor manibus cedidisse virorum

---

[1] accensas *V* accensa *O*
[2] perenni *V* perhenni *O*

confess the secrets of your mind; and you alone, stripped naked in front of men, resolutely refused to reveal your crimes. Glowing charcoal had already burnt your feet, and vile-smelling fumes had driven away the *podestà* and the rest, when you, fixing your fierce gaze on the man who was scorching your feet with lighted charcoal, called him a butcher! There was no longer any hope of Brünnlein being conquered by torture, or of any truth being wrung from her lips; still kept in jail, she was no longer interrogated, nor, having conquered all forms of punishment, was any more being inflicted on her.

Touched by God, she changed her mind, repented of the crime she had committed, and now took thought for her soul and her salvation; now she believed Christ to be God and Lord of salvation; she intended, when washed in baptism, to take a Christian name. She herself begged for the priest-in-charge of the church of Peter the key bearer[1] to be called to her. When he came, she said contritely to him: "Venerable priest of Christ (for you are now my [spiritual] father), hitherto, being of Hebrew birth, I have lived subject to [Jewish] parental law, and I was resolved to die under our law. [sig. cvv] But, I see, God does not wish me to leave this life a Hebrew, nor, I think, does he wish tortures like those I have conquered—or the dark jail's blackness and filth—to have any power. I must surely have done something good, for which I am now being granted such a favor—not to die an everlasting death!

"I confess. When I was ruled by evil error and by long-outmoded Jewish marital and parental law, I always pitied the tribulations of poor Christ-worshipers, and always liked helping those in need. And often, I remember, I quarreled with my husband Samuel when he had demanded too much interest on loans; and when, under interrogation, I was racked by dreadful pain, as I prayed for God's help I seemed to hear in my heart a voice saying: 'Thanks to my mother (who is holy), by God's will you shall be saved, if you confidently pray aloud to God's holy and spotless mother Mary.' Now I condemn evil and pursue good;[2] I ask for baptism as Christ's faithful servant. In the name of him and his gore, may I earn forgiveness of my offense! I confess that Simon fell at the hands of our men.

---

[1] Cf. Matthew 16: 19 (Christ's words to Peter): "et tibi dabo claves regni caelorum."

[2] Reversing Ovid, *Metamorphoses* 7.20–21: "video meliora proboque: / deteriora sequor . . .".

nostrorum. Mihi visum est hoc[1] crudele[2] ferumque,
quod non praetori sum ullo confessa dolore.
Paenitet erroris, piget ac me criminis huius."   940
    Haec audita pio actutum fert ordine ad aures
Hinderbach gaudens,[3] nec enim sine praesulis illam
iussu fas duxit sacrato aspergere rore.
Ut mentem agnovit princeps animumque volentis
baptismum, non victa metu (cui cesserat omne [sig. evir]   945
tormentum) quod sponte sacram sibi postulet undam,
quodque mori cupiat numero conscripta fideli,
mandat aquis illam, sacris sollenniter actis,
perfundi, inque gregem recipi baptismate Christi
illam.[4] Quae[5] vultu laeto devota salubres   950
acceptavit aquas; posuit nomen Caterinae
martyris ipsa sibi. "Nomen placet hoc mihi," dixit,
"namque ambae passae tormenta et vicimus ambae."
    Tu felix, Brunetta, quidem pro munere tanto,
quo donata viam verae[6] es sectata salutis —   955
quod de Iudaea infida caligine pulsa
facta es serva Dei Christi — quod luce recepta
tendis iter caelo rectum, victura beata!
Sed quoque — si fas est dici — felicior aucto
munere: quod miseram haud multo[7] post tempore vitam   960
linquis, et accepto sacrato corpore Christi
illi animam reddis purgata labe nitentem.
    Quam pius Hinderbach[8] decoravit honore supremo
elatam populi turba comitante. Canensque
ordo sacer, Regisque ferens vexilla Superni,   965
ordine flammarum longo procedit; et aedis
clavigeri ante fores Petri deposta quiescunt
ossa, locum fama sacrum sortita perenni[9]
Hinderbach iussu divini antistitis urbis.

---

[1] hoc *O om. V*
[2] crudele *V* fidele *O*
[3] Hinderbach gaudens *V* praesulis exultans *O*
[4] *correxi*: illa *VO*
[5] *correxi*: quod *VO*
[6] verae *V* vere *O*
[7] haud multo *O* multo haud *V*
[8] Hinderbach *V* antistes *O*
[9] perenni *V* perhenni *O*

This deed, which no amount of pain made me confess to the *podestà*, I now consider cruel and brutal. I repent of my error, and I am sickened by this crime."

Delighted to hear these words, straightway the priest dutifully reported them, in order, to Hinderbach, for indeed he thought it wrong to sprinkle her with consecrated water unless the bishop ordered it. The prince, recognizing that, unconquered by fear (having overcome [sig. evir] every torture), she longed heart and soul for baptism— for of her own accord she asked to be washed in the sacred stream, and wanted to die enrolled in the company of the faithful—ordered that at a solemn service she be washed clean with water, and received into Christ's flock by baptism. Smiling happily, she devoutly accepted the saving waters; she named herself after the martyr Catherine.[1] "I like this name," she said, "for both of us suffered torture, and both of us conquered it."

You were blessed indeed, Brünnlein, to receive a gift so great, whereby you pursued the path of true salvation—for, banished from the faithless Jewish fog, you became the slave of Christ our God—for, having received the light, you are now winging your way straight up to heaven, to dwell there in bliss! But also—if one may say it—you were more blessed still when the gift was increased: for not long afterwards you left this miserable life and, after receiving the consecrated body of Christ, gave him back your soul shining, purged of its taint.

Pious Hinderbach accorded her supreme honor when, escorted by a thronging crowd, she was carried out [for burial]. A holy order [of monks], chanting and carrying banners of the Heavenly King,[2] processed in a long candle-lit line; and her bones were laid to rest before the door of the church of Peter the key-bearer, having acquired a sacred place of everlasting fame at the command of Hinderbach, the city's godly bishop.

---

[1] St Catherine of Alexandria, traditionally held to have protested against the persecution of Christians by Maxentius in the early fourth century and, as a result, to have been tied to a wheel, tortured, and beheaded.

[2] Alluding to the Holy Week hymn 'Vexilla regis' by Venantius Fortunatus.

Impressum in Augusta Vindelicorum per magistrum Iohannem Ot[h]mar suis
in aedibus ex transverso sacello Sanctae Ursulae intra rivos Lici. Anno MDXI,
[a. d.] III. Idus Aprilis.[1]

---

[1] Impressum . . . Aprilis *O* Explicit opus Simonidos. *V* Si ducis inuicti populorum
exempla placeret / clara Sygismundi ducibus ipsa sequi, / si gregis et Christi pastoribus
alma sederet / relligio Hinderbach principis eximii, / non auro quassata malo, non mota
labore / iustitia in terris staret, et alma fides. // Ut serpens inimica homini mordere parata
/ in letum semper feruida colla tumet; / sic gens Iudaeum nobis nostraeque saluti / insid-
ians odium non satiata gerit. Idus. V. P. *add. V*

Printed at Augsburg by Master Johannes Othmar at his house beside the shrine of St Ursula between the branches of the River Lech. April 11th, 1511.[1]

---

[1] *V* adds two short poems in conclusion. The second is identical with the six-line poem with which *O* begins. The first, however, is new, and may be translated as follows: "If our leaders agreed to follow those clear precedents set by Sigismund, unconquered leader of peoples, and if the life-giving religion of Hinderbach, excellent prince, were established among the shepherds of Christ's flock, justice, unshaken by evil gold, undisturbed in its work, would stand firm on the earth, and so would the life-giving faith."

APPENDIX 1:
INCUNABULA RELATING TO THE DEATH OF
SIMON OF TRENT

Data taken with adjustments from *ISTC* and Kristeller,
"Alleged Ritual Murder"

1. Giovanni Mattia Tiberino, *Relatio de Simone puero tridentino*
   [Venice]: Gabriele di Pietro, [after 30 Apr. 1475], with additions by Raffaele
   Zovenzoni, and Johannes Hinderbach
   H 15659 = HC 8668; *IGI* 9651; Goff T-480

2. Giovanni Mattia Tiberino, *Relatio de Simone puero tridentino*
   [Venice]: Nicolaus Jenson, [after 30 Apr. 1475], with additions by Raffaele
   Zovenzoni, and Johannes Hinderbach
   IGI 9652

3. Giovanni Mattia Tiberino, *Die geschicht und legend von dem seyligen kind und
   marterer genannt Symon von den Iuden zu Trientt gemarteret und getoetett*
   Augsburg: Günther Zainer, [after 4 Apr. 1475], illustrated with woodcuts
   H 15658; Goff T-489

4. Giovanni Mattia Tiberino, *Relatio de Simone puero tridentino*
   [Nuremberg]: Friedrich Creussner, [after 4 Apr. 1475][1]
   H 15654*; *IGI* 9647; Goff T-485

5. Giovanni Mattia Tiberino, *Die geschicht und legend von dem seyligen kind und
   marterer genannt Symon von den Iuden zu Trientt gemarteret und getoettet*
   [Nuremberg: Friedrich Creussner, after 4 Apr. 1475]
   H 15657*

---

[1] The copy in Munich, Bayerische Staatsbibliothek (shelfmark Rar. 337), and available digitally at www.bsb-muenchen.de/ [consulted on 27 Feb. 2011], has an inserted woodcut image of pilgrims and ex-votos before the injured body of Simon on a table with his attributes, while that in the BL (shelfmark IB.7593) has an illustrated account of the torture of Simon identical to Hartmann Schedel, *Liber Chronicorum* (Nuremberg, 1493), fol. CCLIIIIv, and bound in at the beginning of the text.

6. Giovanni Mattia Tiberino, *Relatio de Simone puero tridentino*
   Sant'Orso: Giovanni da Reno, [after 4 Apr. 1475]
   H 15652*; *IGI* 9649; Goff T-484

7. Giovanni Mattia Tiberino, *Relatio de Simone puero tridentino*
   Treviso: Gerardus de Lisa, de Flandria, [after 4 Apr. 1475]
   H 15653; *IGI* 9650

8. Giovanni Mattia Tiberino, *Relatio de Simone puero tridentino*
   [Augsburg: Monastery of SS. Ulrich and Afra, after 4 Apr. 1475]
   H 15649*; Goff T-483

9. Giovanni Mattia Tiberino, *Relatio de Simone puero tridentino*
   Mantua: [Johannes Schallus, after 4 Apr. 1475]
   H 15651; *IGI* 9646

10. *Historia Sancti Simonis Tridentini interfecti a Iudaeis*
    [no place or date of publication]
    H 14746

11. Matheus Künig, *Gedicht von dem getöteten Knaben Simon von Trient*
    [(Sant'Orso?): Giovanni da Reno, 1475]

12. *Tormenti del beato Simone da Trento*
    [Treviso: Gerardo da Flandria, no date of publication, 1475?], with addition
    by Io. [Giovanni?] Conyl. [da Conegliano?] Fav., *Simone Beato Gloria Laus et
    Honor*
    H 15550

13. Giovanni Mattia Tiberino, *Relatio de Simone puero tridentino*
    Rome: Bartholomaeus Guldinbeck, 19 June 1475
    H 15656; *IGI* 9653; Goff T-486

14. Giovanni Mattia Tiberino, *Relatio de Simone puero tridentino*
    Treviso: G[erardus de Lisa, de] F[landria], 20 June 1475

15. Girolamo Campagnola and Giorgio Summaripa, *Carmina italica de martyrio
    eius et contra Judeos*
    Sant'Orso: Giovanni da Reno, 24 June 1475
    HC 1420

16. Giovanni Mattia Tiberino, *Relatio de Simone puero tridentino*
    Rome: Bartholomaeus Guldinbeck, 24 July 1475
    H 15655*; Goff T-487

17. *Historie von Simon zu Trient*
    [Trent: Albrecht Kunne, 6 Sept. 1475], illustrated with woodcuts
    H 7733

18. Thomas Pratus, *De immanitate Judaeorum in Simonem infantem*
[Treviso: Gerardus de Lisa, de Flandria, Sept? 1475]
IGI 8038

19. Sylvester de Balnoregio, *Conclusiones cum earum declarationibus super canonisatione B. Simonis Tridentini*
[(Trent: Albrecht Kunne, after 6 Dec. 1475)]
H 15203

20. Giovanni Mattia Tiberino, *Relatio de Simone puero tridentino*
[Rome: Bartholomaeus Guldinbeck, 1475–76]
H 15650; *IGI* 9648; Goff T-488

21. Giovanni Mattia Tiberino, *Epitaphium gloriosi pueri Simonis Tridentini novi martyris* (inc. "Sum puer ille Simon")
[Trent: Albrecht Kunne, about 1476], illustrated broadside with Simon seated, crowned by angels, holding martyr's palm and pincers

22. Giovanni Mattia Tiberino, *Historia completa de passione et obitu pueri Simonis*; *Miracula beati Simonis*; *Lamentationes beati Simonis* (inc. "Sum puer ille Simon")
Trent: [Albrecht Kunne for] Hermann Schindeleyp, 9 Feb. 1476
H 15661*; Goff T-481

23. Giovanni Mattia Tiberino, *Relatio de Simone puero tridentino*
[Naples: Arnaldus de Bruxella, about 1477]

24. Johannes Franciscus Pavinis, *Inquisitio et condemnatoria sententia contra Judaeos Tridentinos*
[(Rome: Vitus Puecher, 1478)]
H 12537; *IGI* 7373; not in *ISTC*

25. Giovanni Mattia Tiberino, *Relatio de Simone puero tridentino*
[Cologne: Printer of "Dialogus Salomonis et Marcolfi" (Ludwig von Renchen?), about 1478–81]
H 15648*; *IGI* 9645; Goff T-482

26. Girolamo Campagnola and Giorgio Summaripa, *De Martyrio Beati Simonis pueri Tridentini a Iudaeis trucidati carmina*
[(Verona: Giovanni and Alberto Alvise, after 20 June 1478]), with a poem by Leonardo Montagna
GW 5938; *IGI* 9103

27. Giorgio Summaripa, *Poema in terza rima sopra il martirio del B. Simone da Trento e del B. Sebastiano Novello; tradutto in materno sermone da Zorzi Summaripa*
[Treviso: Bernardinus Celerius de Luere, 14 July 1480]
HC 14888; *IGI* 9104

28. Giovanni Calfurnio, *Mors et apotheosis Simonis infantis novi martiris; Elegia Calphurnii poetae Brix[iensis] ad Franciscum Tronum*
    [Trent: Z. L. (Giovanni Leonardo Longo), about 1481], with additions by Raffaele Zovenzoni
    H 4268; *GW* 5919

29. [Giovanni Calfurnio], Catullus, *Carmina*; Tibullus, *Carmina*; Propertius, *Elegiae*; Statius, *Silvae*; Giovanni Calfurnio, *Mors et apotheosis Simonis infantis novi martiris*, with a preface by Calfurnio addressed to Ermolao Barbaro, and a poem on Simon addressed to Johannes Hinderbach
    [Vicenza: Giovanni da Reno and Dionysius Bertochus, 1481]
    HC 4760; *GW* 6389; *IGI* 2615

30. Giovanni Mattia Tiberino, *Epigrammata aliaque carmina in beatum Simonem* (inc. "Sum puer ille Simon")
    Trent: Giovanni Leonardo Longo, 5 Sept. 1482
    HCR 15660; *IGI* 9644; Goff T-479

31. Quintus Aemilianus Cimbriacus, *Historia beati Simonis Tridentini*
    [Vienna: Johann Winterburg, around 1493], with additions by Paulus Amaltheus and Jacobus Pona
    GW 311

32. *Gedicht von dem Knaben Simon zu Trient*
    [Ulm: Johann Zainer the younger, about 1498], broadside
    HC 5464

33. Pietro Bruto, *Epistola contra Judaeos* [Vicenza: Leonardus Achates de Basilea?, 1477] *IGI* 2213; *GW* 5658

Appendix 2:
A List of Individuals Connected
with the Trent Case

Approvinus de Approvinis: jurist sent by Hinderbach to plead his case in Rome. His letters to Hinderbach from Rome during 1477–1478 record the progress of the case.

Anzelino Austoch (or Henselinus di Termeno): Pusculo suggests that he refused offers of money by the Jews of Trent to throw away the body of Simon. He was placed in prison in Rovereto at the behest of Battista dei Giudici, and accused the 'Schweizer' of murdering Simon and framing the Jews. Pusculo suggests that he was tricked into going to Rome in the hope of a papal pardon, and that he escaped arrest in Verona with the help of the Venetian authorities. Hinderbach alleges that he was corrupted by Jewish bribes, and constricted by force to make his accusation. Battista dei Giudici claimed that Anzelino was convinced by Johannes Alemannus, an innkeeper in Rovereto, to make his accusation, and he denied harming Anzelino. It seems that Battista dei Giudici had Anzelino placed under armed guard to prevent some people from Trent kidnapping him, as they had often attempted. Anzelino fled from Verona but was recaptured with the help of the *podestà* of the city, and he was taken to Rome where he remained for at least two years in Castel S. Angelo, although his statement implicated the Jews in Simon's death.

'M. Aureliam' (Messer Niccoló Aurelio?): unidentified ducal secretary in Venice mentioned by Hinderbach in 1475 as a supporter of his cause.

Giovanni Calfurnio (*c.* 1433–1503): wrote an account of the death of Simon published in 1481 (see Introduction, Section VI/d).

Michele Carcano (1427–1484): Franciscan preacher in Venice, helped establish *monti di pietà* as Christian alternatives to Jewish moneylenders, strongly supported Hinderbach, and was invited to preach in Trent.

Niccolò Cruciger: Franciscan preacher in Vicenza, friend of the poet Raffaele Zovenzoni, in correspondence with Hinderbach, supported cult of Simon, and visited Trent to view the body.

Archangelo dei Balduini: doctor in Trent, testified that Simon died on day of Passover and had not drowned.

Battista dei Giudici (*c.* 1430–1484): Dominican, bishop of Ventimiglia from 1471, and apostolic commissioner appointed by Sixtus IV to investigate Trent case. He was greeted in Trent warmly by Hinderbach but placed in poor accommodation, prevented from interviewing Jewish prisoners alone, and eventually forced by ill health and local ill-feeling to move to Rovereto, in Venetian territory, where he interviewed the advocates for the Jews. He eventually moved back to Rome, but he seems to have been marginalized and harried by accusations of favoring Jews although he asserted that he had often preached against them and had never shared a meal with a Jew in his life.

Bernardino da Feltre (1439–1494): Franciscan preacher who helped establish *monti di pietà* as Christian alternatives to Jewish moneylenders and gave sermons in Trent at Easter 1475 which probably included anti-Jewish themes.

Gabriele di Pietro: printer in Venice and Brescia, *c.* 1472–1482.

Giovanni de Salis: Brescian *podestà* in Trent, excommunicated by Battista dei Giudici, and later involved as witness in Portobuffolè (near Treviso) case of ritual murder (1480).

Frederick III (1415–1493): elected German king in 1440 and in 1452 crowned Holy Roman Emperor in Rome by Pope Nicholas V.

Johannes Hinderbach (1418–1486): born near Kassel in Hesse, enrolled at University of Vienna and obtained Master of Arts, and in 1440 enrolled in Law at University of Padua. From 1449 secretary to Emperor Frederick III, sent on missions to Rome and Bohemia, given title of Count Palatine Lateran of Holy Roman Empire, and elected bishop of Trent in 1465. In 1469 he was imperial ambassador in Rome, in 1471 was imperial legate at Diet of Regensburg and attended Diet of Augsburg in 1474. Supporter of humanism, collector of manuscripts, promoter of cult of Simon.

Nicholas Jenson (1420–1480): French engraver and printer in Venice from 1467, printed accounts of Simon's death by Tiberino and Zovenzoni. The latter addressed couplets to him.

Giovanni Leonardo Longo: printer in Trent, issued Calfurnio's work on Simon in *c.* 1481.

Maximilian (1459–1519): son of Emperor Frederick III, supporter of cult of Simon from 1479; at Hinderbach's urging Pusculo prefaced his verses about Simon with letter to him in 1481. Elected emperor in 1508, and a supporter of moves in the empire to investigate Jewish books for anti-Christians sentiments.

Pietro Mocenigo: Doge of Venice (r. 1474–1476) who instructed subject cities of the empire not to allow violence against the Jews, nor to permit images, texts, or sermons about Simon.

Ottmar Nachtigall (Luscinius) (1480/1–1537): student of the German humanist Jakob Wimpfeling, studied at Paris, returned to Augsburg in 1510, and then moved to Strasburg as organist and vicar of St Thomas' church. He introduced Greek studies to Strasburg, and was a member of the literary society there. He was punningly praised by Erasmus in Sept. 1514: "Do not forget Ottmar, a man who seemed to me well read without ostentation, who with the rapid trilling on his pipes that outdid the very nightingale so ravished me that I seemed rapt in ecstasy."[1] He published works on music and other matters under the name Ottmar Luscinius between 1515 and 1536. His poem was included in the edition of Pusculo's work published in Augsburg in 1511 (see above, Section III).

Johann Othmar: printer active in Augsburg during 1502–1514. Printed Pusculo's poem about Simon in 1511.

Michele Pacis: unidentified Roman supporter of Hinderbach in 1475–1476.

Giovanni Francesco Pavini: canonist and theologian who aided the cardinals sitting in Rome to consider the case of Simon. He wrote two *consultationes* published in 1478 (see Appendix 1, no. 24) in which he supports the legality of the sentences passed against the Jews of Trent, and rejects the authority of the acts of the apostolic commission.

Johann Pinicianus (1478–1542): author of a number of works of poetry, grammar, and conduct published in Augsburg in 1511–1518. His poem was included in the edition of Pusculo's work published in Augsburg in 1511 (see above, Section III).

Bartolomeo Platina (1421–1481): humanist, member of Roman academy, and papal librarian, he was a supporter and correspondent of Hinderbach. Battista dei Giudici composed a work refuting Platina's calumnies against him, including the assertion that he was a supporter of Jews.

---

[1] Erasmus to Wimpfeling, Basel, 21 Sept. 1514: *The Correspondence of Erasmus*, vol. 3, *1514 to 1516*, trans. R. A. B. Mynors and D. F. S. Thomson, annot. James K. McConica (Toronto: University of Toronto Press, 1976), 29.

Ubertino Pusculo (1430–1504): Brescian author of poem in two books about Simon, completed in 1481 and sent to Hinderbach for correction (see Introduction, Section VI/c).

Ludovico Querini: Venetian *podestà* of Rovereto in 1475, considered a supporter of Jews by Hinderbach.

Christopher Romer: possessed a manuscript copy of Pusculo's poem about Simon at some point between 1481 and 1511.

Roper: Christian tailor, Samuel's neighbour and friend, tortured under suspicion of aiding Jews after accusation to this effect made by Schweizer. Spoke to imprisoned Jewish women.

Francesco Sanson (1414–1499): General of the Franciscan order and supporter of Hinderbach.

Johannes 'the Schweizer': laborer and husband of Dorothea, Anna's midwife (and also midwife to household of Engel), he quarreled with Samuel and Israel over fee, sued for payment, harbored a grudge towards them, and was accused by Vital of framing the Jews of Trent for the murder of Simon. Questioned without torture and released without charge.

Sigismund of Tirol (1427–1496): nephew of Emperor Frederick III, archduke until his abdication in 1490, he called a halt to proceedings in Trent in April 1475, but eventually supported trials.

Sixtus IV Della Rovere: Franciscan pope (r. 1471–1484), he instigated investigation into proceedings at Trent.

Giovanni Mattia Tiberino (*c.* 1420–*c.* 1500): friend of Hinderbach, Brescian doctor in Trent, testified that Simon did not drown. Wrote several works about the case which were widely circulated in manuscript and print (see biography in Introduction, Section VI/a and published works listed in Appendix 1).

Francesco Tron: Venetian patrician, supporter of Hinderbach in 1476, ambassador to Hinderbach in 1480; urged Calfurnio to write about Simon and was dedicatee of edition printed in Trent *c.* 1481.

Johannes Kurtz von Eberspach: attested between 1489 and 1512. Around 1500 he seems to have run a Latin school at Munich. He was quite a prolific poet, writing mostly about topical events, also some religious verse. He was instrumental in publication of Pusculo's poem about Simon in Augsburg in 1511.

Christian Umhauser: enrolled at the University of Ingolstadt in 1497 and his *Memoria artificiosa*, which exists in earlier manuscript variants, was published in

Basel after 1500. He lived at Maresco, near Bolzano, and possessed a manuscript copy of Pusculo's poem about Simon at some point between 1481 and 1511.

Andreas Unferdorben (or Garbarius): father of Simon, consulted a wise-woman to find his missing son.

Mary Unferdorben (or Garbarius): mother of Simon, consulted a wise-woman to find her missing son.

Simon Unferdorben (or Garbarius): a young child found dead in Trent in 1475, allegedly murdered by Jews of the city in a ritual associated with Passover. His body was the supposed cause of numerous miracles and the focus for a cult.

Johannes Vögelin Heilbrunnen: professor of mathematics in Vienna, he published or edited several works on geometry, astronomy, and astrology during 1528–1536. His poem was included in the edition of Pusculo's work published in Augsburg in 1511 (see above, Section III).

Jakob von Sporo: captain in Trent in 1475.

Raffaele Zovenzoni (1431–*c*. 1480): poet who wrote verses about Simon's murder at the request of Hinderbach (see biography in Introduction, Section VI/b).

The Jews of Trent:

> **Bonaventura:** *see* Seligman (son of Mayer) and Seligman (cook).

> **Brunetta:** *see* Brünnlein

Household of Samuel

> **Moses (b. 1395):** probably Samuel's uncle, lived in Würzburg, Speyer, and Tirol before he moved to Trent in 1465, spoke German and Yiddish, but Italian only poorly. He was accused of participating in murder of Simon by Tobias, and after confessing he killed himself. Tiberino and Calfurnio suggest that he claimed knowledge of the advent of the Messiah. Pusculo calls him a "high priest". Tiberino, Zovenzoni, Calfurnio, and Pusculo give him the leading role in the attack on Simon, including the act of circumcision.

> **Samuel (b. 1430):** son of Seligman of Nuremberg, educated in Bamberg and Nuremberg, settled in Trent in 1461. Moneylender. Spoke German and Yiddish, but Italian only poorly. Confessed under torture to choking Simon with a handkerchief with the help of Tobias. He subsequently gave a full confession and was executed after his flesh was torn with pincers.

Brünnlein (or Brunetta) (b. 1435): wife of Samuel, arrested, and later voluntarily baptized and taking the name Catherine before execution, according to Pusculo.

Mayer (b. 1435): son of Moses, married Schönlein in 1455 in Hall (Tirol). Confessed and executed.

Schönlein (b. 1439): wife of Mayer, spoke German and Yiddish, but Italian only poorly. Confessed under torture, and was baptized in 1477.

Israel (b. 1450): son of Samuel. Spoke Italian. Under torture accused father of offering money for a Christian child. Executed.

Anna (b. 1452): wife of Israel, mother of a young child. Daughter of Abraham, son of Lazarus of Brescia, grew up near Padua. Spoke and read Italian, read Hebrew. Baptized in 1477.

Seligman (or Bonaventura) (b. *c.* 1455): son of Mayer, cousin of Israel, he discovered body of Simon in the the ditch which ran through the cellar of Samuel's house. He was the first to be tortured and the first to confess that Engel's servant Isaac had told him that he killed Simon with Schweizer as accessory. Later he elaborated on the torture of Simon and the Hebrew words from the *Haggadah* supposedly used in the rite. Baptized and executed.

Vital: son of Seligman of Weissenburg (servant), confessed under torture to torturing Simon. Subsequently elaborated on details of ritual murder. Executed.

Seligman (or Bonaventura): son of Samuel of Nuremberg (cook), under torture supported Tobias's account of tearing of Simon's flesh by Old Moses, Tobias, and Samuel, he subsequently accused Old Moses of cutting the boy's penis. Baptized and executed.

Household of Tobias (next door to Samuel's household)

Tobias of Magdeburg: son of Jordan of Wardburg in Saxony, a doctor specialising in the eye, arrived in Trent in 1462 and treated Christians. Married to Anna by whom he had four sons. After her death he remarried in January 1475 to Sara. Under torture he confessed that Samuel had suggested abducting a child and that he had found and tricked Simon who was then stuck with pins and his flesh torn. Subsequently confessed to buying Christian blood in Venice in *c.* 1469 and was executed, but did not commit suicide as suggested in the edition of Pusculo's poem printed in 1511.

Moses: eldest son of Tobias, sent away to school.

Josche, Haym, and David: young sons of Tobias.

Sara: daughter of Abraham of Schwäbisch Werd, second wife of Tobias, spoke German and did not know Italian, confessed after several torture sessions. Baptized in 1477.

Moses (b. *c.* 1455): son of Salomon of Ansbach, tutor to sons of Tobias, lived in Nuremberg on the charity of the Jewish hospital, learned Hebrew and scriptures, arrived in Trent at Passover 1475. Confessed to knowledge of ritual murder in Nuremberg.

Solomon: formerly of Innsbruck, cook. Baptized in 1477.

Joaff: son of Seligman of Ansbach, a poor relative of Tobias, passing through Trent from Lombardy to Germany. Confessed under torture to witnessing and subsequently to participating in torture and murder of Simon. He elaborated on other cases of ritual murder. Baptized and hanged.

Israel: son of Joaff.

Household of Engel

Engel: moved to Trent in 1471 from Gavardo near Brescia, son of Salomon and Brünnlein of Bern. Confessed under torture that Tobias kidnapped Simon for his blood and that he saw the body on the almemor. Subsequently elaborated on Hebrew prayers and curses on the Egyptians and meaning of blood sacrifice of Simon. Executed.

Brünnlein: mother of Engel.

Süsslein: Engel's wife, and mother of sons Salomon and Moses, she wrote to the Jews of Rovereto informing them of the arrests and accusations against the Jews of Trent.

Gütlein: Engel's sister, with one son Salomon.

Lazarus: Engel's nephew and servant, tortured but did not confess immediately. Subsequently confessed to hearing of ritual murder in Regensburg. Hanged.

Isaac: from Voitsberg near Cleburg, educated at Worms, servant. Confessed under torture, and elaborated on other ritual murder cases, including one at Regensburg. Hanged.

Visitors:

Israel the painter: son of Mayer of Brandenburg, copied and illuminated Hebrew books; on his way to Passau, he was arrested as he fled Trent. He was later baptized Wolfgang and released, held in castle at Trent but rearrested and elaborated on other cases of child murder, including one at Regensburg. Accused of plotting murder of Hinderbach, captain, and *podestà*. Broken on wheel and burned.

Moses of Bamberg: son of Aaron of Bamberg, travelling from Bayreuth to Padua, certified poor pious Jew deserving of alms, stayed with Samuel's household. Confessed under torture and elaborated on involvement in earlier cases. Baptized and hanged.

Isaac: son of Moses of Bamberg, stayed with Engel's household.

APPENDIX 3:
A CHRONOLOGY OF EVENTS

1430		Child murder and execution of Jews in Ravensburg
1440		Earliest evidence of Jews in Trent
		Christian allegedly plants a dead child in house of a Jew in Meran
		Fifty-five Jews burned on a ritual murder charge in Landshut
1461		Child found injured in Trent in the shed of the Jew Samuel
		Child murder and execution of Jews in Pfullendorf
1469		Samuel and household granted rights of residence and moneylending by Hinderbach
1470		Child murder and execution of Jews in Endingen
1472		
	26 November	Birth of Simon
1473		Hinderbach orders body of a dead child to be examined for cut marks
1475		
	21 March	Supposed conspiracy of Jews in Samuel's house in Trent for abduction of Christian child
	26 March	Easter Sunday. Discovery of body of Simon Unferdorben in Trent. The Jews Samuel, Israel, Tobias, Engel, Isaac son of Moses of Bamberg, Joaff, and Seligman arrested
	27 March	Examination of the body of Simon by Tiberino and Archangelo de Balduini. Arrest of Israel son of Samuel, Old Moses, Mayer, Solomon (Tobias's cook), Lazarus of Saravall, Moses of Bamberg, Moses the tutor, Isaac (servant of Engel), Vital, and Brünnlein, Samuel's wife. Depositions taken by the *podestà* Giovanni de' Salis re Jewish

	use of Christian blood and child found in 1461. Seligman brought to torture chamber and confesses
28 March	Seligman the cook confesses under torture
29 March	Vital and Israel tortured. Schweizer accused of murder and arrested
31 March	Samuel and Engel questioned under torture. Schweizer and his wife Dorothea questioned
	First miracle of Simon reported
3 April	Samuel, Engel, Vital, Tobias, Old Moses, and Mayer questioned under torture
4 April	Tiberino writes to the city of Brescia about the murder of Simon
7 April	Samuel tortured and confesses. Tobias tortured. Mayer tortured but does not confess
8 April	Engel and Tobias confess
9 April	Tobias confesses. Israel confesses under torture and implicates father Samuel
10–16 April	Eighteen interrogation sessions, eleven of fifteen men tortured and extensive confessions extracted
17 April	Tobias questioned
18 April	Vital confesses under torture
21 April	Vital confesses under torture
24 April	Venetian doge orders rectors in Brescia, Padua, and Friuli to protect Jews from violence
30 April	Hinderbach writes to Zovenzoni requesting poem about Simon
6 June	Interrogation under torture of Samuel resumes
7 June	Interrogation and confession under torture of Samuel
9 June	Vital and Old Moses tortured
10 June	Old Moses threatened with torture and confesses
11 June	Further confessions of Samuel. Interrogation and torture of Seligman
14 June	Formal charges and sentencing of Samuel, Vital, Old Moses, and Seligman
	Suicide of Old Moses
21 June	Samuel's flesh torn and he is burned at the stake with Israel, Engel, and Tobias

22 June	Vital and Mayer burned at the stake. Seligmans ask for baptism
23 June	Seligmans baptized, beheaded, and burned
2 July	Tiberino composes poem about Simon and punishment of Jews
17 July	Venetian doge orders rectors in Brescia, Padua, and Friuli to protect Jews from violence
23 July	Sixtus IV instructs Hinderbach to suspend trials
2 September	Battista dei Giudici arrives in Trent
6 September	Battista dei Giudici notes putrefaction of the corpse of Simon
23 September	Battista dei Giudici leaves Trent and transfers to Rovereto, in Venetian territory and therefore under the protection of the doge
24 September	Battista dei Giudici meets Jewish representatives in Rovereto
28 September	Anzelino Austoch given safeconduct by Ludovico Querini, *podestà* of Rovereto, in order to give evidence against the Christian Johannes Schweitzer for the murder of Simon before Battista dei Giudici in Rovereto
1 October	Hinderbach writes to Zovenzoni about his suspicions that the *podestà* of Rovereto favors the Jews, and about the need for Venetian patricians to learn the truth about Simon
5 October	Jewish advocates accuse Hinderbach, captain, and *podestà* of Trent of using trial proceedings to rob the Jews
8 October	Giovanni de Salis, *podestà* of Trent, excommunicated
10 October	Sixtus IV instructs Venetian doge to protect Jews and to prohibit sermons about the martyrdom of Simon
12 October	Sixtus IV calls on Hinderbach to release Jewish women and children from prison
13 October	Schweizer interrogated in Trent without torture about death of Simon
20 October	Archduke Sigismund of Tirol authorizes the captain of Trent to interrogate remaining Jews and render justice
24 October	Battista dei Giudici writes to Hinderbach about Jews from Verona in Rovereto pleading for Tridentine Jews

25 October–11 January

    Second round of interrogations begins: Joaff, Isaac, Lazarus, Moses of Bamberg, Moses the tutor, and Israel the painter

26 October   Battista dei Giudici asks Hinderbach to release all Jewish prisoners

29 October   Battista dei Giudici calls on prince-bishop, *podestà*, captain, and city councillors of Trent to release prisoners and transfer trial to Rome

31 October   Hinderbach, captain, and *podestà* accuse Battista dei Giudici of exceeding authority and of being corrupted by Jewish bribery

3 November   Sara, widow of Tobias, questioned. Schönlein questioned without torture

4 November   Sara examined for signs of pregnancy and interrogation resumed, with torture. Schönlein questioned under torture

5 November   Sara confesses under torture. Venetian doge orders rectors in Brescia, Padua, and Friuli to protect Jews from violence, and prohibits images, texts, sermons about Simon

17 November   Sara interrogated

18 November   Israel the painter confesses under torture to child murder in Regensburg in 1467

20 November   Israel the painter confesses to stories of child murder in Mestre, near Venice

22–23 November

    Israel the painter confesses to secret contact with Venetian Jews and Battista dei Giudici to secure release of Jewish women

28 November   Hinderbach writes to pope that Battista dei Giudici has accepted Jewish bribes and falsely imprisoned and tortured Anzelino in order to save Jews

30 November   Moses of Bamberg found dead in his cell—corpse burned

1 December   Battista dei Giudici arrives in Rome after surviving an attempted assault in Verona

18 December   Israel confesses under torture to plot to murder Johannes Hinderbach, the *podestà*, and captain, or to poison well of castle in Trent

1476

13 January	Execution of Lazarus and Isaac by hanging
15 January	Joaff and Young Moses sentenced, and convert
16 January	Joaff and Young Moses hanged
19 January	Israel dragged to execution ground, broken on wheel, and burned

February–March

Sara, Schönlein questioned and confess to other cases of child murder in Trent.

Anna and Gütlein interrogated under torture and confess to other cases of child murder in Trent

3 April	Sixtus IV orders Hinderbach to halt trials against women. Hinderbach complies
14 May	Venetian doge orders rectors in Brescia, Padua, and Friuli to protect Jews from violence
18 August	Venetian doge orders rectors in Brescia, Padua, and Friuli to protect Jews from violence
6 November	The Franciscan preacher Michele Carcano writes to Hinderbach about his supporters in Venice, including Francesco Tron and many other patricians

1477

13 January	Baptism of three Jewish women and one man in Trent
22 August	Venetian doge orders rectors in Brescia, Padua, and Friuli to protect Jews from violence

1478

Tiberino returns to the Bresciano and composes prayer to Simon

20 June — Papal bull clears Hinderbach but admonishes him not to allow anything contrary to the decretum of Innocent IV in 1247 (against ritual murder trials) in promoting cult of Simon. Christians forbidden from killing or harming Jews, extorting money from them, or preventing the practice of their rites

Ritual murder accusations against Jews in Reggio and Mantua

1479

Ritual murder accusations against Jews in Arena, near Milan, and at Bormio

1480

Ritual murder accusations against Jews in Portobuffolè, near Treviso, and in Verona

	10 July	De Salis writes to Hinderbach mentioning his role in Portobuffolè case, and Pusculo's work for Hinderbach to correct
		Francesco Tron appointed Venetian ambassador to Hinderbach
1481		Calfurnio's poem about Simon published in Trent, with help of Francesco Tron
	29 June	Pusculo sends manuscript of poem about Simon to Hinderbach
1482		Ritual murder accusation against Jews at Tortona
		Tiberino returns to Trent from the Bresciano
	5 September	Works by Tiberino and Zovenzoni published in Trent
1483		Tiberino delivers elegy in praise of St Francis in Trent
1486		Ritual murder accusation made at Vicenza and possibly Marostica. Expulsion of Jews from Vicenza
	21 September	Hinderbach dies
1511		
	11 April	Pusculo's poem about Simon published in Augsburg
1588		Cult of Simon officially approved by the pope
1965		Cult of Simon abolished by the pope

Index

Note: In citations of textual material the Arabic page numbers refer only to the English translation since the original Latin text may conveniently be found facing the translation throughout.